We Ride A Whirlwind:

Sherman And Johnston At Bennett Place

Other work by Eric J. Wittenberg:

We Have it Damned Hard Out Here: The Civil War Letters of Sgt. Thomas W. Smith, Sixth Pennsylvania Cavalry (1999)

One of Custer's Wolverines: The Civil War Letters of Brevet Brigadier General James H. Kidd, 6th Michigan Cavalry (2000)

Under Custer's Command: The Civil War Journal of James Henry Avery (2000)

At Custer's Side: The Civil War Writings of James Harvey Kidd (2001)

Glory Enough for All: Sheridan's Second Raid and the Battle of Trevilian Station (2001)

With Sheridan in the Final Campaign Against Lee (2002)

Little Phil: A Reassessment of the Civil War Leadership of Gen. Philip H. Sheridan (2002)

The Battle of Monroe's Crossroads and the Civil War's Final Campaign (2006)

Plenty of Blame to Go Around: Jeb Stuart's Controversial Ride to Gettysburg (with J. David Petruzzi, 2006)

Rush's Lancers: The Sixth Pennsylvania Cavalry in the Civil War (2007)

One Continuous Fight: The Retreat from Gettysburg and the Pursuit of Lee's Army of Northern Virginia, July 4-14, 1863 (with J. David Petruzzi and Michael F. Nugent, 2008)

Like a Meteor Blazing Brightly: The Short but Controversial Life of Colonel Ulric Dahlgren (2009)

The Battle of Brandy Station: North America's Largest Cavalry Battle (2010)

Gettysburg's Forgotten Cavalry Actions: Farnsworth's Charge, South Cavalry Field and the Battle of Fairfield (Second Edition, 2011)

The Battle of White Sulphur Springs; Averell Fails to Secure West Virginia (2011)

Protecting the Flank at Gettysburg: The Battles for Brinkerhoff's Ridge and East Cavalry Field (Second Edition, 2013)

The Devil's to Pay: John Buford at Gettysburg. A History and Walking Tour (2014)

The Second Battle of Winchester: The Confederate Victory that Opened the Door to Gettysburg (with Scott L. Mingus, Sr., 2016)

Out Flew the Sabers: The Battle of Brandy Station, June 9, 1863 (with Daniel T. Davis, 2016)

The Union Cavalry Comes of Age: Hartwood Church to Brandy Station, 1863 (Second ed. 2017)

We Ride A Whirlwind:

Sherman And Johnston At Bennett Place

Eric J. Wittenberg

FOX RUN
PUBLISHING
QUALITY PUBLISHING ONE BOOK AT A TIME

Publisher's Cataloging-in-Publication(Provided by Quality Books, Inc.)

Wittenberg, Eric J., 1961- author.
    We ride a whirlwind : Sherman and Johnston at Bennett
        Place / by Eric J. Wittenberg.
    pages cm
    Includes bibliographical references and index.
    LCCN 2017938074
    ISBN 978-1-945602-02-3 (hardcover : alk. paper)
    ISBN 978-1-945602-03-0 (pbk. : alk. paper)

    1. Sherman's March through the Carolinas.
    2. United States--History--Civil War, 1861-1865--Peace.
    3. Capitulations, Military--Confederate States of America.
    4. Capitulations, Military--United States--History--19th century.
    5. Sherman, William T. (William Tecumseh), 1820-1891.
    6. Johnston, Joseph E. (Joseph Eggleston), 1807-1891.
    7. Bennett Place State Historic Site (N.C.)
    I. Title.

    E477.7.W735 2017   973.7'38
                QBI17-704

Cover design by OctagonLab - http://octagonlab.com/
Historical Painting "The First Meeting" by Dan Nance courtesy of the Artist.
www.dannance.com
Photograph: Bennett Place, 1904 courtesy of the Library of Congress

Published by
Fox Run Publishing LLC
2966 South Church Street, #305
Burlington, NC 27215
http://www.foxrunpub.com/

Respectfully dedicated to the memories of two honorable men, Major General William T. Sherman and General Joseph E. Johnston, who had the vision and courage to make peace and to bring an end to four years of horrific civil war.

Table of Contents

List of Maps

List of Images

Author's Preface

I have long been a student of Major General William T. Sherman's 1865 Carolinas Campaign, and this is my second book on those events. One cannot study the Carolinas Campaign without also studying the remarkable events that occurred in April 1865 at James T. Bennett's hardscrabble farm near Durham Station in North Carolina. There, in three separate meetings, Sherman and his adversary, Confederate General Joseph E. Johnston, met to discuss not only Johnston's army surrendering, but to end to the Civil War and bring peace to a divided nation. In 1882, Johnston succinctly described their efforts:

> I met Gen. Sherman on the 17th of [April] 1865 near Durham, N.C. We made an armistice and agreed upon Terms of Pacification to be suggested to the two governments. They were rejected by Mr. Johnson, President of the U.S. A fact which I was informed by Gen. Sherman on the 24th of the Month. On the 26th we had a second meeting—in which Terms of Capitulation were agreed upon, terminating hostilities in our geographical commands, which happened to be co-extensive. This as we intended and expected, Terminated the war.[1]

The vision and courage of these two old soldiers spared a lot of unnecessary bloodshed and ended the Civil War, once and for all. This book details the story that Johnston clearly and concisely told in his 1882 letter.

A stark and stunning contrast exists between the historic sites where the two primary surrenders of Confederate forces occurred only a few weeks apart in April 1865. In the years after the war, the War Department purchased the entire village of Appomattox Court House and turned it into a shrine. The village is now part of the National Park Service, with many of the buildings, including Wilmer McLean's handsome home, reconstructed as replicas of the original structures. The Appomattox Court House National Historical Park

---

1. Joseph E. Johnston to Edward W. Bok, February 21, 1882, https://www.abaa.org/book/577806772.

consists of 1,800 acres and includes 27 original structures. The park has an ample amount of monuments, and the small battlefield area is well interpreted. General Robert E. Lee briefly fought on the battlefield but aborted the fight upon realizing the Union infantry had arrived, making his plight hopeless. A small military cemetery is located at the site, as well as a large Eastern National Park & Monument Association bookstore and a visitor center with a museum.

In many ways, what happened at Bennett Place is more remarkable, and more important, than what happened at Appomattox Court House. However, the Bennett Place episode has long been downplayed, and even ignored, in light of the more dramatic events at Appomattox. The Bennett Place surrender site is now a North Carolina state park that occupies about four acres, although the state park also consists of a substantial wooded tract located across the road. The original Bennett Place house burned to the ground in 1921, and a replica later replaced it. In 1923, the Unity Monument was erected at the site to pay tribute to the war ending and the nation reuniting. A recently remodeled visitor center includes museum exhibits, a theater, library, and gift shop. The contrast, however, is absolutely shocking when comparing Bennett Place to the plush, huge national park at Appomattox. Bennett Place sits a couple hundred yards from an interstate and is nestled among residential and commercial districts, so the site, realistically, cannot be expanded. Not much else commemorates the location where two of the greatest men of the Civil War era combined efforts to accomplish one of the most astounding events of the American Civil War.

"What happened [at Bennett Place] was far more than a simple military truce," prominent historian James Reston Jr. declared in 1986. Instead, it was the "neck in the hourglass between the war and the Reconstruction period." Reston observed that "the issues of Reconstruction were joined at Bennett Place."[2] The Bennett Place events, despite their significance, have remained secondary in importance to the surrender of General Lee's Army of Northern Virginia at Appomattox.

This book is not intended to be a definitive study of the Carolinas Campaign. Instead, it offers an extremely broad overview of the Carolinas Campaign in order to put those events in their proper context. Nor is it meant to be a definitive study of the last weeks of the Civil War in North Carolina; to those interested in a complete

---

2. Quoted in William M. Vatavuk, *Dawn of Peace: The Bennett Place State Historic Site Durham, North Carolina* (Wake Forest, NC: Scuppernong Press, 2014), 35.

study of the Civil War's final weeks, I recommend my friend Mark L. Bradley's excellent book *This Astounding Close: The Road to Bennett Place* (Chapel Hill: University of North Carolina Press, 2000). Rather, this work will only focus on the extraordinary events that occurred at Bennett Place and give the minimal amount of preliminary detail necessary to set the stage for the drama that played out at the farm. This work arises from the absence of a monograph dedicated to the surrender negotiations at Bennett Place and is intended to demonstrate the significance of these unique events.

The book includes two chapters that establish the scene by bringing the armies to Bennett Place. It then addresses the three meetings between Sherman and Johnston in great detail, followed by a study of the political machinations—both Northern and Southern—that jeopardized the generals' work. It briefly touches on events that happened after Johnston's surrender to Sherman and concludes by examining the role of those events. The epilogue discusses the memory of those events and gives a brief history of the state park at Bennett Place. Four appendices follow the conclusion, which include a detailed order of battle describing the respective Union and Confederate forces, a discussion of the conference between Sherman, Grant, Admiral David D. Porter and President Abraham Lincoln at City Point, Virginia on March 28, 1865, the incredible exchange of correspondence between Confederate President Jefferson Davis and his cabinet when faced with the question of surrender, and the saga of Confederate Lieutenant General Wade Hampton, who refused to surrender with the rest of Johnston's forces.

Any and all errors of interpretation are solely mine.

As with every project of this nature, there are many people to thank. First, and foremost, I am grateful to my friend Mark Bradley, both for blazing the way as the authority on the Carolinas Campaign and for encouraging me to pursue my own studies. J. Keith Jones greatly assisted with the research. My friend Dan Mallock's commentary on the manuscript helped to make this a better book. Dan Nance, a gifted artist, was kind enough to give us permission to use his painting "The First Meeting," which depicts Sherman and Johnston meeting at Bennett Place for the first time, as the cover illustration. Four of Mark Anderson Moore's maps grace this volume's pages. Mark also reviewed the manuscript, and I appreciate his good work.

I am grateful to the good folks at Fox Run Publishing for bringing this project to fruition. This is our first project together, but I doubt that it will be the last. I am particularly grateful to Heather Ammel for her excellent work editing this manuscript. This is a much better book because of her efforts.

Finally, and as always, I remain deeply grateful to my loving and long-suffering wife, Susan Skilken Wittenberg, without whose unflagging support of my historical work, none of this would be possible.

Eric J. Wittenberg
Columbus, Ohio

Prologue

Gen. William Tecumseh Sherman, the second man in the United States Army to don four stars, the insignia of a full general—Sherman's great friend Ulysses S. Grant being the first—died of pneumonia at his home in New York, New York on February 14, 1891, at the age of 71. President Benjamin Harrison, who served under Sherman's command during the Civil War, ordered that the nation's flags be flown at half-staff. "He was an ideal soldier, and shared to the fullest the esprit du corps of the army," President Harrison declared in a message to Congress, "but he cherished the civil institutions organized under the Constitution, and was only a soldier that these might be perpetuated in undiminished usefulness and honor."[1]

After his remains had lain in repose in the family home for two days, Sherman's family held a small funeral at his New York City home, presided over by the general's son Thomas, a Roman Catholic priest.[2] An impressive military procession followed and escorted Sherman's remains to the train that carried him to his final resting place in Calvary Cemetery in St. Louis, Missouri, where he joined his predeceased wife, Ellen. The procession proved to be all of the magnificent Victorian pomp and pageantry one would expect of the obsequies for one of the nation's heroes and the last survivor of the Union's pantheon of Civil War greats. "New-York gave General Sherman yesterday a most impressive farewell," the *New York Times* declared. "The sun at noon shone upon a city draped with the emblems of sorrow. It shed upon the parting at dusk, when the escorting army, with trailing arms and shrouded flags, had discharged its tender office, a glowing benediction. The heart of the community was touched by this event as it had not been since [Grant] passed to his final bivouac at Riverside."[3]

Nearly anyone of national significance, who could find a way to do so, attended. President Harrison led the way to honor his old

---

1. "Sorrow at the Capital: Formal Announcement by the President—Eulogies in the Senate," *New York Times*, February 15, 1891.
2. James Lee McDonough, *William Tecumseh Sherman: In the Service of My Country. A Life* (New York: W. W. Norton, 2016), 720.
3. "On His Way to His Rest. New-York's Sad Farewell to the Great Soldier," *New York Times*, February 21, 1891. If one has a taste for the florid prose of the Victorian era, this article, along with two others that accompanied it, provides a detailed description of the pageantry of the mourning for Sherman's death.

commander, along with virtually all of the important politicians, soldiers, and surviving veterans of the Late Unpleasantness who were able to brave the harshness of a New York City winter. A number of Sherman's former colleagues and friends served as honorary pallbearers, including former Confederate Gen. Joseph E. Johnston, who was Sherman's respected opponent on many a Civil War battlefield, from the first combat at Bull Run in July 1861 to one of the last, in Bentonville, North Carolina in 1865.

"There was another face among them—that of Johnston, the same Joseph E. Johnston who threw himself and his army before Sherman in the march to the sea—the same Johnston who, in 1865, surrendered to the soldier whose corpse he was following in sorrow," the *New York Times* observed.[4]

It was bitterly cold and wet on February 19, 1891. Johnston, who had previously served as a pallbearer at the funerals of Grant and another former adversary Maj. Gen. George B. McClellan, was now 84 years old and frail. Johnston not only insisted on attending Sherman's funeral, but he also insisted on removing his hat as a sign of respect. As they stood bareheaded watching as the flag-draped coffin was carried from the Sherman residence to the caisson that would carry it, a friend, fearing that the old general would contract an illness in the severe cold, suggested that Johnston wear a hat Johnston responded, "If I were in [Sherman's] place, and he were standing in mine, he would not put on his hat."[5] In not doing so, the Virginian fulfilled a promise that he and his great adversary and friend had made to each other years earlier—that whichever of them died first, the other would serve as a pallbearer.[6]

Unfortunately, Johnston's companion's fears proved prescient. The old general indeed caught a cold that day that continued to worsen. By mid-March, it had become an infection and pneumonia, and after lingering for a few more weeks, Joe Johnston followed his friend Sherman to the grave on March 21. Former Generals William S. Rosecrans and John M. Schofield, who had also led Civil War armies in the field against Johnston, were among the first to call on the Johnston family to pay their respects.[7] "General Joseph E. Johnston occupied the same relative position in the Confederate army that

---

4. Ibid.
5. Gilbert E. Govan and James W. Livingood, *A Different Valor: The Story of General Joseph E. Johnston, C.S.A.* (Indianapolis: Bobbs-Merrill, 1956), 397; Craig L. Symonds, Joseph E. Johnston: A Civil War Biography (New York: W. W. Norton, 1992), 380.
6. "Gen. Joseph E. Johnston," *The Scranton Republican*, March 24, 1891.
7. Symonds, *A Different Valor*, 381.

General William T. Sherman did in the Union army," a Pennsylvania newspaper reported. "Johnston surrendered to Sherman as [Gen. Robert E.] Lee had surrendered to Grant. The warm friendship maintained ever afterwards has become almost historical."[8]

Although these two old warriors had clashed on the battlefield many times over the course of four years of hard war, Sherman and Johnston had never met each other in person until April 17, 1865, when they convened to make peace in farmer James Bennett's hardscrabble little wooden roadside house, not far from Durham Station, North Carolina. This is the story of the remarkable events conducted by two remarkable men drawn together by fate at Bennett Place.

---

8. "Gen. Joseph E. Johnston." For a detailed examination of the warm relationship between these two great adversaries, see Edward G. Longacre, *Worthy Opponents: William T. Sherman and Joseph E. Johnston: Antagonists in War-Friends in Peace* (New York: Thomas Nelson, 2006).

CHAPTER ONE

WILLIAM T. SHERMAN AND THE CAROLINAS CAMPAIGN

Major General William Tecumseh Sherman and his army group—the Military Division of the Mississippi, which consisted of three different armies—had just completed one of the most remarkable campaigns in military history. At 45 years old, the intense, brilliant Sherman was at the height of his power and fame. Born in Lancaster, Ohio, on February 8, 1820, he was one of eleven children and named for the great Shawnee war chief Tecumseh. When his father, a justice of the Ohio Supreme Court, died unexpectedly in 1829, various family friends took in the Sherman children. Thomas Ewing, who served as both a U.S. Senator and cabinet officer, took in Sherman and his brother John, a future U.S. Senator. The Ewings raised the two Sherman boys as if they were the couple's own children, and Sherman eventually cemented the bond between the families by marrying the senator's daughter Ellen.

Maj. Gen. William T. Sherman, commander of all Union forces in North Carolina.

In 1836, Senator Ewing arranged for Cump, as Sherman was known to his friends, an appointment to the United States Military Academy at West Point. He graduated sixth in the class of 1840. Sherman earned a brevet to captain for his gallantry in the Mexican-American War and served in the Regular Army for 13 years. In 1853, he resigned his commission to enter the banking business in San Francisco. After the bank failed, Sherman took up the study of law and opened a law office with two of his brothers-in-law in Leavenworth, Kansas. Unhappy with practicing law, he sought and obtained an appointment as superintendent of the Louisiana State Seminary of Learning and Military Academy, which is now known as Louisiana State University. When the secession crisis broke out in 1861, Sherman resigned his position at the seminary in order to avoid opposing the government of the United States. Sherman moved to St. Louis, Missouri, and headed a streetcar company for a few months. He then accepted a commission as a colonel in the Regular Army and was assigned to command the newly organized 13th U.S. Infantry.[1]

Shortly thereafter, Sherman then led a brigade of infantry that took the heaviest casualties at the July 1861 Battle of Bull Run, and he became the seventh highest-ranking brigadier general of volunteers in August, even ahead of Grant. In September, he was sent to Kentucky to assist in holding the state in the Union. The general's notorious temper got him into trouble in Kentucky, and he was ordered to St. Louis to report to Maj. Gen. Henry W. Halleck. At the Battle of Shiloh in April 1862, Sherman commanded a division of the Army of the Tennessee and was promoted to major general of volunteers to rank from May 1, 1862. Sherman and Grant developed a deep and abiding friendship during the time that he served under Grant's command.[2]

Once Grant assumed command of the newly-formed Department of the Mississippi after his Vicksburg victory, Sherman became commander of the Army of the Tennessee. After Grant's decisive triumph at the Battle of Chattanooga in November 1863, he was promoted to lieutenant general and became the commander of all Union armies. Sherman's 1864 campaign to take the critical railroad town of Atlanta, Georgia took all summer, but Sherman seized it in September.[3]

"Sherman was tall, lithe, and active, with light brown hair, close-cropped sandy beard and mustache, and every motion and expression indicated eagerness and energy," Maj. Gen. Jacob D. Cox, who commanded one of Sherman's army corps in 1865, recalled. "His head

1. Ezra J. Warner, *Generals in Blue: Lives of the Union Commanders* (Baton Rouge: Louisiana State University Press, 1964), 441-442.
2. Sherman may have suffered a nervous breakdown in 1861 and was accused of being crazy, but Grant stood by him. Later, Sherman stood by Grant when Grant was accused of being a drunk, prompting Sherman to famously declare, "Grant stood by me when I was crazy, and I stood by him when he was drunk, and now we stand by each other." For a discussion of the relationship between Grant and Sherman, see Charles Bracelen Flood, *Grant and Sherman: The Friendship That Won the Civil War* (New York: Farrar, Straus and Giroux, 2005).
3. Warner, Generals in Blue, 442-443.

was apt to be bent a little forward as if in earnest or aggressive advance, and his rapid incisive utterance hit off the topics of discussion in a sharp and telling way. His opinions usually took a strong and very pronounced form, full of the feeling that was for the moment uppermost, not hesitating even at even a little humorous extravagance if it added point to his statement; but in such cases the keen eye took a merry twinkle accentuated by the crow-foot lines in the corner, so that the real geniality and kindliness that underlay the brusque exterior were sufficiently apparent. The general effect was a nature of intense, restless activity, both physical and mental."[4]

Maj. Gen. Jacob D. Cox, commander of the 23rd Corps of Schofield's command.

(Library of Congress)

Sherman was a brilliant strategist, but he was not a great tactician. "Sherman's own knowledge of his own impulsive nature made him unduly untrustful of his own judgment when under great responsibility in emergencies, and this in spite of his unusual intellectual activity and his great confidence in his deliberately matured judgment," Maj. Gen. John M. Schofield, who commanded one of Sherman's armies, observed. "For this reason Sherman's capacity as a tactician was not by any means equal to his ability as a strategist. He lacked the element of confident boldness or audacity in action which is necessary to gain the greatest results by taking advantage of his adversary's blunders."[5]

After a summer-long campaign to capture Atlanta, Sherman's troops took a break for a few weeks to rest and refit. Then, on November 15, 1864, his grand army shook loose from Atlanta and spent the next five weeks on its legendary March to the Sea. The only

4. Jacob D. Cox, *Reminiscences of the Civil War*, 2 Vols. (New York: Charles Scribner's Sons, 1900), 2:203.
5. John M. Schofield, Forty-Six Years in the Army (New York: The Century Co., 1897), 341-342.

organized Confederate resistance came from Maj. Gen. Joseph Wheeler's dogged cavalry corps, but there was little that the badly outnumbered horse soldiers could do to prevent Sherman's troops from having their way.

Along the way, Sherman "made Georgia howl," as he put it. Sherman believed that the only way to end the Civil War was to break the will of the Southern populace, and he set out to do so. After fanning across Georgia like a plague of locusts, the blue-clad horde arrived at Savannah, Georgia, about a month after setting out from Atlanta. Lieutenant General William J. Hardee, the Confederate commander at Savannah, abandoned the town and led his troops to Charleston, South Carolina, on December 20. The next day, the Savannah mayor surrendered the city in return for Sherman's promise not to destroy it, and thus ended an incredible campaign that only foreshadowed what was yet to come.[6]

On December 25, a victorious Sherman telegraphed President Abraham Lincoln: "I beg to present you as a Christmas gift the City of Savannah, with one hundred and fifty guns and plenty of ammunition, also about twenty-five thousand bales of cotton."[7] Delighted, Lincoln responded the next day:

Executive Mansion, Washington, Dec. 26, 1864.

My dear General Sherman.

Many, many, thanks for your Christmas-gift---the capture of Savannah.

When you were about leaving Atlanta for the Atlantic coast, I was anxious, if not fearful; but feeling that you were the better judge, and remembering that ``nothing risked, nothing gained'' I did not interfere. Now, the undertaking being a success, the honor is all yours; for I believe none of us went farther than to acquiesce. And, taking the work of Gen. Thomas into the count, as it should be taken, it is indeed a great success. Not only does it afford the obvious and immediate military advantages; but, in showing to the world that your army could be divided, putting the stronger part to an important new service, and yet leaving enough to

---

6. For the best detailed discussion of Sherman's March to the Sea, see Noah Andre Trudeau, *Southern Storm: Sherman's March to the Sea* (New York: Harper, 2007).

7. Roy Basler, ed., *Collected Works of Abraham Lincoln*, 18 Vols. (New Brunswick, NJ: Rutgers University Press, 1953), 8:181.

vanquish the old opposing force of the whole---Hood's army---it brings those who sat in darkness, to see a great light. But what next? I suppose it will be safer if I leave Gen. Grant and yourself to decide.

Please make my grateful acknowledgments to your whole army, officers and men.

Yours very truly,

A. LINCOLN.[8]

Lieutenant General Ulysses S. Grant, the commander of the Union armies, moved his army group to the sea with little resistance and wanted Sherman's army to embark on ships to join the Army of the Potomac and the Army of the James in the trenches around Petersburg, Virginia. Sherman, however, had other ideas. On January 5, he declared to his wife, Ellen, "I do think that in the several grand epochs of this war, my name will have a prominent part."[9] After the last Confederate ocean-going port, Wilmington, North Carolina, fell to Union forces in February 1865, Sherman, determined to etch his name in history, proposed to Grant that his army should instead march through the Carolinas and destroy everything of military value along the way, just as he had done during the March to the Sea. Sherman had his eye on South Carolina, which he blamed for triggering the rebellion and was the first state to secede from the Union. Sherman correctly assumed that wreaking havoc upon South Carolina would shatter Southern morale.[10]

Sherman's combined command began its movement toward South Carolina's capital, Columbia, at the end of January. He commanded 60,079 men who were divided into three wings: the Army of the Tennessee, commanded by Maj. Gen. Oliver O. Howard[11], the Army of the

8. Ibid., 181-182. Lincoln referred to Gen. John B. Hood's Army of Tennessee, which at the time operated in northwest Georgia after being driven away from Nashville, Tennessee, when it was defeated in the November 15-16, 1864, Battle of Nashville.

9. M. A. DeWolfe Howe, ed., *Home Letters of General Sherman* (New York: Charles Scribner's Sons, 1909), 325.

10. *The War of the Rebellion: A Compilation of the Official Records of the Union and Confederate Armies*, 128 volumes in 3 series (Washington, D.C.: United States Government Printing Office, 1889), vol. 47, part 2, 154-156, hereinafter referred to as OR. All further references are to Series 1 unless otherwise noted.

11. Oliver Otis Howard was born in Leeds, Maine, on November 8, 1830. He studied at an academy in North Yarmouth, Maine, and put himself through Bowdoin College by teaching school during the off seasons. He graduated from Bowdoin in 1850 and then appointed to West Point, where he graduated in the class of 1854, along with Robert E. Lee's son Custis Lee, J.E.B. Stuart, Stephen D. Lee, William D. Pender, and Stephen H. Weed. Howard spent

Ohio, commanded by Maj. Gen. John M. Schofield, and the Army of Georgia, commanded by Maj. Gen. Henry W. Slocum.[12] Sherman received reinforcements as he made his way north, and by April 1, 1865, his army group numbered nearly 90,000 men.[13]

Sherman intended to bypass small Confederate garrisons at Augusta, Georgia, and Charleston, South Carolina, and to arrive at Goldsboro, North Carolina, by mid-March. In order to deceive the Confederates of his intention, he simultaneously sent his armies in different directions. The maneuver confused the Confederates and concealed Sherman's first objective, Columbia. Instead, the Southerners expected Sherman to inflict revenge on the rebellion's birthplace, Charleston.[14]

Maj. Gen. Oliver Otis Howard, commander of the Army of the Tennessee

(Library of Congress)

most of his pre-war career as a mathematics instructor at West Point, where he was serving as a first lieutenant of ordnance at the outbreak of the Civil War. He was elected colonel of the 3rd Maine at the end of May 1861 and resigned his regular commission on June 7. He commanded a brigade in Samuel P. Heintzelman's division at First Bull Run and was promoted to brigadier general, even though his command was driven from the field in a rout. During the Peninsula Campaign, he commanded a Second 2nd Corps brigade and lost his right arm to a combat wound in Virginia at the Battle of Seven Pines in May 1862. Eighty days later, he returned to duty and commanded the army's rear guard during the retreat from Second Bull Run. At Antietam, he succeeded to command of the 2nd Division, Second 2nd Corps after Sedgwick was wounded and led the division at Fredericksburg, Virginia. On November 29, 1862, he was promoted to major general. On March 31, 1863, he was given command of the Eleventh Corps, which was poorly led and subsequently routed at Chancellorsville, Virginia, and Gettysburg, Pennsylvania, making his command the butt of the entire army's jokes. When the Eleventh and Twelfth Corps were sent to Chattanooga, Tennessee, that fall, Howard remained in command of his corps, and after the death of McPherson, assumed command of the Army of the Tennessee, which was Sherman's right wing during the Carolinas Campaign. He was commissioned brigadier general in the Regular Army at the end of the war and appointed first commissioner of the Freedmen's Bureau, an organization that became rife with fraud, corruption, and inefficiency under his leadership. He was acquitted by a court of inquiry in 1874 and then helped to found Howard University in Washington, D. C. During the 1870s and 1880s, he served in the Indian Wars, and he was superintendent of West Point for a time. When he was promoted to major general in 1886, he commanded the Division of the East until his retirement in 1894. He spent the rest of his life, writing, speaking, and engaging in religious and educational activities. In 1893, he was awarded the Medal of Honor for bravery at Seven Pines. He died on October 26, 1909. Biographer Ezra J. Warner said of Howard's career that it "must constitute one of the great paradoxes of American military history: no officer entrusted with the field direction of troops has ever equaled Howard's record for surviving so many tactical errors of judgment and disregard of orders, emerging later not only with increased rank, but on one occasion with the thanks of Congress." Warner, Generals in Blue, 237-239.

12. Henry Warner Slocum was born on September 27, 1827, at Delphi, Onandaga County, New York. He attended Cazenovia Seminary, taught school for several years, and then entered West Point, graduating in 1852. After serving in Florida in the Seminole Wars and garrison duty in Charleston Harbor, he resigned his commission in 1856 to begin the practice of law, a profession he had prepared himself for during his army career. He served as the county treasurer in Syracuse, New York, as a state legislator, and served as a colonel and artillery instructor in the New York State Militia. On May 21, 1861, he was commissioned colonel of the 27th New York, which fought at First Bull Run, where Slocum received a thigh wound. He was promoted to brigadier general of volunteers on August 9, 1861. When he returned to duty, he took command of a brigade of Gen. William B. Franklin's division, and when Franklin became a corps commander, Slocum assumed command of the division. On July 25, 1862, he was promoted to major general and led his division through the Peninsula Campaign and at Second Bull Run, where he helped to cover Major General John Pope's retreat. He took command of the Twelfth Corps after the Battle of Antietam. The Twelfth Corps took heavy losses at Chancellorsville and at Gettysburg. In September 1863, the Eleventh and Twelfth Corps were ordered to report to Chattanooga, under command of Joseph Hooker. Slocum tendered his resignation, but President Lincoln refused it. He served in the District of Vicksburg in Mississippi for a time, and then, after the death of Army of the Tennessee commander Maj. Gen. James B. McPherson during the Atlanta Campaign, Slocum was called to join the army as commander of the Twentieth Corps (which consisted of the combined Eleventh and Twelfth Corps). During the March to the Sea, Slocum commanded the Army of Georgia and Sherman's left wing. On September 28, 1865, he resigned his commission and returned to Syracuse, New York. He lost an election for Secretary of State and moved to Brooklyn, New York, and resumed practicing law after refusing a commission as colonel in the Regular Army. Slocum served in Congress for three terms as a Democrat and on the Board of Gettysburg Monument Commission. He died on April 14, 1894. Warner, *Generals in Blue*, 451-453. Thus, two of Sherman's army commanders—Howard and Slocum—were refugees from the Army of the Potomac.

13. The best narrative of Sherman's Carolinas Campaign is Mark L. Bradley, *The Battle of Bentonville: Last Stand in the Carolinas* (Mason City, IA: Savas, 1996).

14. OR 47, 2:155.

Major General Lafayette Mc-Laws' Confederate infantry made a stand against Sherman's right wing at Rivers Bridge, across the Salkehatchie River, on February 3. Major General Francis P. Blair's division of the Army of the Tennessee outflanked McLaws' division and drove his troops off, leaving the door to Columbia open. The city of Columbia surrendered to Sherman on February 17, as Lt. Gen. Wade Hampton's Confederate cavalry retreated from the city. Throngs of liberated prisoners and freed slaves overwhelmed Sherman's troops. Overjoyed Federal soldiers helped themselves to supplies of liquor in the city and became intoxicated. Fires started throughout Columbia; fanned by high winds, the flames quickly engulfed most of the city.

Maj. Gen. Henry W. Slocum, commander of the Army of Georgia.

(Library of Congress)

Although many Union soldiers fought the fires, others apparently prevented civilians from extinguishing the flames. Most of the downtown was destroyed, triggering a war of words between Hampton and Sherman and a controversy that still rages.[15]

That same day, February 17, the Confederate garrison evacuated Charleston and made its way into North Carolina. The next day in Columbia, Sherman's forces completed the destruction of anything maintaining military value, which included railroad depots, warehouses, machine shops, and arsenals. Then, on February 22, the Confederate stronghold of Wilmington finally fell. The walls began to close in on the remaining Southern forces in the Carolinas, as one disaster after another befell them.[16]

15. Looking to capitalize on the tragedy, Sherman wrongfully blamed Hampton and his troops for starting the fires, when it was clear that Sherman's soldiers were to blame. Hampton was rightfully angry and bitter about it, and a series of incendiary letters were exchanged between the two generals For a detailed discussion of the burning of Columbia, see William Gilmore Simms, *A City Laid Waste: The Capture, Sack, and Destruction of the City of Columbia* (Columbia: University of South Carolina Press, 2005).
16. For the best account of the protracted Union effort to seize the seaside bastion of Fort Fisher and to close the South's final remaining ocean-going port, see Chris E. Fonvielle, The Wilmington Campaign: Last Rays of Departing Hope (Mason City, IA: Savas Publishing, 1997).

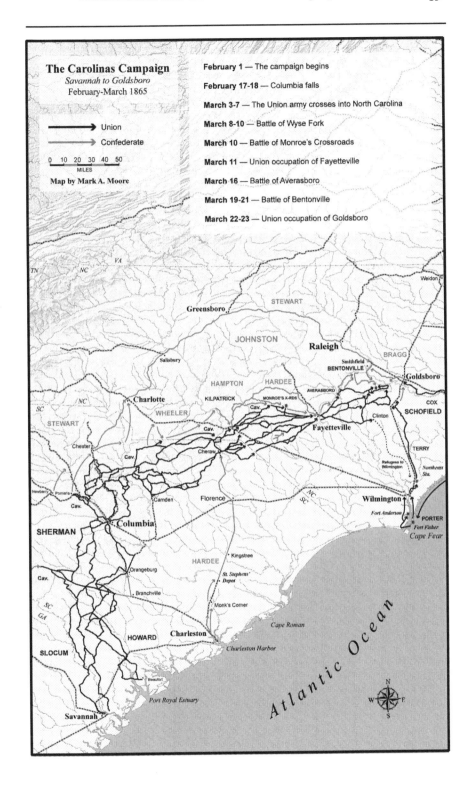

The Carolinas Campaign
Savannah to Goldsboro
February-March 1865

Union
Confederate

0 10 20 30 40 50
MILES

Map by Mark A. Moore

February 1 — The campaign begins

February 17-18 — Columbia falls

March 3-7 — The Union army crosses into North Carolina

March 8-10 — Battle of Wyse Fork

March 10 — Battle of Monroe's Crossroads

March 11 — Union occupation of Fayetteville

March 16 — Battle of Averasboro

March 19-21 — Battle of Bentonville

March 22-23 — Union occupation of Goldsboro

The Confederates continued to resist Sherman's advance. Wheeler's cavalry ambushed Bvt. Maj. Gen. Judson Kilpatrick's Union cavalry at Aiken, South Carolina, on February 11, soundly defeating the troopers. However, there was little that the severely outnumbered Confederates could do to impede Sherman's advance. In the meantime, Sherman's infantry made its way across five major rivers and swamps in South Carolina, building and corduroying roads as they went and scarcely allowing the numerous rivers and typically impenetrable swamps to hinder their progress.[17] They prompted Confederate Gen. Joseph E. Johnston to admiringly declare that "when I heard that Sherman had not only started, but was marching through those very swamps at the rate of thirteen miles a day, making corduroy road every foot of the way, I made my mind that there was no such army since the days of Julius Caesar."[18]

On March 2, Sherman's army entered Cheraw, South Carolina, after driving some of Hampton's cavalry away. Sherman's men set a large ammunition dump ablaze and much of the town was destroyed. The Federals marched again the next day. They crossed the Great Pee Dee River and then into North Carolina with Kilpatrick's horse soldiers leading the way. The Union horsemen constantly skirmished with Wheeler's troopers as they headed north.

"We swept through South Carolina, the fountain-head of rebellion, in a broad, semi-circular belt, sixty miles wide, the arch of which was the capital of the state, Columbia," Bvt. Maj. Gen. Alpheus S. Williams told his daughter in a letter. "Our people, impressed with the idea that every South Carolinian was an arrant Rebel, spared nothing but the old men, women, and children. All materials, all vacant houses, factories, cotton-gins, and presses, everything was swept away. The soldiers quietly took the matter into their own hands."[19]

Again looking to deceive the Confederates of his intent, Sherman feinted toward Charlotte and then changed direction; instead, he headed for Fayetteville, the northern fall line of the Cape Fear River,

---

17. Corduroy, or log, roads are made by placing sand-covered logs perpendicular to the direction of a road over a swampy area. Corduroying improves impassable mud or dirt roads, but they remain rough in the best of conditions and are a hazard to horses because of loose and shifting logs. Building such roads requires the felling of many trees and a great deal of hard work by those tasked to do so. Maxwell G. Lay, *Ways of the World: A History of the World's Roads and of the Vehicles that Used Them* (New Brunswick, NJ: Rutgers University Press, 1992), 43.

18. Michael C. Garber, Jr. "Reminiscences of the Burning of Columbia, South Carolina," *Indiana Magazine of History*, Vol. 11, No. 4 (1915), 287.

19. Milo M. Quaife, ed., From the Cannon's Mouth: The Civil War Letters of General Alpheus S. Williams (Detroit: Wayne State University Press, 1959), 373.

which could be resupplied by boats coming up from Wilmington. Responding, and uncertain whether Sherman was headed for Raleigh or Goldsboro, Johnston divided his forces. Those under General Johnston's command stayed in the Smithfield area, while a significant portion of his command, under Gen. Braxton Bragg, headed toward the important railroad town of Goldsboro, which is northeast of Raleigh.

Hardee's infantry also headed toward Fayetteville, hoping to link up with other troops Johnston commanded, which were gathering near Smithfield.[20] By the night of March 9, Kilpatrick's horsemen, screening Sherman's left flank and closely pursuing Hardee's infantry, encamped around Charles Monroe's house at a crossroads in Cumberland County, not far from Fayetteville. Thanks to shoddy dispositions, Hampton and nearly 5,000 Confederate cavalrymen of his and Wheeler's commands were able to launch a surprise attack on the sleeping Federal camp, routing the blue-clad troopers and nearly capturing Kilpatrick, who had fled into a nearby swamp clothed only in his nightshirt. Kilpatrick eventually rallied his troops and counterattacked, and Hampton eventually broke off and withdrew; he had accomplished his goal of keeping the Union cavalry tied up for an entire day. Kilpatrick had to endure the hoots of Sherman's infantrymen, who quickly dubbed the episode "Kilpatrick's Shirt-tail Skedaddle."[21]

The next day, March 11, Hardee's troops crossed the Cape Fear River and burned the bridge behind them just as pursuing Union troops reached it. Sherman had to halt for a few days until bridging materials could be floated up the river from Wilmington. He finally crossed the Cape Fear River on March 15 and continued toward Smithfield. That afternoon, Kilpatrick's troopers found Hardee's corps deployed in three lines of battle across the Raleigh Road, located not far from Smithville.[22] After determining that the Confederate defenses

20. Smithfield, North Carolina, was approximately halfway between Raleigh and Goldsboro. Johnston chose Smithfield because it placed his army in a position where it could either move toward a junction with Lee's army in Virginia or could cover either Raleigh or Goldsboro, as needed. Thomas Lawrence Connelly, *Autumn of Glory: The Army of Tennessee, 1862-1865* (Baton Rouge: Louisiana State University Press, 1971), 529.

21. The Monroe's Crossroads battlefield sits in the middle of modern-day Fort Bragg, North Carolina. Because of its location, it is perhaps the most preserved and least visited Civil War battlefield in the country. For a detailed discussion of the Battle of Monroe's Crossroads, see Eric J. Wittenberg, *The Battle of Monroe's Crossroads and the Civil War's Final Campaign* (El Dorado Hills, CA: Savas-Beatie, 2006).

22. Hardee deployed his troops in a classic defense in depth, which is a military strategy that seeks to delay, rather than prevent, the advance of the attacker and uses fortifications and field works that rely on a series of prepared positions. A well-known example of a defense in depth in American history is the 1781 Battle of Cowpens, fought in South Carolina.

Bvt. Maj. Gen. Judson Kilpat-
rick, commander of the caval-
ry division assigned to serve
with Sherman's armies in
North Carolina.

Lt. Gen. William J. Hardee,
known as "Old Reliable," com-
mander of the Department of
South Carolina, Georgia, and
Florida of Johnston's army.

(Library of Congress)

(Alabama Dept. of Archives and History)

were too strong, Kilpatrick withdrew and called for infantry support. That night, four divisions of the Army of Georgia's 20th Corps arrived.

At dawn on March 16, the blue-clad infantry advanced, driving back the enemy skirmishers. It took all day for the Federal troops to drive the Confederates from their first two prepared positions. Hardee repulsed an assault on the third line that afternoon. As dusk fell, Slocum's 14th Corps arrived to reinforce the 20th Corps, but it failed to deploy before dark because of the swampy ground that fronted Hardee's main line of battle. After holding up Sherman's advance for two days despite 35,000 Federals outnumbering his 8,500 men, Hardee withdrew under the night's cover so that Sherman found empty works the next morning. Hardee's troops joined with Johnston's growing army at Smithfield.[23]

---

23. The Battle of Averasboro is a fascinating engagement. For an excellent detailed monograph on this battle, see Mark A. Smith and Wade Sokolosky, *"No Such Army Since the Days of Julius Caesar": Sherman's Carolinas Campaign from Fayetteville to Averasboro, March 1865* (El Dorado Hills, CA: Savas-Beatie, 2017). This book also addresses the fighting in Fayetteville on March 11, 1865.

While Hardee's men tangled with Slocum's wing at Averasboro, North Carolina, Sherman's right wing, under General Howard's command, continued its march toward Goldsboro. In the meantime, Johnston had forged an army by absorbing forces from all over North Carolina, including troops from Wilmington commanded by Gen. Braxton Bragg. Sherman hoped to reach Goldsboro in time to unite with Schofield's army, which included forces from Wilmington, and then turn on Johnston before Johnston could complete concentrating his army. Johnston, by contrast, had no intention of permitting Sherman to unite with Schofield. The race was on.

Employing a brilliant plan of battle designed by Hampton, Johnston dug his troops in at Bentonville, North Carolina, and awaited the arrival of Slocum's army. Late on the afternoon of March 19, Johnston unexpectedly attacked, crushing a 14th Corps line. Only the Federal's heavy counterattacks and determined fighting prevented the rout of Slocum's men Elements of the 20th Corps reinforced the 14th Corps; five determined Confederate attacks failed to dislodge the Yankee defenders before nightfall ended the day's heavy fighting.[24]

Realizing that he had lost the initiative, Johnston pulled his troops back into a V-shaped line intended to protect his flanks, with Mill Creek to his rear. On March 20, Howard's Army of the Tennessee arrived to reinforce Slocum, but little fighting occurred that day, and Sherman was inclined to allow Johnston to escape if he chose to

Gen. Braxton Bragg, commander of the Department of North Carolina.

(USAHEC)

---

24. The best account of the Battle of Bentonville is found in full in Bradley's The Battle of Bentonville. Nathaniel Cheairs Hughes, Jr. also has written a good account of the battle, but it fails to credit Hampton for developing the brilliant plan of battle. See Nathaniel Cheairs Hughes, Jr., Bentonville: The Final Battle of Sherman and Johnston (Chapel Hill: University of North Carolina Press, 1996). For an interesting and useful map study of the battle, see Mark Anderson Moore, Moore's Historical Guide To The Battle Of Bentonville (New York: DaCapo, 1997).

do so. But Johnston, who had retreated in Sherman's front many times before, did not leave this time. Instead, his ragtag army held its positions while he removed his wounded from the field.

On March 21, skirmishing up and down the lines intensified in the afternoon. Major General Joseph Mower led his division along a narrow trace across Mill Creek and into Johnston's rear. Ferocious Confederate counterattacks halted Mower's advance, preserving Johnston's only retreat route. Mower withdrew, ending the day's fighting, and Johnston retreated across the bridge at Bentonville that night with some Union forces in pursuit, driving back Wheeler's rearguard. The Federal pursuit finally ended at Hannah's Creek after a severe firefight. "Johnston's effort—a well conceived, bold and well executed blow—was a failure, and their last chance of destroying Sherman and his army was lost," one of Sherman's staff officers correctly observed.[25] "Of course, General Johnston's only object in making this fight was to cripple the enemy and impede his advance," Lt. Gen. Wade Hampton, who designed Johnston's excellent battle plan for Bentonville, recounted.[26] With such terrible odds, Johnston's desperate gamble failed.

Johnston escaped toward Smithfield while Sherman's army marched to its original destination, Goldsboro. Sherman's troops reached Goldsboro on March 23. Despite suffering a defeat at Bentonville, the Confederate infantry remained optimistic. "We are fast concentrating our resources in men and material and if we can gain three weeks, I believe Genl Sherman will be chased out of the state," General McLaws declared.[27]

Sherman's Carolinas Campaign ended when his armies arrived at Goldsboro after marching 425 miles in just 50 days; his troops forced their way through the swamps of South Carolina and captured all of the large cities in the state, except for Charleston, destroyed the railroad, and desolated a swath of the countryside fifty miles wide. The Carolinas Campaign was longer than the March to the Sea and far more demanding. Sherman, quite rightly, was proud of his men. "I heard General Sherman remark today that that the march of this Army

25. M. A. DeWolfe Howe, ed., *Marching with Sherman: Passages from the Letters and Campaign Diaries of Henry Hitchcock, Major and Assistant Adjutant General of Volunteers November 1864-May 1865* (New Haven: Yale University Press, 1927), 282.
26. Wade Hampton, "The Battle of Bentonville," included in Robert U. Johnson and Clarence C. Buel, eds., *Battles and Leaders of the Civil War*, 4 vols. (New York: Century Publishing Co., 1884-1889), 4:705.
27. John C. Oeffinger, ed., A Soldier's General: The Civil War Letters of Major General Lafayette McLaws (Chapel Hill: University of North Carolina Press, 2002), 271.

from Savannah to [Goldsboro], the consequent [fall] of Charleston, without going within a hundred miles of it, and the junction of this Army with a column moving from Kinston, and another one from Wilmington, would be considered by able military men as one of the most perfect military movements in history," a Northern officer reported on March 25.[28] By the time Sherman and his troops arrived in Goldsboro, they needed to rest and refit.

Goldsboro was an important railhead. Major General John M. Schofield's Army of the Ohio had seized and held it after a vicious fight with Bragg's troops at Wyse Fork, near Kinston, North Carolina, from March 7 to 10.[29] Bragg withdrew and joined Johnston's command at Smithfield. Meanwhile, Schofield marched to Goldsboro to seize and hold the town and to oversee the construction and extension of the military railroad that would provide Sherman's army with supplies. Sherman's engineers completed the railroad work on March 25.

"As the troops passed through town, they passed in informal review before General Sherman at his headquarters," artillery officer Maj. Thomas Osborn noted. "They are certainly the most ragged and tattered looking soldiers I have ever seen belonging to our army. It is almost difficult to tell what was the original intention of the uniform. All are very dirty and ragged, and nearly one quarter are in clothes picked up in the country, of all kinds gray and mud color imaginable." Osborn continued, "Physically, they are in excellent condition, and only need new uniforms and rest and regular food for two weeks, when they will be equal to any labor that may be imposed on them. The morale is perfect."[30]

Schofield placed guards around Goldsboro to prevent Sherman's troops from looting and destructing the town, something they were notorious for doing. The blue-clad troops seized provisions and turned them over to officials, and Sherman's infamous "bummers" returned to the ranks, restoring discipline to the army. These precautions saved the town from the devastation that most of the cities in Sherman's path endured.[31]

28. Richard Harwell and Philip N. Racine, eds., *The Fiery Trail: A Union Officer's Account of Sherman's Last Campaigns* (Knoxville: University of Tennessee Press, 1986), 203.
29. For a detailed discussion of the Battle of Wyse Fork, see Wade Sokolosky and Mark A. Smith, *"To Prepare for Sherman's Coming": The Battle of Wise's Forks, March 1865* (El Dorado Hills, CA: Savas-Beatie, 2015).
30. Harwell and Racine, *The Fiery Trail*, 204-205.
31. Diary of Capt. Ferdinand F. Boltz, entry for March 25, 1865, Ferdinand F. Boltz Papers, Special Collections, Perkins Library, Duke University, Durham, North Carolina.

"What a camp we had on all the slopes around Goldsboro," a soldier of the 52nd Ohio noted. "In the solemn forests and spreading fields, the tents of the army were pitched, and the toil-worn veterans took a long holiday." The men received new uniforms and shoes, and observed for the first time the spectacle of watching African-American troops drilling as they prepared to join the ranks of Sherman's army.[32]

On March 25, Sherman boarded a train and went to visit Grant at his headquarters at City Point, Virginia. While there Sherman also met with President Abraham Lincoln and Admiral David Dixon Porter, and the four men plotted out the end of the rebellion and discussed a strategy for reconstructing the Union once the Confederate armies in the field were neutralized. These events are the subject of Appendix B to this book. By March 30, Sherman had returned to Goldsboro to begin planning the final campaign of the war.[33]

Gen. Robert E. Lee, Confederate general-in-chief and commander of the Army of Northern Virginia, who surrendered at Appomattox Court House on April 9, 1865.

(Library of Congress)

After Grant shattered Lee's lines at Petersburg, Virginia, on April 2, Confederate President Jefferson Davis ordered the evacuation of Richmond, and Lee's troops, with three Union armies in pursuit, raced toward Danville, Virginia, near the North Carolina state line, where Lee hoped to link up with Johnston. After shattering the Confederate lines at Petersburg and pursuing the broken Army of Northern Virginia southwest across the Virginia countryside, Grant jubilantly told Sherman on April 6, "We have Lee's army pressed hard, his men scattering and going to their homes by the thousands. He is endeavoring to reach Danville, where Davis and his cabinet have gone.

32. Nixon B. Stewart, *Dan McCook's Regiment: 52nd O.V.I.-1865. A History of the Regiment, Its Campaigns and Battles. From 1862 to 1865* (Alliance, OH: Review Print, 1900), 167-168.
33. For an excellent discussion of the conferences at City Point, Virginia, see Noah Andre Trudeau, *Lincoln's Greatest Journey: Sixteen Days that Changed a Presidency, March 24 – April 8, 1865* (El Dorado Hills, CA: Savas-Beatie, 2016).

I shall press the pursuit to the end. Push Johnston at the same time and let us finish up this job all at once."[34]

"The news of the battles about Petersburg reached me at Goldsborough on the 6th of April," Sherman wrote. "Up to that time my purpose was to move rapidly northward, feigning on Raleigh and striking straight for Burkeville, thereby interposing between Johnston and Lee. But the auspicious events in Virginia had changed the whole military problem, and in the expressive language of Lieutenant-General Grant, the Confederate armies of Lee and Johnston became the strategic points. General Grant was fully able to take care of the former, and my task was to capture or destroy the latter. Johnston at that time, April 6, had his army well in hand about Smithfield, interposing between me and Raleigh." Sherman thought that Johnston had about 35,000 infantry and artillery and an addition 6,000 to 10,000 cavalry, while the Union general had nearly 90,000 men in his command. He prepared to march on April 10.[35]

"About this time came the news that the Confederate Government, with Gen. Lee's army, had hastily abandoned Richmond, fled in great disorder toward Danville, and that Gen. Grant's whole army was in close pursuit. We inferred that Lee would succeed in uniting with Johnston somewhere in our front, where a great and decisive battle would he fought, for, 'When Greek meets Greek then comes the tug of war,'" a captain of the 10th Ohio Cavalry observed. "Thus, while we rejoiced over the good news, our hopes became mingled with fear."[36] Another Union officer wrote in his diary on April 4, "Anxiety and solicitude increase as we approach the crisis of the Rebellion! Bets offered that the Rebellion will go down in from three to five months. Gen. Sherman says this army will be mustered out in five months."[37]

Sherman's adjutant general, Maj. Henry Hitchcock, penned on April 7, "The fact is—though this is nobody's guess but my own—I do not see how it is possible for another great battle to be fought. We know that after Hood's defeat, which was not—on account of weather and roads—followed up with anything like the vigor Sheridan is now using, nor with anything like the force,--his army almost fell to pieces, though pursuit soon ceased, and his men went back without

---

34. *OR* 47, 3:109.
35. Ibid., 1:30.
36. "A 10th Ohio Cavalryman," "Campaign Through the Carolinas. With Kilpatrick from Goldsboro to the End of the War. Lee's Surrender. Joy in Sherman's Ranks at the Glorious News. The Grand Roundup. Scenes with Wheeler's Cavalry when They Surrendered," *National Tribune*, May 12, 1892.
37. Matthew H. Jamison, *Recollections of Pioneer and Army Life* (Kansas City, MO: Hudson Press, 1911), 325.

molestation to Augusta. Now, what has Lee's shattered and flying remnant to hang a hope on—and if Johnston could not defeat a part of 'Sherman's Army' proper, how will his men face it, largely increased and re-fitted acting in concert with as many more, and they the captors of Richmond!"[38]

"To-morrow we move straight against Joe Johnston wherever he might be," Sherman told Ellen on April 9. "Grant's magnificent victories about Petersburg, and his rapid pursuit of Lee's army, makes it unnecessary for me to move further north, and I expect my course will be Raleigh and Greensboro." The commander continued, "Poor North Carolina will have a hard time, for we sweep the country like a swarm of locusts. Thousands of people may perish, but they now realize that war means something else than vain glory and boasting. If Peace ever falls to their lot they will never again invite War. But there is a class of young men who will never live at peace. Long after Lee's and Johnston's armies are beaten and scattered they will band together as highwaymen and keep the country in a fever, begetting a Guerrilla War."[39] Sherman feared the latter more than anything else, which was why he was so determined to catch Johnston and force him to surrender his army.

On April 9, a Union officer wrote home, "General Sherman leaves again tomorrow moving to the interior in search of General Johnston's Army which now lies about 30 miles west of us. I do not think Johnston will fight." He concluded, "I doubt very much that General Sherman has any clear idea of just what he has to do beyond the one thing of searching for General Johnston's Army."[40]

Because it appeared to Sherman that the end of the war was at hand, he was determined to finish it. He worried that Johnston's army might scatter and form guerrilla bands, extending the war indefinitely. Consequently, his blue-clad horde rapidly made for Johnston's camps at Smithfield. "The occasion was quite like a gala-day performance," according to a Wisconsin soldier. "All the bands of the great army were filling the air with lively music, and the men sang songs and shouted. Two or three of the columns were in sight of one another for some miles on the roads up the valley of the Neuse, presenting a most enlivening spectacle."[41]

A real possibility existed that the Confederate army might actually disintegrate. On April 3, Brig. Gen. William Y. C. Humes, who com-

38. Howe, *Marching with Sherman*, 291-292.
39. Howe, *Sherman's Home Letters*, 342-343.
40. Harwell and Racine, *The Fiery Trail*, 210.
41. *Story of the Service of Company E, and of the Twelfth Wisconsin Regiment, Veteran Volunteer Infantry, in the War of the Rebellion* (Milwaukee, WI: Swain & Tate Co., 1893), 425-426.

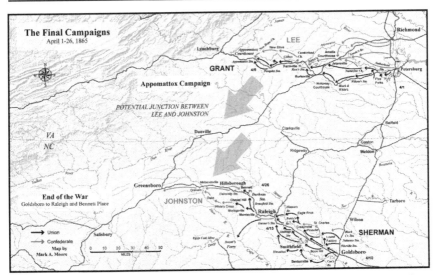

manded a division of Maj. Gen. Joseph Wheeler's Cavalry Corps, forwarded a letter to the War Department in Richmond indicating that the corps was dissatisfied and lacked confidence in Wheeler. Humes indicated that his men were very upset about not being paid, that they were inadequately clothed, and that they had insufficient shoes for the command's horses.[42] Wheeler's corps was on the verge of falling apart.

Sherman's army covered about ten miles on April 10 and another eleven miles the next day.[43] "Eleven months before, Sherman had moved on this same Johnston, many hundred miles from here, when hope was mixed with doubt," an Ohio soldier recalled. "Now with an army almost the same in numbers, he moves in an opposite direction, believing that the remnant of the army of traitors will be ground to powder between the upper millstone, Grant's army, and the nether millstone, the swift-marching legions of Sherman, aided by an almighty providence, thus destroy the image of iron and brass and clay and scattered it to the four winds."[44]

By 10 a. m. on April 11, the 14th Corps entered Smithfield with the 20th Corps close behind. The Federals learned that Johnston had rapidly retreated across the Neuse River, burning the bridge as they went. The Confederates, who used the railroads to transport supplies and baggage, were able to retreat faster than Sherman could pursue

42. Bryan S. Bush, *Terry's Texas Rangers: The 8th Texas Cavalry* (Paducah, KY: Turner Publishing, 2002), 158.
43. John C. Taylor to Lieut. Col. Henry G. Litchfield, May 20, 1865, *Supplement to the Official Records of the Union and Confederate Armies*, 100 vols. (Wilmington, NC: Broadfoot Publishing, 1994), 7:860.
44. Stewart, *Dan McCook's Regiment*, 168.

them. Furthermore, it began raining; the Federals would have to corduroy the roads to make them passable, which would force Sherman to wait for his pontoon bridges to come up. Once they came up and a bridge was built, Slocum placed a division of the 14th Corps across the Neuse River, but his efforts came too late. Johnston was already gone, heading straight for Raleigh.[45]

"I cannot see how Johnston can give battle unless we succeed in catching him and forcing it, and as to that, 'a stern chase is a long chase' on land as well as at sea." Major Hitchcock observed. "Possibly this may be a long march into the interior, possibly a short campaign—nobody can tell."[46]

In the meantime, Johnston's infantry struggled across the North Carolina countryside, fighting heavy rains, bad roads, and lethargy. "Troops out of marching condition from even the short rest at Smithfield," Capt. W. E. Stoney, who served on the staff of Brig. Gen. Johnson Hagood's brigade commanded by Maj. Gen. Robert F. Hoke's division, noted on April 11, "straggled badly." On April 12, Johnston's column reached Raleigh. Johnston wisely deployed his troops in a fashion that prevented Sherman from going to Virginia without exposing his flanks; the Confederate general also placed his own army in a position where he could facilitate a junction with Lee if the opportunity arose. "The city was being rapidly evacuated and immense quantities of stores destroyed and abandoned," Captain Stoney also reported. "Rumors in regard to General Lee assuming an unpleasant air of probability."[47]

"We there heard of the surrender of Lee's army at Appomattox Court-House, Va., which was announced to the armies in orders, and created universal joy," Sherman reported. "Not an officer or soldier of my armies but expressed a pride and satisfaction that it fell to the lot of the Armies of the Potomac and James so gloriously to overwhelm and capture the entire army that had held them so long in check, and their success gave new impulse to finish up our task."[48]

"I have never seen Sherman so elated," Bvt. Maj. Gen. Alpheus Williams remarked. "He called out to me from a bevy of mules and as soon as I could reach him through the kicking animals he grabbed my hand and almost shook my arm off, exclaiming, 'Isn't it glorious? Johnston must come down now or break up!' I confess that I felt and

45. OR 47, 1:30.
46. Howe, *Marching with Sherman*, 293.
47. Ulysses R. Brooks, ed., *Memoirs of the War of Secession from the Original Manuscripts of Johnson Hagood, Brigadier-General, C.S.A.* (Columbia, SC: The State Co., 1910), 368.
48. OR 47, 1:30-31.

expressed a pretty large sized 'Laus Deo' at the prospect of an early end of this great Rebellion and a return to my family."[49]

"Of course, this created a perfect furor, of rejoicing, and we all regarded the war as over, for I knew well that General Johnston had no army with which to oppose mine," Sherman penned in his memoirs. "So that the only questions that remained were, would he surrender at Raleigh? or would he allow his army to disperse into guerrilla bands, to 'die in the last ditch,' and entail on his country an indefinite and prolonged military occupation, and of consequent desolation? I knew well that Johnston's army could not be caught; the country was too open; and, without wagons, the men could escape us, disperse, and assemble again at some place agreed on, and thus the war might be prolonged indefinitely."[50]

When Sherman heard the news of Lee's surrender at 5:00 a.m. on April 12, he quickly dashed off a note to Grant:

> I have this moment received your telegram announcing the surrender of Lee's army. I hardly know how to express my feelings, but you can imagine them. The terms you have given Lee are magnanimous and liberal. Should Johnston follow Lees example I shall of course grant the same. He is retreating before me on Raleigh, but I shall be there to-morrow. Roads are heavy, but under the inspiration of the news from you we can march twenty-five miles a day. I am now twenty-seven miles from Raleigh, but some of my army is eight miles behind. If Johnston retreats south I will follow him to insure the scattering of his force and capture of the locomotives and cars at Charlotte; but I take it he will surrender at Raleigh. Kilpatrick's cavalry is ten

Bvt. Maj. Gen. Alpheus S. Williams, commander of a division of the 20th Corps.

(Library of Congress)

---

49. Quaife, *From the Cannon's Mouth*, 381.
50. William T. Sherman, *Memoirs of Gen. W. T. Sherman*, 2 vols. (New York: Charles L. Webster & Co., 1891), 2:344.

miles to the south and west of me, viz, on Middle Creek, and I have sent Major Audenried with orders to make for the south and west of Raleigh to impede the enemy if he goes beyond Raleigh. All the infantry is pointed straight for Raleigh by five different roads. The railroad is being repaired from Goldsborough to Raleigh, but I will not aim to carry it farther. I shall expect to hear from General Sheridan in case Johnston does not surrender at Raleigh. With a little more cavalry I would be sure to capture the whole army.[51]

Gov. Zebulon B. Vance, the wartime Confederate governor of North Carolina.

(Library of Congress)

Sherman was now determined to end the war.

That same day, North Carolina Governor Zebulon B. Vance reached out to Sherman under a flag of truce to see whether he could negotiate peace. Sherman responded, "I doubt if hostilities can be suspended as between the army of the Confederate Government and the one I command, but I will aid you all in my power to contribute to the end you aim to reach, the termination of the existing war."[52]

Two commissioners Vance appointed, both former North Carolina governors themselves, boarded a train headed toward Raleigh hoping to meet with Sherman to treat for peace and to plead for the city of Raleigh's safety. Lieutenant General Wade Hampton, however, intercepted the train a few miles from Raleigh and refused to allow Vance's fellow commissioners to pass through his lines in order to continue on to Sherman's headquarters. The South Carolinian ordered that the train reverse course, which it did. However, more bad luck struck the Confederate commissioners when some of Kilpatrick's cavalrymen captured, robbed, and then detained them for two days.

Not knowing what happened to his emissaries, and worried about his own fate, Vance mounted his horse at midnight on April 12 and galloped off to Hillsborough. One of the governor's commissioners found him there two days later and assured him that Sherman would

51. OR 47, 3:177.
52. Ibid., 178.

not molest Vance if he returned to Raleigh and that the Federals had done little damage to the city. Vance did not make it back to Raleigh until after Johnston's army surrendered.[53]

Meanwhile, the Union commander prepared an order to announce to his army the news of Lee's surrender, which was read to the troops on the morning of April 13:

> **The General Commanding announces to the army that he has official notice from Gen. Grant that Gen. Lee surrendered to him his entire army on the 9th instant at Appomattox Courthouse, Va. Glory to God and our country! All honor to our comrades-in-arms, toward whom we are matching. A little more labor, a little more toil on our part, and the race is won and our Government stands regenerated after four long years of war.[54]**

"Our army went wild with excitement when this glorious result was announced, and blessings were showered upon the grand old Army of the Potomac, which, after so many mortifying failures, is thus crowned by Grant's genius with magnificent laurels," Major George Ward Nichols, who served on Sherman's staff, recounted. "Our troops gave cheer after cheer to express their joy and then, when cheers became too feeble an expression, uttered yell upon yell until they waked the echoes for miles around. Then the bands burst forth in swelling strains of patriotic melody, which the soldiers caught up and re-echoed with their voices. Everybody was proud and glad."[55] One of

53. Richard E. Yates, "Zebulon B. Vance as War Governor of North Carolina, 1862-1865," Journal of Southern History, Vol. 3, No. 1 (February 1937), 74. Vance had received an urgent summons from Confederate President Jefferson Davis, and, accordingly, he declined to return to Raleigh. Instead, he went to Charlotte to meet with Davis, who suggested that Vance accompany him to the trans-Mississippi West and continue the war there. Vance, who believed that the Confederacy was doomed, refused to enter into such a hopeless undertaking and instead went to Greensboro with the intention of returning to Raleigh. However, the Confederate officers there would not allow him to pass through the lines while negotiations between Sherman and Johnston were pending, and he remained stranded there for the duration of the war. Ibid., 74-75.

54. John Richards Boyle, *Soldiers True: The Story of the One Hundred and Eleventh Regiment Pennsylvania Veteran Volunteers, and of Its Campaigns in the War for the Union 1861-1865* (New York: Eaton & Mains, 1903), 297.

55. George Ward Nichols, *The Story of the Great March, from the Diary of a Staff Officer* (New York: Harper & Bros., 1865), 293. Nichols, of Tremont, Maine, then 33 years old, was an assistant adjutant general serving on Sherman's personal staff. After the war, he became a journalist and was responsible for creating the legend of "Wild Bill" Hickok with an article that appeared in *Harper's Monthly Magazine*. Later in life he became president of the Cincinnati College of Music. He died of tuberculosis on September 15, 1884. J. G. Rosa, "George Ward Nichols and the Legend of Wild Bill Hickok," *Arizona and the West*, Vol. 19, No. 2 (Summer 1977), 143.

Slocum's Pennsylvanians remembered, "All hardships and suffering were forgotten, and there was no room in the whole world for anything but rejoicing."[56]

"I well remember the next morning as we were advancing on Raleigh, when this news came, how the boys threw away their overcoats and blankets and went into the fight, and how they cheered and swung their hats when it was announced along the line that Lee's army had surrendered," an Ohio cavalryman recalled. "It was about 10 o'clock in the morning, and the 10th Ohio Cav., of the Second Brigade, led the advance, followed by the Third Brigade, while the First brought up the rear. While our skirmish-line was engaged with Wheeler's forces, as they slowly gave ground, we heard a cheer away back in the rear. Col. Sanderson inquired of me what it meant; and as it still continued, said he did not like the looks of things in the rear, and ordered me to hold the skirmishers while he rode back, as the cheer indicated trouble in that direction. The first impression was that Hampton's forces had worked around and struck the column in flank. Soon we heard a fresh outbreak nearer; then nearer, when upon looking back we saw Capt. Cockley, one of Kilpatrick's Aides, riding rapidly up, his horse white with foam. Saluting the Colonel, he said: 'Announce to your regiment that Gen. Lee has surrendered.' The Colonel replied, while his sword dropped by his side, 'My God, is it possible? Then the war is ended.'"[57]

A courier carried this welcome news to the marching soldiers of Sherman's armies. "The procession was halted and the message announced, when a shout went up from thousands of throats; such an acclamation as those 'valleys and rocks never heard,'" a New Yorker reminisced. "And away it rolled back down the winding column, and again it swelled forth, while the air overhead was literally filled with hats, haversacks and belts, and even guns and swords were seen making summersaults at an unusual height. Here and there too might be seen warm handshakings and cordial congratulations at the news, and those who have experienced the privations and perils of soldier life, will not be surprised to learn that there were even tears of joy when those

---

56. Boyle, Soldiers True, 298.
57. "A 10th Ohio Cavalryman," "Through the Carolinas." This was the last combat of the Civil War east of the Mississippi. Kilpatrick was determined to avenge the embarrassment he incurred at Monroe's Crossroads and intent on whipping his old adversary, Hampton, one last time. Hampton, in turn, remained truculent and livid over the burning of his home in South Carolina and the loss of a brother and a son to combat wounds throughout the course of the Civil War. For a detailed discussion of this final combat, see Bradley, This Astounding Close, 121-129.

sturdy soldiers were thus suddenly brought to realize the glorious event of 'Victory at last.'"[58]

Captain George W. Pepper of the 80th Ohio, a gifted writer, left a stirring account of when he first heard the news of Lee's surrender. "We had just left Goldsboro, en route to Raleigh, and were in the very disagreeable business of laying corduroy bridges across a miserable swamp, when a rider was seen in the dim distance waving a flag," Pepper recalled. "General Logan turned, and said to me, 'What does that mean?' The tired soldiers soon caught a glimpse of the man, and then eager eyes turned in his direction. The thousands of troops heaved like the ocean under the throb of a storm." He continued, "The rider came nearer a voice was heard, and every soldier placed his hands behind his ears to catch the distant words, which fell like music upon our ears like blessed music: 'Lee and his whole army have surrendered to General Grant!'"

Furthermore, Pepper wrote, "Cheers greeted the news cheers such as the foreign monarch never heard; cheers that shook the plains; cheers such as the heavens seldom hear. The army was formed into a hollow square, and the chaplain gave out the doxology, 'Praise God, from whom all blessings flow!' O, how they did sing it! I have heard camp-meetings sing, when thousands made the welkin ring; I have heard scores of Englishmen sing 'God Save the Queen!' I have heard Grand Army reunions keep time to the air, 'John Brown's soul is marching on,' but none were ever so sweet, so grand, so overwhelming, as the doxology sung by the soldiers that day in the swamps of North Carolina. The boys hugged and kissed each other. The words, 'Lee and his whole army have surrendered,' were as a fountain of sweet waters in the desert. The soldier thought of home, of wife, of babies, of the bright handsome faces of his boys and girls, of the beloved parents whom he had not seen for years. There were others in that joyous crowd whose thoughts were sad when they remembered vacant chairs and loved ones they would never see again."[59]

"It would be difficult to describe the joy which the news of the surrender of Lee's army excited among us," a soldier of the 68th Ohio recounted. "We had not yet tired of cheering over the fall of Rich-

58. J. A. Mowris, A History of the One Hundred Seventeenth N. Y. Volunteers (Fourth Oneida) from the Date of Its Organization, August 1862, till that of Its Muster Out, June 1865 (Hartford, CT: Case, Lockhart & Co., 1866), 209.
59. George W. Pepper, *Under Three Flags: or, The Story of My Life as Preacher, Captain in the Army, Chaplain, Consul, with Speeches and Interviews* (Cincinnati: Curtis & Jennings, 1899), 98-99.

mond, and upon this last news being imparted to us we just let out another notch."[60]

When word reached the 3rd Wisconsin of the 20th Corps, veterans of the Army of the Potomac who came west in the fall of 1863, a man cried out to the staff officer carrying the news, "You are the man we have been looking for, for four years." They cheered, hugged, and clapped each other on the back. But then word flew up and down their ranks: "We must push Joe Johnston now."[61]

Despite this wonderful news, hard work remained to be done. Wheeler's horse soldiers resisted Kilpatrick's advance, skirmishing as they fell back toward Raleigh. Finally, the determined Federal cavalry shoved the Confederate horse out of its way, and Sherman's victorious army entered Raleigh after a marching twenty miles that day. "Gen. Kilpatrick immediately sent the Fifth Ohio Cavalry into the town, and their colors were the first to grace the dome of the Capitol," the *New York Times* reported.[62] 'The troops were elated at the sight of the capital," a Yankee soldier recalled. "The city presented a pleasant contrast with the scenes afforded by the last journey; the sight was cheering also, as the evidence of our military progress."[63]

The general established his headquarters in the governor's mansion, and before long, the stars and stripes fluttered over the state capital for the first time in four years.[64] "We entered Raleigh this morning. Johnston has retreated westward," Sherman told Grant. "I shall move to Asheville [Ashborough] and Salisbury or Charlotte. I hope Sheridan is coming this way with his cavalry. If I can bring

---

60. Myron B. Loop, *The Long Road Home: Ten Thousand Miles Through the Confederacy With the 68th Ohio*, Richard A. Baumgartner, ed. (Huntington, WV: Blue Acorn Press, 2006), 204.
61. Edwin E. Bryant, *History of the Third Regiment of Wisconsin Veteran Volunteer Infantry, 1861-1865* (Madison, WI: Veterans Association of the Regiment, 1891), 329.
62. "The North Carolina Campaign; Occupation of Smithville and Capture of Raleigh. The Negotiation Between Sherman and Johnston. Their Commencement and Ending. Clayton Reached--Skirmishing. Raleigh Occupied by Kilpatrick--The Colors of the Fifth Ohio Cavalry the First in the Capital. The Delegation to Sherman--The Proposed Surrender of the State--Wade Hampton Opposed to the Movement--Gov. Vance-- Newspapers--The Legislature," *New York Times*, April 30, 1865. The veterans of the 5th Ohio Cavalry proudly claimed the honor of capturing Raleigh for the rest of their lives.
63. Mowris, *History of the One Hundred Seventeenth Regiment*, 210.
64. Nichols described it as "a musty old brick building, which, in derision, has been called the 'Palace.' When the frightened Rebel Governor Vance ran away, he managed to carry off all the furniture of this 'palace' with him, so that, uncomfortable at any time, it was almost uninhabitable when General Sherman took possession and established his headquarters there." Nichols, *Story of the Great March*, 297-298.

officers and troops."[5]   However, trying to halt Sherman with meager resources proved to be a daunting task, at best.

"In appearance, General Joseph E. Johnston is rather below the middle height, spare, soldierlike, and well set up; his features are good and he has lately taken to wear a grayish beard," Lt. Col. Arthur Fremantle, a British officer who spent several months in 1863 as a military observer in the Confederacy, observed. "He talks in a calm, deliberate and confident manner...but he certainly possesses the power of keeping people at a distance when he chooses, and his officers evidently stand in great awe of him. He lives very plainly...he has undoubtedly acquired the entire confidence of all the officers and soldiers under him...General Johnston is a very well-read man and very agreeable to converse with."[6]

Lieutenant General James Longstreet, who served under Johnston's command in Virginia, echoed Fremantle's sentiments. "I am inclined to think that General Joe Johnston was the ablest and most accomplished man that the Confederate armies produced," Longstreet claimed. "He never had the opportunity accorded to many others, but he showed wonderful power as a tactician and commander. I do not think we had his equal for handling an army and conducting a campaign. General Lee was a great leader—wise, deep and sagacious. His moral influence was something wonderful. But he lost his poise in certain occasions...He was a great man, a born leader, a wise general, but I think Johnston was the most accomplished and capable commander we had."[7]

Vastly outnumbered, Johnston couldn't defeat Sherman's vastly larger army at the Battle of Bentonville. Once Sherman drove Johnston's army off the field on March 21, the Confederate commander was left with very few options to stop the blue-clad juggernaut making its way across North Carolina. Johnston hoped to link up with Lee's army near the Virginia and North Carolina state line, but once Lee surrendered, the general had difficult choices to make.

On April 9, Lieutenant General Wade Hampton, the Confederate chief of cavalry, advised Johnston that local residents were reporting that Sherman's soldiers expected to march toward Raleigh the following morning. The next day, Hampton confirmed that the

---

5. Oeffinger, *A Soldier's General*, 255.
6. Arthur J. L. Fremantle, *Three Months in the Southern States* (Edinburgh: William Blackwood & Sons, 1863), 116-117, 120.
7. Henry W. Grady, "An Interview with General Longstreet," included in Peter Cozzens, ed., *Battles and Leaders of the Civil War*, Vol. 5 (Urbana: University of Illinois Press, 2002), 691-692.

movement was underway. Responding, Johnston ordered all of his available infantry, along with Maj. Gen. Matthew C. Butler's cavalry division, to march to Raleigh.[8] Also on April 9, President Jefferson Davis had ordered that Johnston and his second-in-command, Gen. P. G. T. Beauregard, travel to Danville, Virginia, for a meeting with Davis and his cabinet.[9] Both men left the next day, Johnston from Smithfield and Beauregard from his headquarters in Raleigh.[10]

On the afternoon of April 9, a courier from Lee's Army of Northern Virginia arrived at Davis' temporary office, bearing the unwelcome news of Lee's surrender.[11] "It fell upon the ears of all like a tire ball in the night," Confederate Secretary of the Navy Stephen R. Mallory recalled. "The president received the unexpected blow about 4:00 p.m. at

Lt. Gen. Wade Hampton of South Carolina, commander of the large force of cavalry assigned to Johnston's army.

(Library of Congress)

8. Joseph E. Johnston, Narrative of Military Operations, Directed, During the Late War Between the States (New York: D. Appleton & Co., 1874), 396.
9. OR 47, 3:774. Pierre Gustave Toutant Beauregard was born on May 28, 1818, at his father's Louisiana plantation south of New Orleans. He attended a school in New York operated by two brothers who had learned to speak French, served under Napoleon, and gained a lifelong admiration for the French emperor. Beauregard graduated second in the class of 1838, and he was commissioned a second lieutenant in the 1st Artillery. A week later, he was assigned to the engineers. He was promoted to first lieutenant in 1839 and fought with rank Winfield Scott in the Mexican-American War, earning brevets at Contreras, Churubusco, and Chapultepec. He was promoted to captain in 1853 and spent most of the decade doing engineering duty in New Orleans. Beauregard accepted an appointment as superintendent at West Point in January 1861, but he resigned his commission when Louisiana seceded three days later. He was appointed a brigadier general in the Confederate army and was assigned to command the forces at Charleston, South Carolina. In that capacity, Beauregard oversaw the surrender of Fort Sumter, a fort located in Charleston Harbor, and then he joined Johnston's army at the First Battle of Bull Run in Virginia. Promoted to general on August 13, 1861, he was the fourth highest-ranking officer in the Confederacy. He was Gen. Albert Sidney Johnston's second-in-command, but Beauregard then assumed command of Johnston's army when he was mortally wounded in action at the Battle of Shiloh. Davis then removed Beauregard from command and replaced him with Gen. Braxton Bragg.

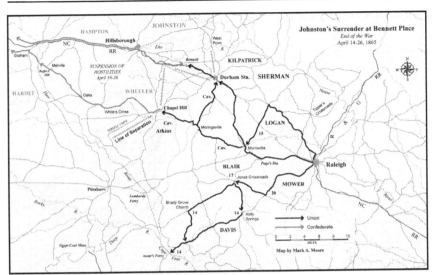

his office, where several members of his cabinet and staff were assembled. They carefully scanned the message as it passed from hand to hand, looked at each other gravely and mutely, and for some moments a silence, more eloquent of great disaster than words could have been, prevailed." Davis decided that he and his entourage would

Beauregard spent much of the war commanding Charleston's defenses; he also served with great distinction in the defense of Petersburg in the summer of 1864. On February 16, 1865, Davis assigned him to command the troops in South Carolina, and Beauregard soon found himself as Johnston's second-in-command. Like Johnston, Beauregard was utterly unable to get along with President Jefferson Davis, and his considerable talents were underutilized during the Civil War. Gary W. Gallagher, "Pierre Gustave Toutant Beauregard," included in Davis and Hoffman, *The Confederate General*, 1:84-93. Beauregard has not had a `modern full-length biographical treatment since T. Harry Williams, *P.G.T. Beauregard: Napoleon in Gray* (Baton Rouge: Louisiana State University Press, 1955).

10. A third Confederate full general, Braxton Bragg, was also assigned to Johnston's department. Johnston had replaced Bragg as the commander of the Army of Tennessee. After the Battle of Wyse Fork, Bragg had commanded only a small force that he felt was beneath him. Consequently, after the Battle of Bentonville, and at his own request, he was relieved of command of that force and established his headquarters in Raleigh on March 25. He constantly complained to Davis. He wrote to Davis, "I have retired to this point where I have nothing to do but mourn over the sad spectacle hourly presented of disorganization, demoralization and destruction....With no duty to perform, I shall remain quietly here awaiting events, and fall back toward the south as necessity may require. My position is both mortifying and humiliating." *OR* 47, 3:686 and 53:415-416. Furthermore, Bragg and Johnston disliked each other, which only added to the friction between the officers.

11. For a detailed discussion of the travails of the 18th Virginia courier, Capt. William P. Graves, see William D. Coleman, "Jefferson Davis' Week at Danville," *Philadelphia Weekly Times*, May 28, 1881.

Confederate Secretary of the Navy Stephen Mallory.

(Library of Congress)

depart Danville for Greensboro, North Carolina, at 8:00 p.m., although their actual departure was delayed nearly two hours.[12]

On April 11, as his troops arrived in Raleigh, Johnston received a horrifying telegram from Davis: "A scout reports that General Lee surrendered the remnant of his army near to Appomattox Court-House yesterday. No official intelligence of the event, but there is little room for doubt as to result...I will have need to see you to confer as to future action." First, though, Johnston's troops were to march to Greensboro and head to Danville afterward.[13] The report of Lee's surrender was, of course, true. Lee's surrender changed everything; now, no reason existed for Johnston to attempt linking up with Lee's army in Virginia.

On the morning of April 12, Johnston boarded a train and traveled to Greensboro where he joined Beauregard. An hour or two later, the two generals received a summons to Davis's office. When they arrived, they found not only Davis awaiting them, but also Secretary of State Judah P. Benjamin, Secretary of the Navy Stephen Mallory, and Postmaster General John H. Reagan with him. Given the long history of conflict between Davis and both Johnston and Beauregard, the tension in the room hung thickly.

Johnston and Beauregard expected questions about the Confederacy's remaining military resources and their ability to continue the war. To their surprise, Davis's "object seemed to be to give, not to obtain information," as Johnston later put it. The Confederate president claimed that in two to three weeks he could field a large army by bringing back into the ranks those who had deserted and through conscription, a prospect that Johnston found "inexpressibly wild." Davis neither sought nor obtained the opinions of the two generals as to the feasibility of such an exercise. Before leaving the

12. Stephen R. Mallory, "The Last Days of the Confederate Government," included in Peter Cozzens, ed., *Battles and Leaders of the Civil War.* Vol. 5 (Urbana: University of Illinois Press, 2002), 675-676.
13. *OR* 47, 3:776.

room, they learned that the Secretary of War, Maj. Gen. John C. Breckinridge, would arrive that afternoon and had information regarding the state of affairs in Virginia.[14]

Davis later explained his reasoning. "Though I was fully sensible of the gravity of our position, seriously affected as it was by the evacuation of the capital, the surrender of the Army of Northern Virginia, and the consequent discouragement which these events would produce, I did not think we should despair," he wrote. "We still had effective armies in the field, and a vast extent of rich and productive territory both east and west of the Mississippi, whose citizens had evinced no disposition to surrender. Ample supplies had been collected in the railroad depots, and much still

Gen. P. G. T. Beauregard, Johnston's deputy commander.

(Valentine Museum)

14. Major General John C. Breckinridge was born in Lexington, Kentucky, on January 16, 1821. He came from an old-line, prominent Kentucky family that included President Thomas Jefferson's attorney general. He attended Centre College and the College of New Jersey (now Princeton), but he ultimately graduated from Transylvania University with a law degree. Breckinridge set up a law office in Kentucky and eventually became active in the Democratic Party. He served as a major in the Mexican-American War in a Kentucky volunteer regiment, but he saw no combat. He was elected to the state legislature in 1848 and then to Henry Clay's old Congressional district in 1851. The Kentuckian served two terms in Congress before accepting the Democratic Party's vice presidential nomination in 1856 and, at 35 years old, was elected the youngest vice president in American history to date. He served one term as vice president and then ran for president in 1860, finishing second to Lincoln in the electoral vote. Learning he was to be arrested for treason, he fled Washington, D.C., and accepted a commission as a brigadier general in the Confederate service in November 1861. In May 1862, he was promoted to major general and continuously headed a division in various commands until Davis nominated him to become Secretary of War in January 1865. Breckinridge was appointed in February 1865 and helped improve Confederate supply and logistics. The Breckinridge family has a long and honorable history of public service; the general's grandson became a lieutenant general in the U.S. Army and his great-great grandson was killed in action during the Korean War. William C. Davis, "John Cabell Breckinridge," included in The Confederate General, 1:126-127. For a full-length biographical treatment, see William C. Davis, *Breckinridge: Statesman, Soldier, Symbol* (Baton Rouge: Louisiana State University Press, 1974).

remained to be placed at our disposal when needed by the army in North Carolina." Davis claimed, "My motive...in holding an interview with the senior generals of the army in North Carolina was not to learn their opinion as to what might be done by negotiation with the United States Government, but to derive from them information in regard to the army under their command, and what it was feasible and advisable to do as a military problem."[15]

Neither Johnston nor Beauregard believed that it was possible to persuade men who had already deserted from the army to return to their ranks, and both leaders said so. As one Confederate officer noted, "The result was so unsatisfactory to the two generals that they had about concluded to undertake in their own hands negotiations with Sherman for the protection of their soldiers."[16] The conference was adjourned to await the arrival of Breckinridge, since his crucial intelligence was needed for the meeting to continue.[17]

When Breckinridge arrived, he confirmed the reports of Lee's surrender. "Generals Johnston and Beauregard were now more than ever convinced that the prolongation of hostilities with any hope of success was an impossibility," Col. Alfred Roman, Beauregard's nephew and biographer, observed.[18] Johnston and Breckinridge then discussed the state of the Confederacy's military resources and came to the inevitable conclusion "that the Southern Confederacy was overthrown." Johnston noted, "In conversation with General Breckinridge afterward, I repeated this, and said that the only power of government left in the President's hands was that of terminating the war, and that this power should be exercised without more delay." Johnston also indicated that he was ready to advise Davis of the necessity of doing so if the opportunity presented itself. Breckinridge promised to give the general that opportunity.[19]

When Mallory approached Johnston on the subject, he asked, "What in your judgment do the best interests of our people require of the government?"

---

15. Davis, *The Rise and Fall of the Confederate Government*, 2:679-680.
16. "Notes Personal of Lt. Col. Alex Robt. Chisholm Relative to the War Of Secession," Manuscripts Division, New York Historical Society, New York, New York, 85.
17. Alfred Roman, *The Military Operations of General Beauregard in the War Between the States 1861-1865* (New York: Harper & Bros., 1884), 394. Colonel Alfred Roman was Beauregard's nephew. Beauregard was actively involved in the writing of Roman's biography, and many historians treat Roman's biography as if it is actually Beauregard's memoirs.
18. Ibid., 394-395.
19. Johnston, *Narrative of Military Operations*, 397-398.

Johnston replied, "We must stop fighting at once, and secure peace upon the best terms we can obtain."

"Can we secure terms?" Mallory inquired.

"I think we can," Johnston responded. "At all events, we should make the effort at once, for we are at the end of our row."

"General Johnston, your position as the chief of this army and as military commander of this department demands from you a frank statement of your views to the President," Mallory replied. "You believe that our cause is hopeless, and that further resistance with the means at our command would not only be useless, but unjustifiable, and that we should lay down our arms and secure the best terms we can get for our people. I will, if you please, state all this to the President; but I think you had better do so at once, and explicitly."

"General Beauregard and I have been requested to meet the President this evening," Johnston said, "and I will give him my opinions very explicitly. You will not find me reticent upon them." However, Johnston believed that the suggestion would be better received coming from one of the cabinet officers.[20]

"Our meeting at Colonel Wood's home the next morning was one of the most solemnly funereal I ever attended, as it was apparent that we must consider the probable loss of our cause," Secretary of the Navy Stephen R. Mallory noted, describing the cabinet meeting. "When we were convened, a general conversation was indulged in for some time. No one seemed disposed to take up the business for which we were assembled. With feelings I cannot well describe, I stated that if we were to proceed as in a council of war, where the youngest spoke first, I was prepared to give my views. The President and the other members of the Cabinet suggested that I should proceed."[21]

Mallory penned a memorandum for his colleagues' consideration:

I. **The disbanding of the military forces of the Confederacy.**

II. **The recognition of the Constitution and authority of the Government of the United States.**

III. **The preservation and continuance of the existing State Governments.**

IV. **The preservation to the people of all their political**

---

20. Mallory, "The Last Days", 677-678; *Johnston, Narrative of Military Operations*, 398.
21. John H. Reagan, *Memoirs with Special Reference to Secession and the Civil War* (New York: Neale Publishing Co., 1906), 199.

rights and the rights of person and property secured
to them by the Constitution of the United States and
of their several States.

V. Freedom from future prosecution or penalties for
participation in the present war.

VI. Agreement to a general suspension of hostilities
pending these negotiations.

When Mallory circulated his memorandum, Breckinridge,
Mallory, and George Davis, the attorney general, all approved it, while
Benjamin expressed his disapproval, preferring to continue the
struggle. "The Cabinet realized the hopelessness of such a course and
decided against him," Reagan recalled.[22]

Breckinridge delivered on his promise to Johnston the next
morning. Davis summoned Johnston and Beauregard to his office after
his morning cabinet meeting. "I have requested you and General
Beauregard, General Johnston, to join us this evening, that we may
have the benefit of your views upon the situation of the country,"
Davis began. "Of course we all feel the magnitude of the moment. Our
late disasters are terrible; but I do not think we should regard them as
fatal. I think we can whip the enemy yet if our people will turn out.
We must look at matters calmly, however, and see what is left for us to
do. Whatever can be done must be done at once. We have not a day to
lose."

Johnston held his tongue, unsure whether he should speak. Sensing
his hesitation, Davis said, "We should like to have your views, General
Johnston."

Without preface or hesitation, Johnston spoke in his "terse,
concise, demonstrative way." "My views are, sir, that our people are
tired of the war, feel themselves whipped, and will not fight. Our
country is overrun, its military resources greatly diminished, while the
enemy's military power and resources were never greater and may be
increased to any extent desired. We cannot place another large army in
the field, and, cut off as we are from foreign intercourse, I do not see
how we could maintain it in fighting condition if we had it." Johnston
continued, "My men are daily deserting in large numbers, and are
stealing my artillery teams to aid their escapes to their homes. Since
Lee's surrender they regard the war as at an end. If I march out of
North Carolina her people will all leave my ranks. It will be the same
as I proceed south through South Carolina and Georgia, and I shall
expect to retain no man beyond the by-road or cow path that leads to

---

22. Ibid., 200.

his home. My small force is melting away like snow before the sun, and I am hopeless of recruiting it."

Johnston's tone and demeanor stunned Mallory. "The tone and manner, almost spiteful, in which General Johnston jerked out these brief, decisive sentences, pausing at every period, left no doubt as to his own convictions," the Navy secretary remarked. A hush fell over the room after Johnston's delivery. Davis silently fiddled with a piece of paper and then turned to Beauregard, who had been listening intently, and asked, "What do you say, General Beauregard?"

The Creole wasted no time in responding. "I concur in all General Johnston has said," Beauregard stated. A thick silence fell over the room.

"Well, General Johnston, what do you propose?" Davis asked. "You speak of obtaining terms. You know, of course, that the enemy refuses to treat with us. How do you propose to obtain terms?"

"I think the opposing generals in the field may arrange them," Johnston replied.

"Do you think Sherman would treat with you?"

"I have no reason to think otherwise," Johnston answered. "Such a course would be perfectly legitimate and in accordance with military usage."

"We can easily try it, sir; if we can accomplish any good for the country, heaven knows I am not particular as to form. How will you reach Sherman?"

"I would address him a brief note proposing an interview to arrange terms of surrender and peace, embracing, of course, a cessation of hostilities during the negotiations," Johnston said.

Resigned, Davis replied, "Well, sir, you can adopt this course, though I confess I am not sanguine as to ultimate results."[23]

Because he didn't believe that negotiations would succeed and convinced that the failure of such negotiations could only demoralize the army and the population, Davis was skeptical.[24] Davis polled his cabinet members. Breckinridge, Mallory, and Reagan all agreed that the war had been decided against the Confederacy and that it was absolutely necessary to make peace. Benjamin took the opposition position, urging that the war should continue.

Davis again suggested that he should instead offer terms to the U.S. government and described a letter Johnston would send to Sherman,

---

23. Mallory, "The Last Days," 678-679.
24. Davis, *The Rise and Fall of the Confederate Government*, 2:680.

proposing a meeting to arrange the terms of an armistice to permit the civil authorities to agree upon terms of peace. Davis believed that if circumstances were such that negotiations were necessary, the Confederacy would get better terms by maintaining organized armies in the field rather than surrendering and "trusting to the magnanimity of the victor."[25] Johnston suggested that Davis should dictate the letter to Mallory, who had good penmanship, and that Johnston would sign and send it to Sherman immediately.[26] The letter provided:

> **HEADQUARTERS,**
> **In the Field, April 14, 1865.**
> **Maj. Gen. W. T. SHERMAN,**
> **Commanding U. S. Forces:**
>
> **GENERAL:**
>
> **The results of the recent campaign in Virginia have changed the relative military condition of the belligerents. I am therefore induced to address you in this form the inquiry, whether, in order to stop the further effusion of blood and devastation of property, you are willing to make a temporary suspension of active operations, and to communicate to Lieutenant-General Grant, commanding the Armies of the United States, the request that he will take like action in regard to other armies; the object being to permit the civil authorities to enter into the needful arrangements to terminate the existing war.**
>
> **I have the honor to be, very respectfully, your obedient servant,**
> **J. E. JOHNSTON,**
> **General.**[27]

Johnston instructed his cavalry commander, Hampton, to see that the letter was delivered to the Union lines under a flag of truce.

According to Reagan, before leaving Greensboro, Johnston told President Davis that Sherman had authorized him to say that Davis might leave the country on a United States vessel and take with him whomever and whatever he pleased. Davis responded, "I shall do no act which will put me under obligations to the Federal Government."[28]

While Johnston was off conferring with Davis and the cabinet, news of Lee's surrender reached the Confederate soldiers on April 9.

25. Davis, *The Rise and Fall of the Confederate Government*, 2:681.
26. Johnston, *Narrative of Military Operations*, 399-400.
27. *OR* 47, 3:206-207.
28. Reagan, *Memoirs*, 200.

Noting that the news was greatly demoralizing, a Texan of the late Brigadier General Hiram S. Granbury's Brigade of the Army of Tennessee declared, "I do hope and believe that we will whip this fight yet." Johnston ordered the army to move toward Raleigh; morale plummeted. Not even receiving new uniforms and other supplies helped. On April 16, the same officer said, "Had Battalion drill today just to see if the men would drill."[29]

When Confederate staff officer Capt. W. E. Stoney learned of Lee's surrender, he lamented, "Great God! Can it be true? I have never for a moment doubted the ultimate success of our cause. I cannot believe it."

Maj. Henry B. McClellan, Wade Hampton's able adjutant, shown as a student at Williams College before the war.

(Williams College)

Stoney certainly echoed the sentiments of many of Johnston's men.[30]

Hampton, without reading the letter and unaware of its contents, sent his very able adjutant general, Maj. Henry B. McClellan, and another staff officer, Capt. Rawlins Lowndes, to deliver the message.[31] Accompanied by a squadron of cavalry, McClellan made for the front lines with a white flag of truce in hand. When he arrived, Sgt. William H. Harding of the 5th Ohio Cavalry, who was doing picket duty that

---

29. Norman Brown, ed., *One of Cleburne's Command: The Civil War Reminiscences and Diary of Capt. Samuel T. Foster, Granbury's Texas Brigade, CSA* (Austin: University of Texas Press, 1980), 166-168.
30. Brooks, *Memoirs of the War of Secession*, 368.
31. Henry Brainerd McClellan was a transplanted Philadelphian and a first cousin of Gen. George B. McClellan. Two of his brothers served in the Union army, and one, Carswell McClellan, served on the staff of Maj. Gen. Daniel E. Sickles, commander of the Army of the Potomac's 3rd Corps. In 1865, 24-year-old McClellan was educated at Williams College in Massachusetts, and he became a schoolteacher before the war. McClellan also served on Maj. Gen. J. E. B. Stuart's staff. After Stuart's death in May 1864, McClellan joined Hampton's staff and served the rest of the war as his adjutant general. McClellan was a gifted staff officer who found himself in the right place at the right time when Hampton opted to let him deliver Johnston's letter to Sherman. Robert J. Trout, *They Followed the Plume: The Story of J.E.B. Stuart and His Staff* (Mechanicsburg, PA: Stackpole Books, 1993), 197-200.

day, received the flag of truce and the letter, which he took to Kilpatrick.[32]

"On the morning of the 14th General Kilpatrick reported from Durham's Station, twenty-six miles up the railroad toward Hillsboro, that a flag of truce had come in from the enemy with a package from General Johnston addressed to me," Sherman recalled. "Taking it for granted that this was preliminary to a surrender, I ordered the message to be sent me at Raleigh."[33]

On reading the note, Sherman immediately responded:

> HDQRS. MILITARY DIVISION OF THE MISSISSIPPI,
> In the Field, Raleigh, N. C., April 14, 1865.
> General J. E. JOHNSTON,
> Commanding Confederate Army:
> GENERAL:
>
> I have this moment received your communication of this date. I am fully empowered to arrange with you any terms for the suspension of further hostilities as between the armies commanded by you and those commanded by myself, and will be willing to confer with you to that end. I will limit the advance of my main column tomorrow to Morrisville, and the cavalry to the University, and expect that you will also maintain the present position of your forces until each has notice of a failure to agree.
>
> That a basis of action may be had, I undertake to abide by the same terms and conditions as were made by Generals Grant and Lee at Appomattox Court-House, on the 9th instant, relative to our two armies; and, furthermore, to obtain from General Grant an order to suspend the movement of any troops from the direction of Virginia. General Stoneman is under my command, and my order will suspend any devastation or destruction contemplated by him. I will add that I really desire to save the people of North Carolina the damage they would sustain by the march of this army through the central or western parts of the State.
>
> I am, with respect, your obedient servant,
> W. T. SHERMAN,
> Major-General.[34]

32. Dave Dougherty, ed., *Making Georgia Howl! The 5th Ohio Cavalry in Kilpatrick's Campaign and the Diary of Sgt. William H. Harding* (Point Pleasant, NJ: Winged Hussar Publishing, 2016), 267-268.
33. Sherman, *Memoirs*, 2:346.
34. *OR* 47, 3:207.

Sherman faced a challenging situation on April 15. Johnston's army was rapidly retreating on the roads from Hillsborough, North Carolina to Greensboro, and the army commander was at Greensboro. "Although out of place as to time, I here invite all military critics who study the problems of war to take their maps and compare the position of my army on the 15th and 16th of April, with that of General Halleck about Burkeville and Petersburg, Va., on the 26th of April, when, according to his telegram to Secretary Stanton, he offered to relieve me of the task of cutting off Johnston's retreat," Sherman later wrote.

Maj. Gen. Henry W. Halleck, Union chief of staff.

(Library of Congress)

Sherman was displeased with his treatment at the hands of Halleck in the coming days and said, "Major-General [George] Stoneman['s Cavalry Division] at the time was at Statesville, and Johnston's only line of retreat was by Salisbury and Charlotte. It may be that General Halleck's troops can outmarch mine, but there is nothing in their past history to show it, or it may be that General Halleck can inspire his troops with more energy of action. I doubt that also, save and except in this single instance, when he knew the enemy was ready to surrender or disperse, as advised by my letter of April 18, addressed to him when chief of staff at Washington City, and delivered into his hands on the 21st instant by Major Hitchcock, of my staff."[35]

Maj. Gen. George Stoneman, commander of a lengthy raid into Virginia and North Carolina that threatened Greensboro.

(Library of Congress)

Sherman took time to update his superiors on this important change of circumstances. He wrote:

---

35. *OR* 47, 1:31.

HDQRS. MILITARY DIVISION OF THE MISSIS-
SIPPI,
Raleigh, N. C., April 15, 1865,
General U.S. GRANT and SECRETARY OF WAR:
(Care of General Easton, New Berne or Morehead.)

I send copies of a correspondence begun with General
Johnston, which, I think, will be followed by terms of
capitulation.* I will accept the same terms as General
Grant gave General Lee, and be careful not to complicate
any points of civil policy. If any cavalry have started
toward me caution them that they must be prepared to
find our work done. It is now raining in torrents, and I
shall await General Johnston's reply here, and will
propose to meet him in person at Chapel Hill. I have
invited Governor Vance to return to Raleigh with the civil
officers of his State. I have met ex-Governor Graham, Mr.
Badger, Moore, Holden, and others, all of whom agree
that the war is over, and that the States of the South must
resume their allegiance, subject to the Constitution and
laws of Congress, and that the military power of the
South must submit to the national arms. This great fact
once admitted, all the details are easy of arrangement.

W. T. SHERMAN,
Major-General.[36]

In the meantime, Capt. Rawlins Lowndes, of Hampton's staff, who
carried the letter to Kilpatrick's headquarters, sat and waited for a
response for nearly eight hours. Lowndes struck up a conversation
with Kilpatrick, who was in a foul mood. Kilpatrick complained that
the attack on his camp at Monroe's Crossroads reflected unfairly upon
him, and he suggested that another battle where his troopers were not
caught by surprise might have a different outcome.

Lowndes replied, "Well, General, I will make you the following
proposition, and I will pledge myself that General Hampton will carry
it out in every respect. You, with your staff, take fifteen hundred men,
and General Hampton, with his staff, will meet you with a thousand
men, all to be armed with the saber alone. The two parties will be
drawn up mounted in regimental formations, opposite to each other,
and at a signal to be agreed upon will charge. That will settle the
question which are the best men." Kilpatrick thanked Lowndes for the
offer but turned it down. Just before leaving, Lowndes repeated the
offer. Kilpatrick again demurred.[37]

---

36. Ibid., 3:208.
37. Edward L. Wells, *Hampton and His Cavalry in '64* (Richmond, VA: B. F.
     Johnson Publishing, 1899), 423; Wiley C. Howard, *Sketch of Cobb Legion*

Determined to put arrangements in place in case Johnston did not surrender, Sherman also sent the following correspondence to his cavalry commander, Kilpatrick:

> HDQRS. MILITARY DIVISION OF THE MISSIS-SIPPI,
> In the Field, Raleigh, April 16, 1865.
> General KILPATRICK,
> Durhams:
> GENERAL:
>
> I have faith in General Johnston's personal sincerity, and do not believe he would use a subterfuge to cover his movements. He could not stop the movement of his troops till he got my letter, which I hear was delayed all day yesterday by your adjutant's not sending it forward. If he gains on us by this time lost we will make up at the expense of North Carolina. Major McCoy will be with you and will receive Johnston's letter, and I will instruct him to open it and send me contents. My orders are for all to be ready to move.
>
> Yesterday the roads were impassable to trains, but if the weather be favorable they will be good to-morrow.
> W. T. SHERMAN,
> Major-General.[38]

The news that Sherman and Johnston were going to meet to discuss an end to the war was warmly received at Sherman's headquarters. "'After so much,' as the President says, it is needless to say that we look for no more fighting hereabouts," an elated Maj. Henry Hitchcock reported on April 15. "Thank God that at the end of all this strife and bloodshed does at least appear,--and that it will be the end, when it does come, and not a mere armed truce. Terrible as the cost has been, the price had to be paid, and it was worth paying."[39]

The news spread rapidly. Cheer after cheer went up among Sherman's troops. The commander of the 68th Ohio, Lt. Col. George E. Welles, gathered his men around him. When they fell silent, Welles said, "Comrades, Johnston has sent in word that he would like to know the terms of surrender." Loud, prolonged cheering burst out among the Buckeye soldiers. One soldier exclaimed, "The victory for which many had hoped and prayed was almost within our reach; h-u-r-

Cavalry and Some Incidents and Scenes Remembered (Atlanta: Atlanta Camp, United Confederate Veterans, 1901), 19.
38. *OR* 47, 3:221.
39. Howe, *Marching with Sherman*, 299-300.

JAMES BENNETT'S HOUSE, ... JOHNST... RENDERED TO SHERMAN—EXTERIOR VIEW.—[Sketched by Davis.]

The Bennett house and grounds as they appeared in April 1865.
(Harper's Weekly)

r-a-h!"[40]

Sherman was confident that the end had indeed come. After sending the telegram to Kilpatrick agreeing to meet with Johnston on April 17, Sherman turned to his adjutant, Hitchcock, and said that "the war is over—occupation's gone!" All believed that the terms would be set the next day, but the men expected that they would match the terms Grant gave to Lee.[41]

Celebrations continued that morning, and a soldier of the 17th Corps recalled that there was quite a bit of cheering. "The cheering seemed to have some regularity about it," he recalled. "One regiment would break forth into joy, then another, and another. This betokened good news, each regiment cheering as the tidings were announced to them." Soon his colonel rode over and beckoned to his command, which eagerly crowded around him. "When we had crowded ourselves into the smallest possible space and got still, the colonel said: 'Boys, Johnston has sent in word that he would like to agree upon terms of surrender; and so we have been halted. It is very likely that our chase after General Joe Johnston is at an end.' And then we shouted; we whooped and hurrahed with all our might, and acted our joy to the best of our ability."[42]

40. Loop, *The Long Road Home*, 204.
41. Howe, *Marching with Sherman*, 302.
42. *Story of the Service of Company E*, 426-427.

In the meantime, Johnston set his troops in motion away from Raleigh and toward Greensboro. He left Greensboro on the night of April 13 and rejoined his army at Hillsborough the following morning. Sherman's response made its way to Johnston. "Supposing that the President was waiting in Greensboro to open negotiations should the armistice be agreed upon, I hastened there to show General Sherman's reply, and to receive any instructions he might have to give," Johnston remembered. Davis, however, was on his way to Charlotte, North Carolina, and unavailable for consultations.[43]

However, a courier sent by Johnston located Davis and announced to the Confederate president "that General Sherman had agreed to a conference, and asking that the Secretary of War, General J. C. Breckinridge, should return to cooperate in it. The application as complied with, and the Postmaster-General, John H. Reagan, also went at my request." Davis and his remaining cabinet members continued on to Charlotte and established their headquarters. They awaited news of Johnston's efforts.[44]

Johnston then telegraphed Hampton to instruct the cavalryman to arrange for the time and place for his meeting with Sherman. Afterward, he rode for his cavalry chief's headquarters two or three miles southeast of Hillsborough. Upon his arrival, Hampton advised Johnston that the meeting would occur at noon the next day at a house on the road to Raleigh near Durham Station, midway between the pickets of the two armies.[45]

That nondescript small wooden house, owned by James Bennett, was about to host two remarkable men determined to undertake remarkable deeds.

---

43. Johnston, *Narrative of Military Operations*, 401.
44. Davis, *The Rise and Fall of the Confederate Government*, 2:683.
45. Johnston, *Narrative of Military Operations*, 401-402.

CHAPTER THREE

APRIL 17, 1865:
THE FIRST MEETING BETWEEN
SHERMAN AND JOHNSTON

In April 1865, Durham, North Carolina, vastly differed from the sprawling metropolitan area that it is today. The North Carolina Railroad connected the state capital, Raleigh, and Hillsborough, North Carolina, and the wood-burning steam locomotives had to stop frequently for wood and water. The railroad required a depot somewhere between Raleigh and Hillsborough, so the Durham area was a prime pit stop. Local businessman Bartlett S. Durham donated land for the construction of a railroad depot in 1849.

"This place was called Durham's Station in honor of a venerable townsman, Dr. B. L. Durham. Ordinarily, about two hundred people resided at this little station. But on this memorable spring day thousands of men swarmed the woods in this vicinity," a local resident recalled about the day Maj. Gen. William T. Sherman and Gen. Joseph E. Johnston met. "General Sherman's army campt just to the south of the station and General Johnston's about three and one half miles west, at the Bennett Place. Soldiers from both sides met at Durham Station and had a genuinely good time." Part of that "genuinely good time" included ransacking a local house filled with smoking tobacco.[1]

Sherman awoke ebullient on April 17, anticipating the end of the war and returning to his family. He had breakfast and then proceeded

---

1. R. McCants Andrews, *John Merrick: A Biographical Sketch* (Durham, NC: The Seeman Printery, 1920), 29. John R. Green owned the house full of tobacco. The soldiers who had helped themselves to the tobacco took it around the country and became quite fond of it. "Thus it happened that the railroad agent, postmaster, and other officials around this little 'burg began to receive letters from various places, asking for more of that Durham tobacco. Mr. Green was quick to see his opportunity and accordingly began to manufacture more tobacco and call it 'Durham Bull Smoking Tobacco.'" Ibid., 29. Durham grew up around the train depot. For an early history of Durham's development, including the story of Durham Bull Smoking Tobacco, see William Kenneth Boyd, *The Story of Durham: City of the New South* (Durham, NC: Duke University Press, 1925).

to the North Carolina Railroad depot in Raleigh for the short trip to Durham Station. As Sherman prepared to board, the station's telegraph operator emerged from his office to inform Sherman that he had received an important cipher dispatch for the army commander. Sherman ordered the train held for nearly an hour while he waited for the dispatch to be deciphered. When the message was finally ready, the content was shocking:

> **Major-General Sherman,**
> **Commanding:**
>
> **President Lincoln was murdered about 10 o'clock last night in his private box at Ford's Theater in this city, by an assassin who shot him through the head with a pistol ball. About the same hour Mr. Seward's house was entered by another assassin, who stabbed the Secretary in several places, but it is thought he may possibly recover; but his son Frederick will probably die of wounds received from the assassin. The assassin of the President leaped from the box, brandishing a dagger, exclaiming, Sic semper tyrannis! and that now Virginia was revenged. Mr. Lincoln fell senseless from his seat, and continued in that state until twenty-two minutes after 7 o'clock, at which time he breathed his last. General Grant was published to be at the theater, but fortunately did not go. Vice-President Johnson now becomes President, and will take the oath of office and assume the duties today.**
>
> **I have no time to add more than to say that I find evidence that an assassin is also on your track, and I beseech you to be more heedful than Mr. Lincoln was of such knowledge.**
>
> **Edwin M. Stanton,**
> **Secretary of War**[2]

This incomprehensible announcement staggered Sherman.[3] The army commander keenly remembered his meeting with President Abraham Lincoln at City Point, Virginia, just two weeks earlier. "Dreading the effect of such a message at that critical instant of time, I asked the operator if anyone besides himself had seen it; he answered no. I then bade him not to reveal the contents by word or look till I came back, which I proposed to do the same afternoon," Sherman

---

2. *OR* 47, 3:220-221.
3. Major General Oliver Otis Howard, who accompanied Sherman that day, recalled, "Sherman was greatly startled" by the news of Lincoln's assassination. Oliver O. Howard, *Autobiography of Oliver Otis Howard*, 2 vols. (New York: Baker & Taylor Co., 1907), 2:155.

recounted. "The train then started, and, as we passed Morris's Station, General [John] Logan, commanding the Fifteenth Corps, came into my car, and I told him I wanted to see him on my return, as I had something very important to communicate. He knew I was going to meet General Johnston, and volunteered to say that he hoped I would succeed in obtaining his surrender, as the whole army dreaded the long march to Charlotte (one hundred and seventy-five miles), already begun, but which had been interrupted by the receipt of General Johnston's letter of the 13th."[4]

The train covered the 26 miles to Durham Station and arrived at about 10:00 a.m. Sherman's cavalry chief, Bvt. Maj. Gen. Judson Kilpatrick, or "Little Kil" as the men knew him, awaited the commander's arrival with a squadron of cavalry drawn up as an escort.[5] The two generals entered a house where Kilpatrick established his headquarters and chatted until horses could be brought up. Once the horses arrived, Sherman and his staff mounted, and the column moved out, with one Union trooper leading the way with a white flag

4. Sherman, *Memoirs*, 2:348.
5. Hugh Judson Kilpatrick, the son of a farmer, was born near Deckertown, New Jersey, on January 14, 1836. Kilpatrick received minimal formal education in the local schools, but he was appointed to the U.S. Military Academy in 1856 and graduated in the May 1861 class (because of the outbreak of the Civil War, the class of 1862 graduated early, in June 1861). He joined the 5th New York Infantry on May 9, 1861, and was wounded in the Battle of Big Bethel in June; Kilpatrick was the first West Point-trained Union officer to be wounded in battle. In September 1861, he was commissioned as a lieutenant colonel in the 2nd New York Cavalry. In 1862, he was briefly imprisoned in the Old Capitol Prison, in Washington, D.C., for conduct unbecoming of an officer. Kilpatrick was promoted to colonel while imprisoned and assumed his post upon his release. In the spring of 1863, he was assigned to command a brigade of the Army of the Potomac's Cavalry Corps, where he performed well. In June 1863, he was promoted to brigadier general, and at the end of the month, Kilpatrick was assigned to command the Army of the Potomac's Third Cavalry Division. By this time, he had earned the unflattering nickname "Kill Cavalry" because of his penchant for using up men and horses; he was known as an overly ambitious, vain, and licentious young man. The general believed that if he found glory in the Civil War, then the White House awaited him, and he was determined to find that glory. Seeking fame, Kilpatrick came up with the idea of leading a raid on Richmond, Virginia, in February 1864, with the intent to free Union prisoners of war, to kidnap and assassinate Confederate President Jefferson Davis and his cabinet, and to burn the city. The expedition failed miserably, at least in part because Kilpatrick lost his nerve; Maj. Gen. Wade Hampton's cavalry defeated him near Atlee's Station on the Virginia Central Railroad. When Col. Ulric Dahlgren, his second-in-command, was killed in action and the true plans were discovered, Kilpatrick disavowed the expedition's real objective. He was then transferred to Sherman's command, prompting Sherman to say, "I know that Kilpatrick is a hell of a damned fool, but I want just that sort of man to command my cavalry in this expedition." Kilpatrick's performance was spotty, and Sherman seems to have lost faith in him during the course of

of truce in hand. "As General Sherman rode past his picket lines upon that sunny spring morning, the ear was not pained by the moans and cries of mangled men, but the fresh breeze came laden with the fragrance of the pines, of apple blossoms, of lilacs, roses, and violets," Sherman's adjutant, Maj. George W. Nichols, recalled. "The eye rested upon a thousand forms of beauty; for the rains and warm sun had quickened into life countless buds and flowering plants, until the hillsides, and glens and bushes were brilliant in their robes of delicate green." Nichols concluded, "The scene was symbolic of the new era of peace then just beginning to dawn upon the nation."[6]

After covering about five miles, the trooper carrying the flag of truce spotted another flag of truce approaching from the opposite direction. The two flag bearers met, and the Confederate horseman told Sherman's rider that Johnston was nearby. Hearing this news, Sherman and Kilpatrick rode forward and met Johnston, who rode alongside his cavalry commander, Lt. Gen. Wade Hampton.

Thus, as one of Sherman's staff officers noted, "two great men came together in the heart of North Carolina, intent, with true

Sherman and Johnston meet for the first time.
(Frank Leslie's Illustrated Newspaper)

the Carolinas Campaign. Between the Eastern and Western Theaters, Kilpatrick and Hampton tangled many times on many different fields and were familiar adversaries. Warner, *Generals in Blue*, 266-267. Only one full-length biography about Kilpatrick is available, and it is largely unsatisfactory. See Samuel J. Martin, *Kill-Cavalry: Sherman's Merchant of Terror: The Life of Union General Hugh Judson Kilpatrick* (Madison, NJ: Fairleigh-Dickinson University Press, 1996).

6. Nichols, *The Great March*, 310.

nobility of soul and in the highest interest of humanity, upon putting a stop to the needless sacrifice of life."[7]

The two generals shook hands, asked about mutual acquaintances, and introduced their respective staffs, although neither Hampton nor Sherman wanted to meet due to Hampton's ongoing bitterness about being wrongfully blamed for the burning of Columbia, South Carolina. Sherman then asked Johnston if there was someplace where they could talk in private. Johnston mentioned that he had passed a small farmhouse a short distance back, and the two opposing army commanders rode side by side toward it, their staffs and escorts following behind.

As one of Johnston's staff officers recalled, Hampton's horse became "fractious" during the introductions and refused to heed Hampton's commands. By the time Hampton had his steed under control, Sherman and Johnston had gone inside James Bennett's house. The staff officer suggested that Hampton, known for being a superb horseman, had prodded the horse to misbehave in order to give him an excuse not to shake Sherman's hand.[8]

"We had never met before, though we had been in the regular army together for thirteen years; but it so happened that we had never before come together. He was some twelve or more years my senior; but we knew enough of each other to be well acquainted at once," Sherman said about his relationship with Johnston.

A correspondent of the *New York Herald* described the appearance of the two generals. "General Sherman, with his coat unbuttoned, his hands in his pockets and smoking his cigar, was quite cheerful and at his ease, having the air of one who felt himself indubitably 'master of the situation.' General Johnston, with his coat carefully buttoned up, his uniform new, and looking every inch the soldier, appeared quite haggard and careworn. It was unquestionably a very unpleasant duty he was performing, and weighed heavily upon him."[9]

"I had a good opportunity to observe Generals Johnston and Wade Hampton," a cavalryman serving as one of Sherman's orderlies recalled. "They were both in full dress uniforms of gray cloth. Johnston was a full general and his badge of rank was three stars in a row, on each end of his coat collar."[10]

---

7. Ibid.
8. John Johnson, "An Incident Under the White Flag," Joseph E. Johnston Papers, American Civil War Museum, Richmond, Virginia.
9. "Mr. O. F. Howe's Dispatches," *New York Herald*, April 27, 1865.
10. Arthur O. Granger, "The 'Fifteenth' at General Joe Johnston's Surrender," included in Charles H. Kirk, ed., *History of the Fifteenth Pennsylvania Volunteer Cavalry* (Philadelphia: Historical Committee of the Society of the Fifteenth Pennsylvania Cavalry, 1906), 593-594.

Hampton, in particular, cut a striking figure.[11] The physically imposing Confederate cavalry chief normally carried a long broadsword. Instead, this day, he carried a switch. Maj. Henry Hitchcock noted that Hampton's "whole demeanor was marked with the easy 'well-bred' essentially vulgar insolence which is characteristic of that type of 'gentleman', a man of polished manners, scarcely veiling the utter arrogance and selfishness which marks his class, and which I hate with a perfect hatred. There is nothing of the true man in such a

11. Wade Hampton III, reputedly was the wealthiest man in the antebellum South. Born in Charleston, South Carolina, on March 28, 1818, he was the scion of one of the richest families in the South. Hampton was a big man, standing about six feet, three inches tall, and weighing about 240 pounds. Strong, brave, and virile, Hampton was proud of hunting and killing bears armed with only a knife. He was credited with killing 13 Yankees in hand-to-hand combat during the Civil War. After graduating from South Carolina College (now the University of South Carolina) in 1836, Hampton managed the family's vast landholdings in South Carolina and Mississippi. He also served in both houses of the South Carolina state legislature between 1852 and 1861. He initially opposed secession, but once South Carolina left the Union, Hampton embraced the Confederate cause. He raised and equipped, by himself and at his own expense, the Hampton Legion, which included six companies of infantry, four companies of cavalry, and a battery of artillery. Hampton was slightly wounded on Henry House Hill, in Virginia, at the First Battle of Bull Run in 1861. When he returned to duty, he was promoted to brigadier general and assigned to command an infantry brigade. On May 31, 1862, he was severely wounded in the Battle of Seven Pines in Virginia. After recovering, Hampton was assigned to command a brigade of cavalry. In September 1863, he was promoted to major general after receiving two serious wounds on East Cavalry Field at the Battle of Gettysburg, in Pennsylvania, on July 3, 1863. Then Hampton was assigned to command a division. After J. E. B. Stuart's death in May 1864, Hampton was assigned to command the Army of Northern Virginia's Cavalry Corps, a position he held until February 1865. When it became obvious that Hampton's native South Carolina was squarely in Sherman's crosshairs, Hampton requested to be transferred to defend his home state. His request was granted, which created a problem. Hampton was junior to Maj. Gen. Joseph Wheeler who commanded a Confederate cavalry corps and refused to serve under the much younger man. To solve the problem, Hampton was promoted to lieutenant general, becoming the highest-ranking cavalry officer in the Confederacy's history. He performed well during the Carolinas Campaign and designed Johnston's battle plan at Bentonville. Despite his successes, Hampton was angry and bitter. His brother Lt. Col. Frank Hampton was mortally wounded in combat at the Battle of Brandy Station, in Virginia, on June 9, 1863. In the fall of 1864, his son Wade Hampton IV was badly wounded in battle near Petersburg, Virginia, and when his other son Preston Hampton, a staff officer, tried to rescue Wade, he was mortally wounded. Worsening matters, Sherman's troops burned Hampton's beautiful plantation home, Millwood, to the ground. And he remained especially bitter about being blamed for the burning of Columbia, South Carolina. Jeffry D. Wert, "Wade Hampton," *The Confederate General*, 3:50-53. For the best full-length biography of Hampton, see Rod Andrew, Jr., *Wade Hampton: Confederate Warrior to Southern Redeemer* (Chapel Hill: University of North Carolina Press, 2009).

'gentleman', their external polish and tact, their knowledge of the world, their easy self-possession...count for just as much as the glitter of paste diamonds and not much more."[12]

"Wade Hampton, a large and powerful man, gave but little opportunity for a critical examination of the graces of his person...either nature or his tailor, or both, gave him an appearance of vulgarity and clumsiness...Hampton's face...seemed bold even beyond arrogance, and this expression was, if possible, intensified by the boastful fanfaronade which he continued during the whole period of the conference," Maj. George W. Nichols, who served alongside Hitchcock as one of Sherman's adjutants.[13] Despite the fact this meeting was for the purpose of treating for peace, there was, nevertheless, a hint of trouble in the air.

The commanders soon reached James Bennett's small wood-framed house.[14] One of Sherman's staff officers remembered it as "a plain, one storied frame, with, apparently, but one room, that in which the conference was held—the out-house, or kitchen detached, after the North Carolina style, and built of logs."[15]

"It is a small and unpretentious country dwelling, with only two rooms, and a small allowance of windows in each room. The house, however, was scrupulously neat, the floors scrubbed to a milky whiteness, the bed in one room very neatly made up, and the few articles of furniture in the room arranged with neatness and taste. The grounds were ornamented with a few flowers and a little shrubbery," another Union soldier observed. "Opposite the house is a fine oak tree casting a broad shadow; and other trees about the premises had been trimmed by the Rebel officers and soldiers to give them an inviting appearance."[16] The small house belied the fact that Bennett owned and farmed more than 300 acres and that he was a middle-class farmer.[17]

---

12. Howe, *Marching with Sherman*, 310-311.
13. Nichols, *The Great March*, 311.
14. Johnston's staff officer Maj. John Johnson claimed that by the time the flags of truce came together, Sherman's staff had already chosen Henry Neal's house, about half a mile away, as the meeting site. Johnston thought that the Bennett house was a better location, and Sherman agreed. Thus, history arrived at James Bennett's door. Johnson, "An Incident Under the White Flag."
15. George W. Pepper, *Personal Recollections of Sherman's Campaigns in Georgia and the Carolinas* (Zanesville, OH: Hugh Dunne, 1866), 415.
16. Edmund M. Hatcher, *The Last Four Weeks of the War* (Columbus, OH: Edmund N. Hatcher, 1891), 300-301.
17. Richard R. Sacchi and Terry H. Erlandson, "An Intensive Archaeological Survey of the Bennett Place," 12, North Carolina Collection, Wilson Library, University of North Carolina, Chapel Hill, North Carolina.

The two generals dismounted and handed their horses off to order-lies. Their officers also dismounted and entered the yard. Sherman and Johnston asked Bennett if they could use his house for a few minutes to speak in private. After agreeing, Bennett and his wife, Nancy, excused themselves and went to their summer kitchen, where they would wait for the generals to finish their meeting.[18]

"There was little cordiality, especially on the part of the rebel officers," *New York Herald* correspondent O. F. Howe noted. "They kept to themselves, for the most part, and seemed little inclined to exchange civilities. Our officers had provided themselves with cigars, wine, and other creature comforts, which they freely offered to their rebel friends, but they were generally declined, and often with an air of haughtiness almost insulting."[19]

Not everyone remembered it that way. "I conversed with several Union officers," Maj. John Johnson, an engineer officer on Johnston's staff, said, which included "Majors Nichols, Hitchcock, Col. [Orlando M.] Poe, Chf. Eng. of Sherman's Army."[20] A Confederate cavalryman recalled that Maj. Gens. Matthew C. Butler and O. O. Howard "sat on stick chairs in the front yard," discussing "politics and the war."[21]

Colonel J. Fred Waring, of the Jeff Davis Cavalry Legion of Mississippi and the Confederate cavalry escort commander that day, engaged Maj. Llewellyn G. Estes, Kilpatrick's assistant adjutant general, in conversation. To his great surprise, Waring found Estes to be "a pleasant, civil gentleman. I was treated civilly by all the officers I met.

---

18. Sherman, *Memoirs*, 2:348-349. Some evidence exists that the Bennett family's last name was actually spelled "Bennitt" and that it had changed throughout the years. James and Nancy Bennett were yeoman farmers who owned small acreage, worked their land themselves, and made money through sewing, making and repairing tools, and other similar skills. The Bennetts were not slave owners. They had three children named Lorenzo Leigh, Eliza Ann, and Alphonzo Jackson. Lorenzo served in the 27th North Carolina Infantry and died of typhoid fever at a Confederate military hospital in Winchester, Virginia. Alphonzo also died in 1862, but he was not a soldier. Like so many other American families, the Bennetts suffered because of the Civil War. After James died in 1878, Nancy lost the farm. James and Nancy were likely buried somewhere on the property, but nobody knows the precise location of their graves. "A Brief History of the Bennett Family," http://www.bennettplacehistoricsite.com/history/bennett-family/ .
19. "Mr. O. F. Howe's Dispatches."
20. John Johnson diary, entry for April 17, 1865, John Johnson Family Papers, Special Collections, Perkins Library, Duke University, Durham, North Carolina.
21. John Witherspoon DuBose, *General Joseph Wheeler and the Army of Tennessee* (New York: Neale Publishing Co., 1912), 461.

Col. J. Frederick Waring, commander of the Jeff Davis Legion Cavalry of Georgia.

(Georgia Historical Society)

We recalled our fights in Virginia." Estes agreed with Waring's point of view, adding that "it seemed like meeting old friends." Waring actually found Estes's warmth a bit unsettling. "Queer expression for a man who is ready to cut my throat when we next meet on the field," the colonel mentioned. "But he is a good fellow, if he is an enemy."[22]

Describing Hampton's staff, Capt. George W. Pepper of the 80th Ohio noted, "I liked the look of Captain [Rawlins] Loundes, who, together with Colonel Waring—a very wide awake and withy little officer—like sensible gentlemen, for the occasion at least, appropriately set aside hostility and reserve, and partook of the courtesies of the conference."[23]

There was quite a contrast in the appearance of the opposing groups of cavalrymen. "The Yanks were in splendid and handsome uniforms of blue," a Confederate horsemen said, and "the 'Johnny Rebs' in torn and sodden suits of gray."[24]

Once the two generals entered the house, Sherman showed Johnston the dispatch announcing Lincoln's assassination, watching his rival's reaction closely. "The perspiration came out in large drops on his forehead, and he did not attempt to conceal his distress," Sherman recalled. "He denounced the act as a disgrace to the age, and hoped I did not charge it to the Confederate Government. I told him I could not believe that he or General Lee, or the officers of the Confederate army, could possibly be privy to acts of assassination; but I would not say as much for Jeff. Davis, George Sanders, and men of that stripe. We talked about the effect of this act on the country at large and on the armies, and he realized that it made my situation extremely delicate. I explained to him that I had not yet revealed the news to my own personal staff or to the army, and that I dreaded the effect when made

22. *Diary of J. Frederick Waring*, entry for April 17, 1865, J. Frederick Waring Papers, Southern Historical Collections, Wilson Library, University of North Carolina, Chapel Hill, North Carolina.
23. Pepper, *Personal Recollections of Sherman's Campaigns*, 409.
24. U. R. Brooks, *Butler and His Cavalry in the War of Secession 1861-1865* (Columbia, SC: The State Company, 1899), 289.

known in Raleigh. Mr. Lincoln was peculiarly endeared to the soldiers, and I feared that some foolish woman or man in Raleigh might say something or do something that would madden our men, and that a fate worse than that of Columbia would befall the place."[25] Johnston told Sherman that, in his opinion, Lincoln's assassination "was the greatest possible calamity to the South."[26]

While waiting for the generals to complete their business, Hampton and his son, Lt. Wade Hampton IV, lounged on a carpenter's bench outside the Bennett house. The elder Hampton wore his best uniform, topped by a black felt hat adorned with a gold braid.

Hampton's escort also remained aloof. A Federal trooper offered to hold the horse of a member of Hampton's staff, but he was told that no damned Yankee could hold that horse. The staffer sniffed and said that his horse could not be trusted with a Yankee, because they were all horse thieves. Some of the Confederate soldiers' suspicions lingered about the opposing party. A Union horse soldier offered Hampton's orderly coffee, but the orderly made the Federal taste it first before he would drink it.[27]

Determined to end the fraternizing between his men and the Unionists, Hampton snarled, "Fall in!" When Kilpatrick approached to protest, one witness remembered, "Wade Hampton looked savage enough to eat 'Little Kil'," which prompted his antagonist to return "his looks most defiantly."[28]

"The war is over," Kilpatrick proclaimed to his old adversary. "Let the men fraternize."[29]

"I do not intend to surrender," Hampton snapped. He added that he would never fraternize with the Yankees "but would retaliate with torch and sword" to avenge the style of war the North had waged.[30] With a stern tone, Hampton again snarled at his troopers, "Fall in!"

"General Hampton, you compel me to remind you that you have no authority here," Kilpatrick shot back.

The South Carolinian, his words dripping with disdain, replied, "Permit me, sir, to remind you that Napoleon said that any general who would permit him to be surprised is a very poor soldier, and I surprised you [at Monroe's Crossroads]."

25. Sherman, *Memoirs*, 2:349.
26. Johnston, *Narrative of Military Operations* 402.
27. Brooks, *Butler and His Cavalry*, 289.
28. "Mr. O. F. Howe's Dispatches".
29. *Sussex Independent*, January 13, 1882.
30. "North Carolina—Sherman and Johnston," *Philadelphia Inquirer*, April 28, 1865.

Hampton and Kilpatrick arguing outside the Bennett House on April 17, 1865.

(*Frank Leslie's Illustrated Newspaper*)

"Yes, but what did Napoleon say of one general who after having surprised another, allowed himself to be whipped by his opposite in his shirt and drawers," Little Kil sneered in return. And so, the two old horse soldiers began refighting their campaigns.[31]

"Well, General, down yonder in Linch's Creek, I gave you a splendid entertainment, but you were too strong for me," Kilpatrick teased his adversary by referring to an incident that happened in February in South Carolina.

"When and where?" Hampton demanded.

"Oh, when I was after your wagon train and fought your cavalry and a regiment of infantry," Kilpatrick replied.

Hampton laughed. "Beg pardon, General, allow me to introduce you to Col. Gib Wright who was in command that day with one regiment of cavalry and twenty dismounted men."[32] With that, barbs really began to fly.

The longer the argument lasted, the more heated and louder it became. "I have heard of your promise to pursue me to the death, General Kilpatrick," an angry Hampton exclaimed. "I only wish to say

31. David P. Conyngham, *Sherman's March Across the South with Sketches and Incidents of the Campaign* (New York: Sheldan & Co., 1865), 365.
32. J. W. Evans, "Reminiscences of J. W. Evans in the War Between the States," included in *Confederate Reminiscences and Letters 1861-1865*, vol. 10 (Atlanta: Georgia Division, United Daughters of the Confederacy, 1999), 22. Hampton referred to Col. Gilbert J. "Gib" Wright, the commander of the Cobb Legion Cavalry of Georgia.

that you will not have to pursue far."

"Well, I'll go where I'm sent," Kilpatrick retorted.

"Oh? You sometimes go where you are not sent?" Hampton retorted, prompting some nearby Federals to chuckle at the reference to Kilpatrick's hasty retreat into the swamp at Monroe's Crossroads.

"You refer to the time you surprised me near Fayetteville?"

"Yes," Hampton answered. "A general surprised is a general disgraced."

"That happened once. It will never happen again," Kilpatrick stated.

"This is the second time. Remember Atlee's Station?" Hampton taunted, referring to a fight during Kilpatrick's aborted February 1864 raid on Richmond, Virginia. "General

Col. Gilbert J. "Gib" Wright of the Phillips Legion Cavalry of Georgia, who commanded Young's Brigade of Butler's Division.

(Georgia Historical Society)

Kilpatrick, when I look at men like you, I feel like Wellington, who said under the circumstances, I thank God for my belief in a hell." The assembled crowd exploded in laughter, which only caused Kilpatrick's already simmering anger to boil.[33]

When one of Kilpatrick's taunts finally drew Hampton's ire, the big Confederate rose from the carpenter's bench, loomed dangerously over his diminutive adversary, and proclaimed, "Well, you never ran me out of Headquarters in my stocking feet!" A Northern horse soldier who overheard the exchange observed that Hampton's retort "was a home thrust and too true to be funny."

Anger clouded Kilpatrick's ruddy face. The Union commander replied that Hampton had to leave faster than he came, and then "words grew hot" with "both parties expressing a desire that the issue of the war should be left between the cavalry." By this time, their row had grown quite loud, such that Sherman and Johnston had to interrupt their discussion to separate the two cavalrymen.[34] "These

33. Memorandum of conversation with Wade Hampton, October 5, 1895, Bradley T. Johnson Papers, Special Collections, Perkins Library, Duke University, Durham, North Carolina.
34. Henry B. McClellan, "The Campaign of 1863—A Reply to Kilpatrick," *Philadelphia Weekly Times*, February 7, 1880.

gentlemen parted with no increased love for each other," a newspaper correspondent, who witnessed the episode, humorously noted.[35] Another observer said that once Sherman and Johnston separated their cavalry commanders, "the conference went on pleasantly enough."[36]

Returning to their conference, Sherman told Johnston that he must be convinced that the Confederate general could not oppose his army, and that, since Gen. Robert E. Lee had surrendered to Gen. Ulysses S. Grant, Johnston could do the same without dishonor. Johnston "plainly and repeatedly admitted this," and he indicated that any further fighting would be equivalent to murder. Johnston then stated that rather than simply surrendering his command piecemeal, they might instead craft terms that would encompass all remaining Confederate armies. Sherman asked whether Johnston could control armies other than his own, to which the Virginian indicated that he could obtain authority to do so from Confederate President Jefferson Davis. Sherman offered that he had recently had an interview with Lincoln and Grant and thought he understood what Lincoln had in mind for the end of the war and the Union's reconstruction—"that with them and the people North there seemed to be no vindictive feeling against the Confederate armies, but there was against Davis and his political adherents; and that the terms that General Grant had given to General Lee's army were certainly most generous and liberal."[37]

Johnston acknowledged that all of this was true, but he kept returning to the idea that he could arrange for the surrender of Lt. Gen. Richard Taylor's forces in Louisiana and the forces under the command of Lt. Gen. Nathan Bedford Forrest and several others in Alabama. "Our conversation was very general and extremely cordial, satisfying me that it could have but one result, and that which we all desired, viz., to end the war as quickly as possible; and, being anxious to return to Raleigh before the news of Mr. Lincoln's assassination could be divulged, on General Johnston's saying that he thought that, during the night, he could procure authority to act in the name of all the Confederate armies in existence, we agreed to meet again the next day at noon at the same place, and parted, he for Hillsboro and I for Raleigh," Sherman recalled.[38] They adjourned after about two hours of earnest conversation in order to give Johnston sufficient time to

---

35. "Mr. E. D. Wesftall's Dispatch," *New York Herald*, April 27, 1865.
36. Conyngham, *Sherman's March Across the South*, 365.
37. Ibid., 349-350. This is a subtle distinction lost on many: politicians brought on the war, and the soldiers fought it. The politicians would have to be part of the process of ending it.
38. Ibid., 350.

communicate with Davis and to permit Sherman to return to his headquarters in Raleigh before word of Lincoln's assassination spread.[39]

When he wrote his after-action report of the final campaign, Sherman respectfully observed that this first meeting with Johnston was "frank and soldier-like."[40]

Johnston and Sherman agreed to meet again at the Bennett house the following day at the same time, noon. Due to the tension between Kilpatrick and Hampton, a newspaper correspondent noted that the parting of the staffs of the two army commanders "was consequently very cool and distant."[41] Watching the two generals mount and ride off, the men wondered what momentous events had transpired inside James Bennett's humble little house. "'What was the result?' each inquired of the other, returning; for nothing could be gathered from the secret face of Sherman," Captain Pepper recalled.[42]

Despite Sherman's best efforts, word of Lincoln's assassination had already spread by the time he arrived in Raleigh. Angry soldiers awaited his arrival at the depot, shouting, "Don't let Johnston surrender! Don't let the Rebels surrender!"[43] A captain of the 103rd Illinois recorded in his diary, "The Army is crazy for vengeance. If we make another campaign it will be an awful one...We hope Johnston will not surrender. God pity this country if he retreats or fights us."[44]

An Ohioan stated that the news of Lincoln's assassination "spread like wildfire, and we were plunged into a moment from the pinnacle of rejoicing to the lowest depths of grief. To every soldier Lincoln's death came as a sore, personal bereavement. For a time we were dazed, then the fountains of the great deep were broken up and hundreds of those bronzed veterans wept like children. It was darkness at noontide. Even the people of the south felt that they had lost a friend."[45]

When Sherman arrived back at his headquarters he told Logan and the other officers the terrible news about Lincoln's assassination. Concerned that his enraged soldiers would blame the civilian population for John Wilkes Booth's despicable act, Sherman instructed

39. "North Carolina—Johnston and Sherman."
40. *OR* 47, 1:32.
41. "North Carolina—Johnston and Sherman."
42. Pepper, *Personal Recollections*, 412.
43. Manning F. Force to a Mr. Kebler, April 18, 1865, Manning F. Force Papers, Special Collections, University of Washington Libraries, Seattle, Washington.
44. Charles W. Wills, *Army Life of an Illinois Soldier* (Washington, DC: Globe Printing Co., 1906), 371.
45. Stewart, *Dan McCook's Regiment*, 170.

his subordinates to watch their men carefully to prevent violent retaliation.[46]

Then Sherman composed and published the following order to his army:

> **Special Field Orders, No. 56**
> **Headquarters Military Division of the Mississippi**
>
> The General commanding announces, with pain and sorrow, that on the evening of the 14th instant, at the theatre in Washington city, his Excellency the President of the United States, Mr. Lincoln, was assassinated by one who uttered the State motto of Virginia. At the same time, the Secretary of State, Mr. Seward, while suffering from a broken arm, was also stabbed by another murderer in his own house, but still survives, and his son was wounded, supposed fatally. It is believed, by persons capable of judging, that other high officers were designed to share the same fate. Thus it seems that our enemy, despairing of meeting us in open, manly warfare, begins to resort to the assassin's tools.
>
> Your general does not wish you to infer that this is universal, for he knows that the great mass of the Confederate army would scorn to sanction such acts, but he believes it the legitimate consequence of rebellion against rightful authority.
>
> We have met every phase which this war has assumed, and must now be prepared for it in its last and worst shape, that of assassins and guerrillas; but woe unto the people who seek to expend their wild passions in such a manner, for there is but one dread result!
>
> By order of Major-General W. T. Sherman,
> L. M. Dayton, Assistant Adjutant-General.[47]

"I watched the effect closely, and was gratified that there was no single act of retaliation," Sherman said, "though I saw and felt that one single word by me would have laid the city in ashes, and turned its whole population houseless upon the country, if not worse."[48]

The gut-wrenching news of Lincoln's assassination was announced to the assembled Union officers, who listened in shocked silence. "In sadness we parted and returned to our tents to announce to our

---

46. Sherman, *Memoirs*, 2:350.
47. *OR* 47, 3:238-239.
48. Sherman, *Memoirs*, 2:351.

companies at roll call the sad news we had learned," a captain of the 10th Ohio Cavalry remembered.[49]

"The soldiers stood around in the camps, in little squads, silent or talking in subdued but bitter tones, and many of them weeping like children, after they heard it," Sherman's adjutant, Maj. Henry Hitchcock, recalled. "I heard officers who, I know, always denounced and strove against violence and outrages in our marches through Georgia and South Carolina swear in bitter terms, that if our army moved again they would never spare nor protect another house or family."[50]

Sherman also reported the day's events to Grant, via one of his subordinates, who maintained his headquarters in New Bern, North Carolina:

> I have returned from a point twenty-seven miles up the railroad, where I had a long interview with General Johnston, with a full and frank interchange of opinions. He evidently seeks to make terms for Jeff. Davis and his cabinet. He wanted to consult again with Mr. Breckinridge at Greensborough, and I have agreed to meet him at noon to-morrow at the same place. We lose nothing in time, as by agreement both armies stand still and the roads are drying up, so that if I am forced to pursue we will be able to make better speed.
>
> There is great danger that the Confederate armies will dissolve and fill the whole land with robbers and assassins, and I think this is one of the difficulties that Johnston labors under. The assassination of Mr. Lincoln shows one of the elements in the rebel army which will be almost as difficult to deal with as the main armies. Communicate substance of this to General Grant, and also that if General Sheridan is marching down this way to feel for me before striking the enemy. I don't want Johnston's army to break up in fragments.[51]

Preventing Johnston's army from breaking up into guerrilla bands remained one of Sherman's primary objectives.

Sherman spent the rest of the day, on April 17, consulting with his generals and discussing the day's momentous events. He wrote that "without exception, all advised me to agree to some terms, for they all dreaded the long and harassing march in pursuit of a dissolving and

---

49. "10th Ohio Cavalryman", "Campaign Through the Carolinas".
50. Howe, *Marching with Sherman*, 307.
51. *OR* 47, 3:234.

Maj. Gen. John A. Logan, commander of the 15th Corps of the Army of the Tennessee. Logan commanded the Army of the Tennessee at the Grand Review in Washington, D.C. in May 1865.

(Library of Congress)

fleeing army—a march that might carry us back again over the thousand miles that we had just accomplished. We all knew that if we could bring Johnston's army to bay, we could destroy it in an hour, but that was simply impossible in the country in which we found ourselves. We discussed all the probabilities, among which was, whether, Johnston made a point of it, I should assent to the escape from the country of Jeff. Davis and his fugitive cabinet; and some one of my general officers, either Logan or [Maj. Gen. Francis P.] Blair, insisted that, if asked for, we should even provide a vessel to carry them to Nassau from Charleston."[52]

Wisely, Sherman increased the guards around Raleigh, put pickets on the roads, and ordered that all stray soldiers be rounded up and arrested. He spent the night riding around his army's camps, helping to calm the fury of his soldiers. The general later claimed, and likely justifiably, if it weren't for his efforts to keep the calm, the city would have been destroyed.[53]   General John Logan also prevented his men from allowing their rage to consume them, in turn helping to save North Carolina's capital from Union soldiers wanting to burn it to the ground. In fact, Logan threatened to use artillery fire on his own troops to get them to stand down. "General Logan saved the City, and it owes him a debt it can never pay," an admiring Indiana sergeant observed.[54]

Instead of boarding a train back to Greensboro, Johnston went to Lt. Gen. Wade Hampton's headquarters in Hillsborough, leaving him with a much shorter trip in the morning. "Thinking it probable that the confidential relations of the Secretary of War with Mr. Davis might enable him to remove the only obstacle to an adjustment, I requested

52. Sherman, *Memoirs*, 2:351-352.
53. John F. Marszalek, *Sherman: A Soldier's Passion for Order* (New York: Free Press, 1993), 344.
54. Bradley, *This Astounding Close*, 163-165; George Francis Dawson, *Life and Services of General John A. Logan as Soldier and Statesman* (Washington, DC: National Tribune, 1884), 344.

him by telegraph to join me as soon as possible," recalled Johnston.[55] Johnston had no way of knowing, but Davis and the rest of his cabinet had departed Greensboro for Charlotte, intending to escape into what remained of the Deep South, followed by heading to safety in Mexico.

"When we had gotten about half way to Charlotte, the President received a dispatch from General Johnston, informing him that he was in communication with General Sherman, and requesting that some one should be sent to assist in the negotiations," Postmaster General John H. Reagan recalled. "Mr. Davis requested the attendance of General Breckinridge and myself, and, stating the substance

Confederate Postmaster General John Reagan.

(Library of Congress)

of the dispatch, observed that as I had proposed the bases for the negotiations, he desired me to go, and that as there might be a refusal to treat with the civil authorities of the Confederacy, he wished General Breckinridge to go to represent the Army."[56] Reagan and Breckinridge hurried to find a train.

After a difficult journey, Reagan and Breckinridge, joined by North Carolina Governor Zebulon Vance, arrived by train from Greensboro, past midnight; much of the railroad track had been torn up and a number of bridges were burned, significantly delaying their arrival.[57] Fortunately, a local family had prepared a sumptuous feast for the Confederate officials—a twenty-five pound turkey, served on fine china, which the weary travelers enjoyed. Johnston used the opportunity to break the news of Lincoln's assassination and to describe the day's events, telling the cabinet officers that Sherman had specifically refused to give amnesty to the civilian authorities. Then Reagan offered to record the proposed surrender terms, and Johnston dictated them to Reagan.

Reagan wrote:

> **As the avowed motive of the Government of the United States for the prosecution of the existing war with the Confederate States is to secure a reunion of all the States**

55. Johnston, *Narrative of Military Operations*, 404.
56. Reagan, *Memoirs*, 201.
57. Ibid.

under one common government, and as wisdom and sound policy alike require that a common government should rest on the consent and be supported by the affections of all the people who compose it:

Now, in order to ascertain whether it be practicable to put an end to the existing war and to the consequent destruction of life and property, having in view the correspondence and conversation which has recently taken place between Maj. Gen. W. T. Sherman and myself, I propose the following points as a basis of pacification:

First. The disbanding of the military forces of the Confederacy; and,

Second. The recognition of the Constitution and authority of the Government of the United States on the following conditions:

Third. The preservation and continuance of the State governments.

Fourth. The preservation to the people of all the political rights and rights of person and property secured to them by the Constitution of the United States and of their several States.

Fifth. Freedom from future prosecution or penalties for their participation in the present war.

Sixth. Agreement to a general suspension of hostilities pending these negotiations.

Copy of a project submitted by General Johnston, being the product of Mr. Reagan, Postmaster-General of the Confederacy.[58]

If Sherman accepted these proposed terms, every Confederate, from Davis down to the lowliest private, would receive full amnesty. Once he finished dictating the terms to Reagan, Johnston suggested that all try to get a few hours of sleep before the next day's travails.

Capt. W. E. Stoney, a staff officer, wrote in his diary on April 17, "Early in the day it was reported our army was to be surrendered. This rumor was at first disregarded, but presently began to assume shape and force. The wildest excitement seized the troops." When Stoney

58. W. J. McMurray, *History of the Twentieth Tennessee Regiment Volunteer Infantry, C.S.A.* (Nashville, TN: Regimental Publication Committee, 1904), 358.

confirmed the report, he asked for and received permission to spread the news. When he arrived at his brigade's camp, he related the news to Lt. Col. James H. Rion, the brigade commander. Rion immediately ordered the brigade into line and urged the men not to leave. "The enemy were now supposed to be not only in rear, but on both flanks, and it would be difficult to escape; that if any considerable number left it might compromise the terms given to those who remained," Rion declared. These soldiers burned their brigade's flags to prevent them from being surrendered. "About dark an order came from army headquarters to keep the men together," Stoney recalled, "but with that day the army perished—a mob remained."[59]

None of this was easy for Johnston. "On the 17th, Johnston's army was confronted with overwhelming numbers, yet his troops were full of fight, for they had just repulsed three times their number at Bentonville," a member of the 20th Tennessee Infantry of Lt. Gen. Benjamin Cheatham's Corps of the Army of Tennessee, observed.[60] While those men were still ready to fight despite the surrender of Lee's army, it was unrealistic to ask the soldiers to make the sort of sacrifices that another battle would require. This all weighed heavily on Johnston.

After dinner, Hampton and Governor Vance had an unpleasant confrontation; the truculent South Carolina cavalryman was vehemently opposed to making peace and wanted the war to continue. Hampton was angry with Vance for attempting to contact Sherman to discuss ending hostilities.[61] The day, which had started with so much promise of peace, ended on a sour note.

Weary from the day's emotional events, Johnston settled down for the night.

---

59. Bradley, *This Astounding Close*, 166-167. Hampton, in fact, had written to Davis to seek permission to take his remaining troopers south, rather than surrender, and an extended correspondence ensued. Davis eventually granted Hampton permission, but by that time, it was too late—Johnston had already surrendered. Instead, Hampton refused to surrender and disbanded his command. See Appendix D to this book.
60. W. J. McMurray, *History of the Twentieth Tennessee Regiment Volunteer Infantry, C.S.A.* (Nashville, TN: Regimental Publication Committee, 1904), 358.
61. Bradley, *This Astounding Close*, 166-167. Hampton, in fact, had written to Davis to seek permission to take his remaining troopers south, rather than surrender, and an extended correspondence ensued. Davis eventually granted Hampton permission, but by that time, it was too late—Johnston had already surrendered. Instead, Hampton refused to surrender and disbanded his command. See Appendix D to this book.

CHAPTER FOUR

APRIL 18: THE SECOND MEETING

" The next morning, the 18th, as bright and propitious as the preceding, smiled upon the continued conference," Capt. George W. Pepper, of Sherman's staff, remembered.[1] The lovely spring day heralded important events to come.

Major General William T. Sherman and Gen. Joseph E. Johnston both set out early again on the morning of April 18. "We had breakfast toward sun-up; and shortly afterward General Johnston suggested that he and General Breckinridge would go to the place of meeting and entertain General Sherman until I could put in writing our proposed terms," Confederate Postmaster General John H. Reagan recalled. "This programme was followed, and I sent the paper to General Johnston, who subsequently stated that it contained with slight variations the terms of the armistice agreed on by those generals. I did not join in the negotiations beyond this, because objection had been made to the recognition of the civil government of the Confederacy."[2]

That morning, Gen. P. G. T. Beauregard sent a note to Johnston that plainly reflected this expectation: "Should your negotiations terminate favorably let me suggest that you secure, if possible, the right to march our troops to their homes and there muster them duly out of service, depositing their regimental colors in their respective State capitols for preservation."[3]

Sherman, accompanied by most of his personal staff and several of his corps commanders, boarded a train headed to Durham Station. After arriving at Bvt. Maj. Gen. Judson Kilpatrick's headquarters, Sherman and his entourage left for the Bennett house. "An escort of two hundred men picked from the 8th Indiana [Cavalry] carried sabers, in two ranks, facing between headquarters and the railroad," Captain Pepper stated. "Behind them, and on the opposite side of the track, thronging the fences, climbing every lookout, pressed the gay and dashing cavalrymen, to view the scene, and catch a glimpse of the grim Sherman, delighted to witness his marks of regard toward their own

1. Pepper, *Personal Recollections of Sherman's Campaigns*, 414.
2. Reagan, *Memoirs*, 201-202.
3. *OR* 47, 3:809.

favorite leader, the bold young raider, whose signed enterprise was now reaping just reward; thus made host of the ceremonies of truce, toward the hastening on of which his own vigor had not failed to contribute."[4] With Kilpatrick at his side, Sherman and his entourage arrived at the Bennett house just before noon.[5]

Johnston arrived soon after. "The brilliantly-costumed crowd of staff officers, in full uniform, paused for a moment, as their chiefs rode forward into the open space, lifting their hats courteously, and then, grasping each other by the hand, Sherman and Johnston dismounted and passed into the house," Sherman's staff officer Maj. George W. Nichols recounted.[6]

Hoping to avoid the difficulties of the previous afternoon, Johnston left his escort out of sight, but it did little good since the men fraternized freely anyway. Lieutenant General Wade Hampton's adjutant, Maj. Henry B. McClellan, advised the Union officers that Hampton "did not see fit to be present today." However, the cavalry chief's son Lt. Wade Hampton IV was present. Captain Pepper conveyed "how sorry I was to find his frank face, so much more genial than his father's covering the same frantic principles of savage, Scotch-Highland inveteracy, and bloodthirsty, clannish hate, then ceases only in death, whose hope is despair, and whose grave is blood." The younger Hampton told Pepper, "I went into this war for independence, and I expected to keep on fighting till I succeeded or was killed. I expect now to fight until I am killed." Pepper related how the general's son did not intend to surrender and instead aimed to go to Mexico to carry on the fight.[7]

"An indescribable gloom was cast over us by the terrible tidings of the assassination of President Lincoln," Major Nichols imparted. "It is but just to say that the Union officers could not have expressed more horror and detestation at that dastardly act than did General Johnston and his friends. They seemed to understand that in Mr. Lincoln the South had, after all, lost the best friend it had in the government and at the North."[8] The staff officers and orderlies passed the afternoon reading newspapers and chatting idly while they waited for the conference to end.

Johnston and Sherman entered the Bennett house, and Sherman closed the door behind them. Johnston began the discussion by assuring the Union general that he possessed full authority over all

---

4. Pepper, *Personal Recollections of Sherman's Campaigns*, 414.
5. Sherman, *Memoirs*, 2:352.
6. Nichols, *The Great March*, 314-315.
7. Pepper, *Personal Recollections of Sherman's Campaigns*, 416-417.
8. Nichols, *The Great March*, 316.

Maj. Gen. John C. Breckinridge, a former Vice President of the United States, who served as the Confederacy's final Secretary of War.

(Library of Congress)

Confederate armies, and they would obey his orders to surrender on the same terms as his own. However, Johnston suggested that Sherman should give the Confederate troops some assurance of their political rights after they surrendered. Sherman elaborated about those concerns in his after-action report: "The points on which he expressed especial solicitude were, lest their States were to be dismembered and denied representation in Congress, or any separate political existence whatever, and that the absolute disarming his men would leave the South powerless and exposed to depredations by wicked bands of assassins and robbers."[9]

Responding, "I explained to him that Mr. Lincoln's proclamation of amnesty, of December 8, 1863, still in force, enabled every Confederate soldier and officer, below the rank of colonel, to obtain an absolute pardon, by simply laying down his arms, and taking the common oath of allegiance, and that General Grant, in accepting the surrender of General Lee's army, had extended the same principle to all the officers, General Lee included; such a pardon, I understood, would restore to them all their rights of citizenship," Sherman reported.[10]

---

9. *OR* 47, 1:32.

10. Sherman, *Memoirs*, 2:352. Sherman testified before the Joint Committee on the Conduct of the War in May 1865 and said: "Then a conversation arose as to what form of government they were to have in the south. Were the States there to be dissevered; and were the people to be denied representation in Congress? Were the people there to be, in the common language of the people of the south, slaves to the people of the north. Of course I said 'No; we desire that you shall regain your position as citizens of the United States, free and equal to us in all respects, and with representation, upon the condition of submission to the lawful authority of the United States as defined by the Constitution, the United States courts, and the authorities of the United States supported by those courts.'" "Sherman-Johnston," *Report of the Joint Committee on the Conduct of the War at the Second Session, Thirty-Eighth Congress* (Washington, DC: Government Printing Office, 1865), 4.

"Something being said about State rights, Sherman made one of his characteristic remarks in reply. Said he: 'The American citizen has some rights too. I have some rights, among them is the right to go where I please, and jump what fences I please.' 'That,' said Johnston, 'is because you have a large force to back you.' Said Sherman, 'That is the identical thing.'"[11]

Johnston insisted that the Confederate officers and enlisted men were very alarmed about the question of a pardon and their ability to vote, "as a sort of bugbear." Johnston told Sherman that Maj. Gen. John C. Breckinridge was nearby, and he thought having him attend the conference would be a good idea. Sherman objected on the grounds that Breckinridge was a member of Davis's cabinet, and the negotiations should be strictly confined to the belligerents. Johnston reminded Sherman that Breckinridge was a major general in the Confederate army, which convinced Sherman to change his mind. Johnston sent a staff officer to find Breckinridge, and the staff officer soon returned with the secretary of war. Without much flourish, Breckinridge clattered into the room, and the conference resumed.[12]

One of Sherman's clerks observed Breckinridge. "I recognized him at once from photographs I had seen," he remembered. "He was a good specimen of a real Southerner. His clothes looked rather seedy; but he was haughty and his manner was proud."[13]

Like many native Kentuckians, Breckinridge appreciated good bourbon. The Confederate cabinet's precipitous flight from Richmond, Virginia, left many staples—such as tobacco and bourbon—in short supply, and Breckinridge missed his bourbon. After a few minutes of pleasantries, someone finally suggested that they should probably get to the matter at hand. "Yes," Sherman agreed, "but, gentlemen, it occurred to me that perhaps you were not overstocked with liquor, and I procured some medical stores on my way over. Will you join me before we begin work?" Sherman pulled a bottle of bourbon and a glass out of his saddlebag. Johnston recollected that "he watched the expression of Breckinridge at this announcement, and it was beatific." Breckinridge tossed his plug of chewing tobacco into the fire, rinsed his mouth, and then, when the bottle and the glass were passed to him, "he poured out a tremendous drink, which he swallowed with great satisfaction. With an air of content, he stroked his mustache and took a fresh chew of tobacco." With that out of the way, they began their work.[14]

11. Hatcher, *The Last Four Weeks of the War*, 294.
12. Sherman, *Memoirs*, 2:352.
13. Granger, "The Fifteenth at General Joe Johnston's Surrender," 594.
14. John S. Wise, *The End of an Era* (Boston: Houghton-Mifflin & Co., 1901), 451. Johnston supposedly related, "'You know how fond of his liquor

For Breckinridge's benefit, Sherman repeated what he had told Johnston, and Breckinridge then echoed what Johnston had said about the Confederate officers' and soldiers' uneasiness regarding the future of their political rights, in case they surrendered. "While we were in consultation, a messenger came with a parcel of papers, which General Johnston said were from Mr. Reagan, Postmaster-General," Sherman recalled. Johnston and Breckenridge looked over the papers, and, after some discussion, Johnston handed one of the papers to Sherman. The handwritten document began with a long preamble and terms "so general and verbose," Sherman stated, "that I said they were inadmissible."[15]

Johnston recalled, "I read this paper to General Sherman, as a basis for terms of peace, pointing out to him that it contained nothing which he had not already accepted, but the language that included the President and cabinet in the terms of amnesty." Breckinridge also spoke fervently about the merits of Reagan's terms for ending the war.[16] Sherman listened carefully. "See here, gentlemen, just who is doing this surrendering, anyhow?" quipped Sherman. "If this thing goes on, you'll have me sending a letter of apology to Jeff Davis."[17]

Recalling his conversations with President Abraham Lincoln, Gen. Ulysses S. Grant, and Admiral David Dixon Porter at City Point, Virginia, Sherman sat down at the table and wrote out the terms, which he thought concisely expressed Lincoln's views and wishes regarding the end of the war. Sherman explained that he was willing to submit the terms to President Andrew Johnson, provided that both armies remained where they were until the truce expired. As Sherman put it, "Neither Mr. Breckenridge nor General Johnston wrote one word of that paper. I wrote it myself, and announced it as the best I could do, and they readily assented."[18]

Johnston absently stared out the window while Sherman rapidly scratched away with his pen. Never seeing one up close and curious about it, Johnston went outside for a few minutes to examine a Spencer carbine carried by one of Kilpatrick's troopers. As Sherman finished, he looked up and declared, "Gentlemen, this is the best I can

---

Breckinridge was?' added General Johnston, as he went on with his story. 'Well, nearly everything to drink had been absorbed. For several days, Breckinridge had found it difficult, if not impossible, to procure liquor. He showed the effect of his enforced abstinence. He was rather dull and, heavy that morning. Somebody in Danville had given him a plug of very fine chewing tobacco, and he chewed vigorously while we were awaiting Sherman's coming.'" Ibid., 451.

15. Sherman, *Memoirs*, 2:353.
16. Johnston, *Narrative of Military Operations*, 405.
17. Wise, *The End of an Era*, 451.
18. Sherman, *Memoirs*, 2:353.

do." He then stepped aside to permit the two Confederates an opportunity to read the remarkable document he had just written—a document that extended even more generous terms than those Reagan proposed.[19]

While the two Confederates reviewed the document, Sherman retrieved the bottle of bourbon from his saddlebag and absent-mindedly poured himself a drink. However, he neglected to offer any to either Johnston or Breckinridge, which deeply offended Breckinridge. "From pleasant hope and expectation the expression on Breckinridge's face changed successively to uncertainty, disgust, and deep depression," an observer recalled. "At last his hand sought the plug of tobacco, and, with an injured, sorrowful look, he cut off another chew. Upon this he ruminated during the remainder of the interview, taking little part in what was said." After the meeting ended, the disgusted former vice president told Johnston, "General Sherman is a hog. Yes, sir, a hog. Did you see him take that drink by himself? No Kentucky gentleman would ever have taken away that bottle...he knew we needed it and needed it badly."[20]

When Johnston and Breckinridge finished reading the draft, Sherman called for his clerk, Pvt. Arthur Granger of the 15th Pennsylvania Cavalry. Sherman directed Granger to make two copies of the document, which his adjutant, Maj. Henry Hitchcock, proofread. Granger later recalled overhearing the generals chatting, making him wish he could put down the pen and listen to their discussions.[21]

Sherman had his reasons for agreeing to a truce. "I had full faith that General Johnston would religiously respect the truce, which he did; and that I would be the gainer, for in the few days it would take to send the papers to Washington, and receive an answer, I could finish the railroad up to Raleigh, and be the better prepared for a long chase," Sherman penned. While their respective staff officers wrote out copies of the document that awaited the participants' signatures, the generals' remaining staff officers mingled in the yard. Sherman introduced all of them to Johnston and Breckinridge. "All without exception were rejoiced that the war was over, and that in a very few days we could turn our faces toward home," Sherman recorded.

"I remember telling Breckenridge that he had better get away, as the feeling of our people was utterly hostile to the political element of the South, and to him especially, because he was the Vice-President of the United States, who had as such announced Mr. Lincoln, of Illinois,

19. Bradley, *This Astounding Close*, 171.
20. Wise, *The End of an Era*, 452.
21. Granger, "The Fifteenth at General Joe Johnston's Surrender," 595.

duly and properly elected the President of the United States, and yet that he had afterward openly rebelled and taken up arms against the Government." Breckinridge assured Sherman that he would give no further trouble to anyone, and suggested that he would soon leave the country permanently. "I may have also advised him that Mr. Davis too should get abroad as soon as possible," Sherman concluded.[22]

"During the interval while the memorandum was being made and signed the staff officers and escort of both Generals commingled together in friendly congratulations that the war was ended," a captain of the 10th Ohio Cavalry recollected.[23]

When the copies were ready, Sherman and Johnston signed them.[24] The scope and breadth of the document far exceeded the terms Grant gave to Gen. Robert E. Lee at the village of Appomattox Court House, in Virginia, just a few days earlier. This is the document drafted by Sherman:

> **Memorandum or basis of agreement made this 18th day of April, A.D. 1865, near Durham's Station, in the State of North Carolina, by and between General Joseph E. Johnston, commanding the Confederate army, and Maj. Gen. William T. Sherman, commanding the army of the United States in North Carolina, both present.**
>
> **First. The contending armies now in the field to maintain the status quo until notice is given by the commanding general of any one to its opponent, and reasonable time, say forty-eight hours, allowed.**

---

22. Ibid., 353-354.
23. "A 10th Ohio Cavalryman," "Through the Carolinas."
24. One of Kilpatrick's officers later reported that Capt. David Cockley of the 10th Ohio Cavalry, who served on Kilpatrick's staff, purchased from James Bennett the plain black walnut table upon which Sherman scrawled the peace terms. Cockley later had an office desk made from the wood, refusing to sell it for the significant sum of $350. Ibid. This is, of course, reminiscent of Maj. Gen. Philip H. Sheridan purchasing Wilmer McLean's table, on which Grant wrote the Appomattox surrender terms. Sheridan gave the table to Bvt. Maj. Gen. George A. Custer as a reward for Custer's valor and successful service. Cockley was later awarded the Medal of Honor for his valor at the December 4, 1864, Battle of Waynesboro in Georgia. His Medal of Honor citation reads: "While acting as aide-de-camp to a general officer, he 3 times asked permission to join his regiment in a proposed charge upon the enemy, and in response to the last request, having obtained such permission, joined his regiment and fought bravely at its head throughout the action." *Civil War (A-F) Medal of Honor Recipients*, http://www.history.army.mil/moh/civilwar_af.html#ALBER; "Over Five Barricades," included in W. F. Beyer and O. F. Keydel, eds., *Deeds of Valor*, 2 vols. (Detroit, MI: The Perrien-Keydel Co., 1907), 1:463-465.

Second. The Confederate armies now in existence to be disbanded and conducted to their several State capitals, there to deposit their arms and public property in the State arsenal, and each officer and man to execute and file an agreement to cease from acts of war and to abide the action of both State and Federal authority. The number of arms and munitions of war to be reported to the Chief of Ordnance at Washington City, subject to the future action of the Congress of the United States, and in the meantime to be used solely to maintain peace and order within the borders of the States, respectively.

Third. The recognition by the Executive of the United States of the several State governments of their officers and legislatures taking the oaths prescribed by the Constitution of the United States, and where conflicting State governments have resulted from the war the legitimacy of all shall be submitted to the Supreme Court of the United States.

Fourth. The re-establishment of all the Federal courts in the several States, with powers as defined by the Constitution and laws of Congress.

Fifth. The people and inhabitants of all the States to be guaranteed, so far as the Executive can, their political rights and franchises, as well as their rights of person and property, as defined by the Constitution of the United States and of the States, respectively.

Sixth. The Executive authority of the Government of the United States not to disturb any of the people by reason of the late war so long as they live in peace and quiet, abstain from acts of armed hostility, and obey the laws in existence at the place of their residence.

Seventh. In general terms, the war to cease, a general amnesty, so far as the Executive of the United States can command, on condition of the disbandment of the Confederate armies, the distribution of the arms, and the resumption of peaceful pursuits by the officers and men hitherto composing said armies.

Not being fully empowered by our respective principals to fulfill these terms, we individually and officially pledge ourselves to promptly obtain the necessary authority and to carry out the above programme.

W. T. SHERMAN,

Major-General, Comdg. Army United States in North Carolina.

J. E. JOHNSTON,
General, Commanding C. S. Army in North Carolina.[25]

When he wrote his after-action report about the war's final campaign a few weeks later, Sherman correctly noted, "It was designed to be, and so expressed on its face, as a mere basis for reference to the President of the United States and constitutional commander-in-chief, to enable him, if he chose, at one blow to dissipate the military power of the Confederacy which had threatened the national safety for years. It admitted of modification, alteration, and change," he wrote. "It had no appearance of an ultimatum; and by no false reasoning can it be construed into an usurpation of power on my part."[26]

When asked why the document did not address the abolition of slavery, Sherman responded, "There was nothing said about slavery, because it did not fall within the category of military questions, and we could not make it so. It was a legal question which the President had disposed of, overriding all our action. We had to treat the slave as free, because the President, our commander in-chief, said he was free. For me to have renewed the question when that decision was made would have involved the absurdity of an inferior undertaking to qualify the work of his superior."[27]

Johnston later recalled that Sherman "had accepted, virtually, the terms that I had offered in writing. They included general amnesty without naming individuals or classes." In short, the terms Sherman offered were even more generous than those Reagan proposed.[28]

Theo Davis, an artist for Harper's Weekly, was assigned to Sherman's army. Sherman trusted him, so he called for the artist to join him and Johnston inside the house. The two generals wanted the

25. *OR* 47, 3:244.
26. Ibid., 1:33; Sherman, *Memoirs*, 2:354. Jefferson Davis wrote that "the proposition for a suspension of hostilities to allow the civil authorities to negotiate was not even entertained; that the agreement was, in fact, a military convention, in which all references to the civil authorities was excluded, except by the admission that the negotiators respectively had principals from whom they must obtain authority, i.e., ratification of the agreement into which they had entered. There seemed to be a special dread on the part of the United States officials lest they should do something which would be construed as the recognition of the existence of a government which for four years they had been vainly trying to subdue." Davis, *Rise and Fall of the Confederate Government*, 2:688.
27. "Sherman-Johnston," 14.
28. Joseph E. Johnston to Alexander H. Stephens, April 29, 1868, Alexander H. Stephens Papers, Manuscripts Division, Library of Congress, Washington, DC.

INTERIOR OF JAMES BENNETT'S HOUSE—SCENE OF JOHNSTON'S SURRENDER, April 26, 1865.
Sketched by Davis.]

Sherman and Johnston conferring inside the Bennett house.

(Harper's Weekly)

artist to sketch their conference for posterity, so they sat down at the table Sherman used to write the accord. Accustomed to working fast, Davis quickly sketched the seated generals, as if in deep thought. Years after the war, Johnston visited Theo Davis's studio. While looking at the sketch for the first time in years, Johnston noted that posterity would probably construe the bottle on the table to be a whiskey bottle, and likely his own because it was closer to him than Sherman. However, when Davis asked Sherman about it later, he not only remembered the bottle, but he claimed "it was good whiskey, some of my own," vindicating Johnston's fears.[29]

Johnston and Breckinridge emerged from the Bennett house together. "At the gate they both took leave of Sherman, the latter courteously lifting his hat again, as the day before, also to the rest of us," Captain Pepper recalled. "Breckinridge, however, very stiffly parted with Sherman only, and then strode on and through the gate

29. Theo R. Davis, "With Sherman in His Army Home," *The Cosmopolitan* 12 (December 1891), 205.

toward his horse, without so much as a glance deigned to meaner mortals."[30]

Colonel Orlando M. Poe, Sherman's chief engineer, had spent a pleasant afternoon chatting with Maj. John Johnson, Johnston's chief engineer. Sherman's adjutant, Major Hitchcock, had also visited with Johnson, and as Hitchcock passed through the Bennett's front gate, Johnson said, "Good-bye, Major—hope we shall meet again." Softly, Johnson added, "in the right way."[31]

Dusk fell as the three generals departed the Bennett property. When Johnston arrived at Hampton's headquarters in Hillsborough, he instructed Major Johnson to make two copies of the document signed at the Bennett house. Meanwhile, Johnston wrote a synopsis to be telegraphed to Beauregard. Johnston, Breckinridge, and, Reagan had dinner together and then left to board a train headed for Greensboro. The gentlemen expected to find Governor Vance waiting for them at the depot, but Vance was not there as arranged. They waited for 45 minutes, and when Vance did not appear, the train pulled out of the station without him. Johnston arrived at his headquarters in Greensboro about 2:00 a.m.[32]

Lieutenant General Stephen D. Lee and some of his staff awaited Johnston's arrival. Johnston informed Lee that he had surrendered the army, showing him a copy of the agreement. Lee read them aloud, "and as he did so the tears which had been gathering in Johnston's eyes burst bounds and trickled down his cheeks." Lee asked Johnston whether such liberal terms would be approved in Washington, D.C., and Johnston replied that he had asked Sherman the same question. Johnston reported that Sherman had confirmed that the terms were the same ones Lincoln had authorized, and the Union general was acting in good faith.[33]

"Demoralization...is utter and complete; there is no spark of fight left in the troops," Captain W. E. Stoney lamented in his diary that night. "General Johnston expresses, we are told, great displeasure at the report." And it would only get worse.[34]

30. Pepper, *Personal Recollections of Sherman's Campaigns*, 420.
31. John Johnson diary, entry for April 18, 1865; Howe, *Marching with Sherman*, 311.
32. Johnston, *Narrative of Military Operations*, 405. Quite a drama developed after Vance had been left behind. For a detailed discussion of those events, see Bradley, *This Astounding Close*, 180-182.
33. J. W. Ratchford, *Some Reminiscences of Persons and Incidents of the Civil War* (Reprint edition. Austin, TX: Shoal Creek Publishers, 1971), 45-46.
34. Brooks, *Memoirs of the War of Secession*, 369.

Meanwhile, Sherman and his officers arrived at Durham Station, which was packed with Union soldiers waiting to hear whether Johnston had surrendered. When the news spread, cheering erupted. "All the troops are jubilant and talked of going home," a New York artillerist said. "God be praised for the glorious termination of this war."[35] The Northern generals arrived at Kilpatrick's headquarters in time to have dinner before boarding the train to Raleigh.[36]

Major General Henry W. Slocum, commander of the Army of Georgia, had accompanied Sherman to the Bennett house that day, returning to his own headquarters near midnight. "After the proposed terms had been made known to the leading officers of Sherman's army, I conversed with nearly all of these officers, among them Logan, Howard, and Blair, and heard no word

Maj. Gen. Carl Schurz, Slocum's acting chief of staff, shown as Secretary of the Interior during the Grant administration.

(Library of Congress)

of dissent from any of them," Slocum recounted. "I can now recall to mind but one general officer who, at the time, questioned the wisdom of General Sherman's action, and that was General Carl Schurz." Formerly a division commander in the Eleventh Corps, General Carl Shurz was acting as Slocum's temporary chief of staff. Schurz was waiting for Slocum when he arrived at his headquarters. Slocum wrote, "He was eager to learn the terms, and when I stated them to him he expressed regret and predicted...the public mind of the North would be inflamed by the assassination of Lincoln, and now that the armies of the Confederacy were virtually crushed, anything looking toward leniency would not be well received." Schurz's rationale proved prophetic.[37]

---

35. Joseph Kittinger, *Diary, 1861-1865* (Buffalo, NY: Kittinger Co., 1979), 206.
36. Pepper, *Personal Recollections of Sherman's Campaigns*, 420.
37. Henry W. Slocum, "Final Operations of Sherman's Army," included in Robert U. Johnson and Clarence C. Buel, eds., *Battles and Leaders of the Civil War*, 4 vols. (New York: Century Publishing Co., 1884-1889), 4:736. In fact, Schurz declared that "its provisions were astonishing to the last degree." He noted, "It required no extraordinary political foresight to predict the prompt rejection of the Sherman-Johnston agreement by the government, as well as by the public opinion of the country. I remember the midnight scene spoken of by General Slocum very vividly. I was very much distressed—not as if there could have been any doubt as to the final outcome of the matter,

Maj. Gen. Francis P. Blair, Jr., commander of the 17th Corps of the Army of the Tennessee.

(Library of Congress)

When Sherman arrived at his headquarters in Raleigh, he realized that he required direction from the civil authorities. "I cared little whether they were approved, modified, or disapproved in toto; only I wanted instructions," he explained in his post-war memoirs. Slocum, who was a lawyer, expressed doubt that the agreement would be approved. "In fact his legal mind saw objections to its approval on account of Sherman having permitted civil questions to be embodied with the military," Slocum's son observed years later.[38] Some of his officers, including Generals John Logan and Francis P. Blair, urged Sherman to simply accept the terms on his own authority without referring to Washington, but Sherman chose to submit the document to the civil authorities instead.[39] As a great soldier, like Ulysses S. Grant and Robert E. Lee, Sherman understood that in the American system the military was subordinate to the civil authority. Knowing this, Sherman elected to subordinate himself to the politicians' wishes, even if it meant that they repudiated what he had so boldly done.

The general sat down at his desk and wrote a letter to Grant:

HDQRS. MILITARY DIVISION OF THE MISSISSIPPI,
In the Field, Raleigh, N. C., April 18, 1865.
Lieut. Gen. U. S. GRANT, or
Major-General HALLECK,
Washington, D. C.

GENERAL: I inclose herewith a copy of an agreement

---

but on account of General Sherman. With all his companions in arms, I esteemed him very highly, and cherished a genuine affection for him. And now, to think that, at the very close of his splendid career in the war for the Union, he should by one inconsiderate act bring upon himself the censure of the government and of the country, was sad indeed. And this one inconsiderate act was so foreign to what had been, and were again, his natural tendencies." Carl Schurz, *The Reminiscences of Carl Schurz*, 4 vols. (London: John Murray, 1909), 3:113-115.

38. Charles Elihu Slocum, *The Life and Services of Major-General Henry Warner Slocum* (Toledo, OH: The Slocum Publishing Co., 1913), 309.
39. Sherman, *Memoirs*, 2:354.

made this day between General Joseph E. Johnston and myself which, if approved by the President of the United States, will produce peace from the Potomac and the Rio Grande. Mr. Breckinridge was present at our conference in his capacity as major-general, and satisfied me of the ability of General Johnston to carry out to the full extent the terms of this agreement, and if you will get the President to simply indorse the copy and commission me to carry out the terms, I will follow them to the conclusion. You will observe that it is an absolute submission of the enemy to the lawful authority of the United States, and disperses his armies absolutely, and the point to which I attach most importance is that the dispersion and disbandment of these armies is done in such a manner as to prevent their breaking up into guerrilla bands.

On the other hand, we can retain just as much of an army as we please. I agreed to the mode and manner of the surrender of arms set forth, as it gives the States the means of repressing guerrillas, which we could not expect them to do if we stripped them of all arms. Both Generals Johnston and Breckinridge admitted that slavery was dead, and I could not insist on embracing it in such a paper, because it can be made with the States in detail.

I know that all the men of substance South sincerely want peace, and I do not believe they will resort to war again during this century. I have no doubt that they will in the future be perfectly subordinate to the laws of the United States.

The moment my action in this matter is approved I can spare five corps, and will ask for orders to leave General Schofield here with the Tenth Corps, and to march myself with the Fourteenth, Fifteenth, Seventeenth, Twentieth, and Twenty-third Corps, via Burkeville and Gordonsville, to Frederick or Hagerstown, there to be paid and mustered out. The question of finance is now the chief one, and every soldier and officer not needed should be got home at work. I would like to be able to begin the march north by May 1.

I urge on the part of the President speedy action, as it is important to get the Confederate armies to their homes as well as our own.

I am, with great respect, your obedient servant,
W. T. SHERMAN,
Major-General, Commanding.[40]

With the letter, Sherman enclosed a copy of Reagan's document that set forth the Confederate government's proposed terms. He sent them to Washington, D.C., in the hands of his able adjutant, Major Hitchcock.[41]

Sherman then sent out other important correspondences before retiring for the night. He sent a letter to General Henry Halleck dismissing purported assassination threats against him, and suggested a different course of action:

HDQRS. MILITARY DIVISION OF THE MISSIS-SIPPI,
In the Field, Raleigh, N. C., April 18, 1865.
General H. W. HALLECK,
Chief of Staff Washington, D. C.:

GENERAL: I received your dispatch describing the man Clark detailed to assassinate me. He had better be in a hurry or he will be too late. The news of Mr. Lincoln's death produced a most intense effect on our troops. At first I feared it would lead to excesses, but now it has softened down and can easily be guided. None evinced more feeling than General Johnston, who admitted that the act was calculated to stain his cause with a dark hue, and he contended that the loss was most serious to the people of the South, who had begun to realize that Mr. Lincoln was the best friend the South had. I cannot believe that even Mr. Davis was privy to the diabolical plot, but think it the emanation of a set of young men of the South who are very devils. I want to throw upon the South the care of this class of men, who will soon be as obnoxious to their industrial classes as to us. Had I pushed Johnston's army to an extremity these would have dispersed and would have done infinite mischief.

Johnston informed me that Stoneman had been at Salisbury and was now about Statesville. I have sent him orders to come to me. General Johnston also informed me that Wilson was at Columbus, Ga., and he wanted me to arrest his progress. I leave that to you.

Indeed, if the President sanctions my agreement with

---

40. OR 47, 3:243.
41. Sherman, *Memoirs*, 2:356.

Johnston, our interest is to cease all destruction. Please give all orders necessary according to the views the Executive may take, and influence him, if possible, not to vary the terms at all, for I have considered everything and believe that the Confederate armies once dispersed we can adjust all else fairly and well.

I am, yours, &c.,

W. T. SHERMAN,

Major-General, Commanding.[42]

He then composed a telegram to Maj. Gen. George G. Meade, commander of the Army of the Potomac, announcing the results of the day's meeting:

HDQRS. MILITARY DIVISION OF THE MISSISSIPPI,

In the Field, Raleigh, N. C., April 18, 1865.

COMDG. GENERAL ARMIES OF THE UNITED STATES IN VIRGINIA:

GENERAL: I have agreed with General Joseph E. Johnston for a temporary cessation of active hostilities, to enable me to lay before our Government at Washington the agreement made between us, with the full sanction of Mr. Davis and in the presence of Mr. Breckinridge, for the disbandment of all the armies of the Confederacy from here to the Rio Grande. If any of your forces are moving toward Johnston I beg you to check them where they are or at the extremity of any railroad where they may be supplied until you receive orders from General Grant, or until I notify you that the agreement is at an end and hostilities resumed.

I have the honor to be, your obedient servant,

W. T. SHERMAN,

Major-General, Commanding.[43]

Finally, Sherman wrote to his wife, Ellen. He could not hide his excitement. "I have just got back from a long interview with General Johnston and Breckenridge, Secretary of War to the Confederacy, in which we arranged terms for the disbandment of all the Confederate

---

42. *OR* 47, 3:245. For an outstanding detailed discussion of Maj. Gen. George Stoneman's month-long raid that eviscerated much of what remained of the Confederate forces in western Virginia and North Carolina, and which also closed in on Greensboro in the waning days of the war, see Chris J. Hartley, *Stoneman's Raid, 1865* (Winston-Salem, NC: John F. Blair, 2010).

43. Ibid.

armies from this to the Rio Grande, the submission to the national authority, etc., which I send at once to Washington for ratification, when this cruel war will be over. I can hardly realize it, but I can see no slip," he penned.

"The terms are all on our side. If approved I can soon complete the details, leave Schofield here and march my army for the Potomac, there to be mustered out and paid. If I accomplish this I surely think I will be entitled to a month's leave to come and see you," he continued. "The assassination of Mr. Lincoln is most unfortunate, but we ride a whirlwind and must take events as they arise. I have notice that I was embraced in the [assassination conspiracy], but the fellow who was to do the job did not appear, and if he is not in a hurry he will be too late. I don't fear an assassin, though I would prefer, for the name of the thing, to get my quietus in a more honest way, in open manly fight."[44]

Relieved that he and Johnston had established a preliminary framework for ending the war, William T. Sherman slept well that night, blissfully unaware that he was about to ignite a political firestorm.

---

44. Howe, *Home Letters of General Sherman*, 344-345.

CHAPTER FIVE

RIDING THE WHIRLWIND

On April 20, Maj. Gen. William T. Sherman sent his adjutant, Maj. Henry Hitchcock, to Washington, D.C., to hand deliver to Gen. Ulysses S. Grant the document he and Gen. Joseph E. Johnston signed on April 17. Hitchcock was to wait for instructions from the War Department.[1] While Sherman waited for Hitchcock to return with instructions, the Union commander rode the whirlwind he had described in a letter to his wife, Ellen, the night before. "Major Hitchcock got off on the morning of the 20th," Sherman wrote, "and I reckoned that it would take him four or five days to go to Washington

---

1. *OR* 47, 1:33. Henry Hitchcock was the great-grandson of the Revolutionary War general Ethan Allen, from Vermont. His paternal grandfather, Samuel Hitchcock, also from Vermont, was a member of the Vermont convention that approved the U.S. Constitution; he also served as attorney general of Vermont and as a U.S. District Judge. Hitchcock's father, also named Henry Hitchcock, was born in Vermont but moved to Alabama, where he served as Attorney General, United States District Attorney, and Chief Justice of the Supreme Court of Alabama. Finally, he was a nephew of Brig. Gen. Ethan Allen Hitchcock, who commanded U.S. Army Regular troops during the Civil War. Hitchcock was born near Mobile, Alabama, on July 3, 1829. His father died in 1839, and his mother took Henry to live in Nashville, Tennessee. He graduated from the University of Nashville at 17 years old and then enrolled at Yale College, from which he graduated two years later. He spent a year teaching, followed by an apprenticeship in a Nashville law office. Hitchcock settled in St. Louis, Missouri, and was admitted to the Missouri bar. In 1852, he was a delegate for the Whig Party national convention in Baltimore, Maryland, and in 1858, he joined the Republican Party. In 1860, he made his first political speech, and then served as a delegate for the Missouri state secession convention as one of its few Republican delegates. When the war broke out, he wanted to enlist. His uncle persuaded him to wait, though, because he would be of greater service at the state convention. Finally, in September 1864, Hitchcock applied to Secretary of War Edwin M. Stanton for a commission; he was appointed assistant adjutant general with the rank of major, in October 1864. At Sherman's request, Hitchcock was assigned to his staff. His legal training and skills meshed well with Sherman's own, and they were close friends. Hitchcock found prominence as a lawyer after the Civil War. He helped found a St. Louis law school, becoming its first dean. Hitchcock was also a co-founder and the twelfth president of the American Bar Association. John Green, "Henry Hitchcock," *American Antiquarian Society* 17 (October 1895), 253-262.

and back. During that time the repairs on all the railroads and telegraph-lines were pushed with energy, and we also got possession of the railroad and telegraph from Raleigh to Weldon, in the direction of Norfolk." Major General Judson Kilpatrick's horsemen occupied Durham Station and Chapel Hill, Major General Henry W. Slocum's command was at Avent Ferry on the Cape Fear River, Major General O. O. Howard's command was strung along the railroad toward Hillsborough, and the rest of the army remained at Raleigh.[2] In short, Sherman used the time precisely as he said he would—the general positioned his army to deliver a coup de grace to Johnston's army, in case their deal collapsed.

Sherman discussed his and Johnston's peace terms with Bvt. Maj. Gen. Alpheus S. Williams, who commanded a 20th Corps division. "The only point of probable difficulty to an agreement is that the state authorities shall resume their powers on taking an oath of allegiance, or something to that effect," Williams recounted. "Nothing is said about Jeff Davis or his government. All troops and munitions of war to the Rio Grande are to be surrendered. But for the unfortunate and damnable murder of Lincoln...I think, and Sherman thinks, the whole subject would be peacefully settled, so far as the military authorities are concerned, within twenty days. Of course, there will be the great swell of the storm for years to come," he ominously, but correctly, concluded.[3]

"In the meantime we waited, and hoped that the surrender of Johnston would soon become a settled fact," a member of the 12th Wisconsin of the 17th Corps recalled. "We went into camp in a better place, and soon had everything about us convenient and pleasant. Yet we lived for a few days in a sort of suspense that was not very pleasant. We half feared that affairs would take some turn to set us off on another long campaign. We knew well that, if Johnston should undertake it, he could lead us on a lively race clear to the Mississippi. We hoped he would not do so—did not believe he would—yet we did not know."[4]

"When we left Goldsboro, we contemplated a campaign of 30 days," a surprised 33rd Massachusetts soldier of the 20th Corps declared, "but we were happily disappointed, for in four days we overtook Johnston's army and penned them."[5]

"The Angel of Peace has spread his wings over our country once

2. Sherman, *Memoirs*, 2:357.
3. Quaife, *From the Cannon's Mouth*, 384.
4. *Story of the Service of Company E*, 429.

more," a soldier of the 3rd Wisconsin jubilantly stated. "The glad tidings were announced to the army last night by General Sherman in general orders. As soon as the agreement which he had made with General Johnston and higher authorities could be ratified at Washington, peace would be restored from the Potomac to the Rio Grande. It was a glorious day for us who have seen the thing through from the beginning to the end. General Sherman also says that he expects 'soon to have the pleasure of conducting this army to its homes,' and I believe that within six weeks you will see me in Chicago 'home from the wars.'"[6]

Sherman reviewed the Tenth Corps, which included the first division of the United States Colored Troops that the general had ever seen on April 20. The next day he reviewed the Twenty-third Corps. "Nothing of interest happened at Raleigh till the evening of April 23d, when Major Hitchcock reported by telegraph his return to Morehead City, and that he would come up by rail during the night," Sherman recorded.[7]

The men remained uncertain. "Considerable anxiety prevails in the army for the administration of Pres. Johnson," a soldier of the 20th Illinois noted. "He is deemed as too passionate dissipated and unstable for so responsible a position at so critical a period." They also worried about whether the war was actually going to end this time, or whether they would have to take the field again.[8] After hearing that Sherman and Johnston had agreed on the terms of surrender, a trooper of the 10th Ohio Cavalry probably spoke for all of his comrades when he succinctly wondered in his diary, "What will we do next?"[9]

A member of the 117th New York of Maj. Gen. Alfred Terry's command, which had arrived from Wilmington, North Carolina, described the soldiers' frustration. "There being still no news of results in the matter pending between Sherman and Johnston, and it being a question in which the humblest and the greatest had an equal interest, the troops again began to murmur. 'How long,' it was petulantly and perhaps pertinently asked, 'does it take a rebel General to surrender?'

5. Andrew J. Boies, *Record of the Thirty-Third Massachusetts Volunteer Infantry, From Aug. 1862 to Aug. 1865* (Fitchburg, MA: Sentinel Printing Co., 1880), 122.
6. Julian Wisner Hinkley, *A Narrative of Service with the Third Wisconsin Infantry* (Madison: Wisconsin History Commission, 1912), 173-174.
7. Sherman, *Memoirs*, 2:357.
8. Mary Ann Andersen, ed., *The Civil War Diary of Allen Morgan Geer Twentieth Regiment, Illinois Volunteers* (Denver, CO: R. C. Appleman, 1977), 216.
9. George E. Carter, ed., *The Story of Joshua D. Breyfogle, Private, 4th Ohio Infantry (10th Ohio Cavalry) and the Civil War* (Lewiston, NY: Edward Mellen Press, 2001), 336.

The dissatisfaction would have been much more marked, had the matter not been in the hands of General Sherman, who, up to that time, among the soldiers I think, was the most popular man in the United States. But when the troops began to suspect that this great commander had assumed, with the duty of restoring the authority of the government, the gratuitous job of preserving the self-respect of the traitors, they seemed to admire more moderately."[10]

Sherman spent the next day, April 21, catching up on his correspondences. Major General James H. Wilson's 16,000-man cavalry army captured Macon, Georgia, prompting Sherman to advise Wilson that a truce had gone into effect and that he should stand down until further orders arrived.[11] Throughout the day, Sherman also traded several letters with Johnston. Sherman informed the Confederate general that he expected Hitchcock to return in a few days and addressed an important issue: "It may be the lawyers will want us to define more minutely what is meant by the guaranty of rights of person and property," he wrote. "It may be construed into a compact for us to undo the past as to the rights of slaves and leases of plantations on the Mississippi, of vacant and abandoned plantations. I wish you would talk to the best men you have on these points and if possible let us in the final convention make these points so clear as to leave no room for angry controversy."

Sherman continued, "I believe, if the South would simply and publicly declare what we all feel, that slavery is dead, that you would inaugurate an era of peace and prosperity that would soon efface the ravages of the past four years of war. Negroes would remain in the South and afford you abundance of cheap labor which otherwise will be driven away, and it will save the country the senseless discussions which have kept us all in hot water for fifty years. Although strictly speaking this is no subject of a military convention, yet I am honestly convinced that our simple declaration of a result will be accepted as good law everywhere. Of course I have not a single word from

---

10. Mowris, *A History of the One Hundred Seventeenth Regiment*, 212.
11. *OR* 47, 3:266. Instructing Wilson, Sherman wrote, "A suspension of hostilities was agreed on between General Johnston and myself on Tuesday, April 13, at 12 noon. I want that agreement religiously observed, and you may release the generals captured at Macon, occupy ground convenient, and contract for supplies for your command, and forbear any act of hostility until you hear or have reason to believe hostilities are resumed. In the meantime, it is also agreed the position of the enemy's forces must not be altered to our prejudice. You know by this time that General Lee has surrendered to General Grant the rebel Army of Northern Virginia, and that I only await the sanction of the President to conclude terms of peace co-extensive with the boundaries of the United States, You will shape your conduct on this knowledge unless you have overwhelming proof to the contrary."

Washington on this or any other point of our agreement, but I know the effect of such a step by us will be universally accepted."[12]

The Union general also answered a letter from a Regular Army comrade, S. L. Fremont, of Wilmington, who was president of a railroad. Sherman's response was later published in the Official Records of the Civil War due to its content regarding the end of slavery:

> HDQRS. MILITARY DIVISION OF THE MISSIS-SIPPI,
> In the Field, Raleigh, N.C., April 21, 1865.
> S. L. FREMONT, Esq.
> Wilmington, N.C.:
>
> SIR: I have before me your letter addressed to General Hawley, inclosing a paper signed by John Dawson, Edward Kiddon, and others testifying to your feelings of loyalty and attachment to the Government of the United States. Of course I am gratified to know the truth as to one for whom I entertained friendship dated far back in other and better days. I will be frank and honest with you. Simple passive submission to events by a man in the prime of life is not all that is due to society in times of revolution. Had the Northern men residing at the South spoken out manfully and truly at the outset the active secessionists could not have carried the masses of men as they did. It may not be that the war could have been avoided, but the rebellion would not have assumed the mammoth proportions it did. The idea of war to perpetuate slavery in the year 1861 was an insult to the intelligence of the age. As long as the South abided by the conditions of our fundamental contract of government, the Constitution, all law-abiding citizens were bound to respect the property in slaves, whether they approved it or not, but when the South violated that compact openly, publicly, and violently, it was absurd to suppose we were bound to respect that kind of property or any kind of property. I do have a feeling allied to abhorrence toward Northern men resident South, for their silence or acquiescence was one of the causes of the war assuming the magnitude it did, and in consequence we mourn the loss of such men as John F. Reynolds, McPherson, and thousands of noble gentlemen, any one of whom was worth all the slaves of the South and half

---

12. Ibid.

of the white population thrown in. The result is nearly accomplished, and is what you might have foreseen, and in a measure prevented desolation from the Ohio to the Gulf and mourning in every household. I am not made of stone, and can not help indulging in a feeling toward the Union men South who failed at the proper time to meet the storm and check it before it gained full headway. I have a right to speak thus, because I was South in 1861 and saw myself such men as Duncan, Bush Johnson, and others join in the popular sneer at Yankees when they knew better. For them I have not a particle of sympathy, and for the other classes of Northern men who were coerced or wheedled into acquiescence or neutrality, all I can say is that I will not sit in judgment on them, but I shall never confide in their courage, manliness, or virtue.

I am, with respect,
W. T. SHERMAN,
Major-General.[13]

Sherman's feelings shone through. He could be sympathetic, but he also carried a grudge against those men who had brought about the war.

In the interim, while Johnston waited for Sherman to receive the administration's response, Confederate morale collapsed. "The meeting between General Sherman and my-self, and the armistice that followed, produced great uneasiness in the army," Johnston recollected. "It was very commonly believed among the soldiers that there was to be a surrender, by which they would be prisoners of war, to which they were very averse. This apprehension caused a great number of desertions between the 19th and 24th of April—not less than four thousand in the infantry and artillery, and almost as many from the cavalry; many of them rode off artillery horses, and mules belonging to the baggage-trains."[14]

"Desertion every night is frightful," a staff officer penned in his diary. Two days later, the same officer noted, "Our army is getting demoralized. A band of marauding soldiers visited our camp this morning and coolly helped themselves to some leather and goods that we had quietly secured from the Quartermaster's Department."[15]

On April 17, an entire brigade and another regiment of Mississippians deserted, despite Maj. Gen. William W. Loring's pleas

13. Ibid., 271-272.
14. Johnston, *Narrative of Military Operations*, 410.
15. "Captain Ridley's Journal," *Confederate Veteran* 3 (1895), 99.

not to go.[16] Rather than wait to be surrendered, these men simply left without their paroles and returned home to their families, disregarding consequences. Apparently, these soldiers had seen and experienced enough. "My heart is heavy," Capt. William M. Kelly of the 30th Alabama lamented on April 19. "I cannot write."[17]

"This is a critical time with us up here," a Confederate soldier remarked, "we have no hope of getting out of this place. Our army is nearly surrounded by overwhelming forces. For the last few days we have been waiting for Genl Johnston to surrender this army. There is no other hope but for it to surrender eventually. I am firmly convinced of that fact." The soldier, an artillerist, attempted to escape by riding one of the artillery horses away; however, he changed his mind and returned to camp, preferring to face his fate with comrades.[18]

On April 20, another woeful Confederate inscribed in his diary, "I went to the first consolidated Arkansas regiment on dress parade, as I thought it would be my last opportunity to see a Confederate regiment on dress parade. As I thought of the past and looked into the future, I could scarcely keep back the tears." The same soldier recalled that he spent April 21 guarding his unit's horses to keep them from being stolen.[19]

Johnston's troops were not keen about waiting anymore. "They regretted to have to remain in camp a few days longer, although the difference was between going home as prisoners of war on parole or as freemen under an honorable peace," Capt. W. E. Stoney stated. "This was undoubtedly the prevailing statement with the mass," he said on April 19. A few days later, Stoney reported, "There being reason to think that many of the brigade were contemplating leaving for home, Colonel Rion issued a circular advising them to remain to the end. Immediately the whole command collected at headquarters to hear more fully from him. He addressed them at length. He stated that position of affairs as far as it was known to him, and urged that their departure would be a violation of the truce, compromising their personal safety, compromising General Johnston, and finally

16. Larry J. Daniel, *Soldiering in the Army of Tennessee: A Portrait of Life in a Confederate Army* (Chapel Hill: University of North Carolina Press, 1991), 167.

17. William M. Kelly to his wife, April 19, 1865, quoted in William Milner Kelly, "A History of the Thirtieth Alabama Volunteers (Infantry) Confederate States Army," *The Alabama Historical Quarterly*, Vol. 9, No. 1 (Spring 1947), 167.

18. "Henry" to his sister, April 20, 1865, Mark Bradley Collection, Bentonville Battlefield Archives, Four Oaks, North Carolina.

19. Diary of H. M Pollard, entries for April 20 and 21, 1865, Confederate Collection, Tennessee State Library and Archives, Nashville, Tennessee.

Maj. Gen. Joseph Wheeler, commander of the Army of Tennessee's Cavalry Corps.

(Library of Congress)

compromising their personal honor." The colonel's words did no good, however. "They are going in large bodies at all hours without an effort being made to stop them," Stoney recollected the next day.[20]

Colonel J. Fred Waring, a Georgian who commanded the Jeff Davis Legion Cavalry of Maj. Gen. Matthew C. Butler's division, had seen a lot of war after serving with the Army of Northern Virginia's Cavalry Corps. "I fear that the war is over & that all our sacrifices are in vain," Waring entered in his diary. "We shall be betrayed by our own leaders."[21]

One of Maj. Gen. Joseph Wheeler's Southern cavalrymen noted that from the moment Johnston began deliberating with Sherman, "it was impossible for Gen. J. to back out from his negotiations with S. never mind what terms S. dictated, because his army would no longer fight." He continued, "Thousands under the pretense of not being willing to remain to be surrendered stole mules from the wagons & horses from artillery & deserted their colors endeavoring to get home."[22] When Col. W. W. Allen, who commanded one of Wheeler's cavalry regiments, heard that Johnston intended to surrender, he "wrote an earnest letter to General Wheeler in protest."[23]

Another one of Wheeler's horse soldiers said, "It would be impossible to describe the surprise created from the highest ranking officer to the humblest private by [the news of the armistice]. They were dazed, and had never thought of a surrender. It is surprising, too, that they had not; for they were too intelligent not to know of the disastrous condition of affairs, and that they were fighting a force numerically larger than their own by at least ten to one." In summary, he asked, "Had they not concluded that all left to them was to remain

20. Brooks, *Memoirs of the War of Secession*, 370.
21. Waring diary, entry for April 16, 1865.
22. W. W. Gordon diary, entry for April 17, 1865, Gordon Family Papers, Southern Historical Collections, Wilson Library, University of North Carolina, Chapel Hill, North Carolina.
23. DuBose, *General Joseph Wheeler*, 465.

to the end and to let consequences take care of themselves—in other words, that honor dictated that there was nothing for them to do but, if need be, to die with the harness on?"[24]

A Confederate officer who had witnessed the surrender of Gen. Robert E. Lee's army observed that "the spirit of General Johnston's men was much finer than, under the circumstances, anybody would have expected. They were defiant, and more than ready to try conclusions with Sherman in a pitched battle." He elaborated, "Many expressed disgust and indignation when the surrender of the army was announced. An epidemic of drunkenness, gambling, and fighting prevailed while we were waiting for our final orders. Whatever difficulty General Breckinridge may have experienced in procuring liquor, the soldiers seemed to have an abundance of colorless corn-whiskey and applejack, and the roadsides were lined with 'chuck-a-luck' games. The amount of Confederate money displayed was marvelous. Men had it by the haversackful, and bet it recklessly upon anything. The ill-temper begotten by drinking and gambling manifested itself almost hourly in free fights." This situation threatened to spiral out of control.[25]

Lieutenant General William J. Hardee, who was Johnston's senior subordinate and who remained with the main body of the army at Greensboro, North Carolina, wrote to Gen. P. G. T. Beauregard: "We are all agog respecting the object [of the truce], and surmises are that negotiations are afoot between Johnston and Sherman. If such be not the case, it would be well for me to know it as soon as practicable, that I may contradict it. The report, as you may well conceive, can do our troops no good."[26] One of Hardee's staff officers commented, "Rumors of capitulation very demoralizing to troops."[27] A Rebel soldier recorded in his diary, "Thousands under pretense of not being willing to remain to be surrendered, stole mules...and horses...& deserted their colors, endeavoring to get home."[28]

Johnston's men harbored no illusions. "Everything seems to indicate a speedy termination of the Confederacy & a restoration of the old state of affairs which though it is very humiliating to us still has its pleasant features," staff officer G. P. Collins admitted on April

24. George B. Guild, *A Brief Narrative of the Fourth Tennessee Cavalry Regiment, Wheler's Corps, Army of Tennessee* (Nashville: n.p., 1913), 145.
25. Wise, *The End of an Era*, 454-455.
26. *OR* 47, 3:807.
27. Thomas Benton Roy diary, entry for April 16, 1865, Thomas Benton Roy papers, Illinois Archives and Manuscripts Department, Chicago Historical Society, Chicago, Illinois.
28. William M. Gordon diary, entry for April 17, 1865, William M. Gordon papers, Southern Historical Collection, Wilson Library, University of North Carolina, Chapel Hill, North Carolina.

22. "Everyone is so worn out with war & I am almost inclined to believe that our people scarcely deserve freedom or they would stand up better."[29]

Civilian morale fared no better. Elizabeth Collier, who lived in Hillsborough, despaired in her diary, "Gen Johnston has surrendered his army! We have no army now-We have been overpowered-outnumbered, but thank God we have not been whipped—Did I ever think to live to see this day! After all the misery & anguish of the four past years-Think of all our sacrifices—of broken hearts, & desolated homes-of our noble, glorious dead--, & say for what? Reconstruction! How the very word galls—Can we ever live in peace with the desecrators of our homes & the murderers of our Fathers, Brothers & Sons—Never—We are bound to rise again—My God is it thy will that we should be conquered?" She reflected, "Oh I had such supreme faith—such profound belief in the justice of our cause—that I thought it impossible for us to be vanquished—Surely oh My God thine our hast not ben deaf to the fervent prayers for our success which have ascended nigh & day? Teach us to say They will be done on earth—Good may yet result from evil—God has some wise, & hidden purpose in thus punishing us—Perhaps we were too presumptuous—we relied too much upon his favor when we had no right to expect it—God knows what is best for as a people as well as individuals."[30]

Confederate Secretary of State Judah P. Benjamin.

(Library of Congress)

Confederate President Jefferson Davis also took the opportunity to poll his cabinet regarding their views about whether to approve the terms Sherman and Johnston negotiated at the meeting on April 18, and, if so, how the negotiations should be handled. Each of the remaining cabinet members wrote lengthy letters to Davis explaining their opinions. All favored making peace on the best terms possible, including Confederate Secretary of State Judah P. Benjamin, who had previously supported any attempts to continue the

---

29. G. P. Collins to Anne Cameron Collins, April 22, 1865, Anne Cameron Collins Papers, Southern Historical Collection, Wilson Library, University of North Carolina, Chapel Hill, North Carolina.
30. Diary of Elizabeth Collier, entry for April 25, 1865, Elizabeth Collier diary 1861-1865, Southern Historical Collection, Wilson Library, University of North Carolina, Chapel Hill, North Carolina.

war. These unique letters are set forth, verbatim, in Appendix C.

Major Hitchcock arrived in Washington, D.C., on April 21. Hitchcock, aware of the document's contents he had delivered, told his uncle, Maj. Gen. Ethan Allen Hitchcock, who was then stationed at the nation's capital, that "President Johnson would not approve or carry out certain points submitted to him." That afternoon, Grant told Hitchcock "that a cabinet meeting would probably have to be held, and it might be forty-eight hours before" the adjutant would have answers.[31]

Grant promptly forwarded Sherman's package to Secretary of War Edwin Stanton. "I have received and just completed reading the dispatches brought by special messenger from General Sherman," Stanton wrote. "They are of such importance that I think immediate action should be taken on them and that it should be done by the President in council with his whole cabinet. I would respectfully suggest whether the President should not be notified and all his cabinet, and the meeting take place to-night."[32]

Grant was invited to attend the cabinet meeting. Secretary of State William H. Seward was still recovering from being wounded in the failed assassination attempt less than a week earlier. Grant read Sherman's communications to a stunned cabinet; only a few days earlier, Sherman had assured Stanton, "I will accept the same terms as General Grant gave General Lee, and be careful not to complicate any points of civil policy."[33]

"Among the Cabinet and all present there was but one mind on this subject," Secretary of the Navy Gideon Welles recorded in his diary. "The plan was rejected, and Sherman's arrangement disapproved. Stanton and [Joshua] Speed were emphatic in their condemnation, though the latter expressed personal friendship for Sherman. General Grant, I was pleased to see, while disapproving what Sherman had done, and decidedly opposed to it, was tender to sensitiveness of his brother officer and abstained from censure. Stanton came charged with specified objections, four in number, counting them off on his fingers. Some of his argument was apt and well, some of it not in good taste nor precisely pertinent. It was decided that General Grant should immediately inform General Sherman that his course was disapproved, and that generals in the field must not take upon themselves to decide on political and civil questions, which belonged to the executive and civil service."[34]

31. Howe, *Marching with Sherman*, 304.
32. *OR* 47, 3:263.
33. Ibid., 221.
34. John T. Morse, ed., *The Diary of Gideon Welles, Secretary of the Navy*

Secretary of War Edwin M. Stanton, whose actions in rejecting the agreement of April 18, 1865 offended Sherman.

President Andrew Johnson.

(Library of Congress)

(Library of Congress)

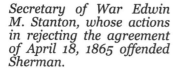

Later, Grant said, "There seemed to be the greatest consternation, lest Sherman would commit the government to terms to which they were not willing to accede to and which we had no right to grant."[35]

Stanton responded quickly and ominously. "The memorandum or basis agreed upon between General Sherman and General Johnston having been submitted to the President, they are disapproved. You will give notice of the disapproval to General Sherman and direct him to resume hostilities at the earliest moment. The instructions given to you by the late President Abraham Lincoln on the 3d of March by my telegraph of that date, addressed to you, express substantially the views of President Andrew Johnson and will be observed by General Sherman. A copy is herewith appended. The President desires that you proceed immediately to the headquarters of General Sherman and direct operations against the enemy."[36]

Under Lincoln and Johnson, 3 vols. (New York: Houghton-Mifflin, 1911), 2:294.

35. Ulysses S. Grant, *Personal Memoirs of U. S. Grant,* 2 vols. (New York: Charles L. Webster & Co., 1892), 2:516.

36. *OR* 47, 3:263. Stanton also sent this note to Halleck: "The memorandum or basis of arrangement made between General Sherman and General Johnston are disapproved by the President period? General Sherman is ordered to resume hostilities." Ibid., 264.

The March 3 letter by Lincoln referenced by Stanton provided: "The President directs me to say to you that he wishes you to have no conference with General Lee, unless it be for the capitulation of General Lee's army or on some minor and purely military matter. He instructs me to say that you are not to decide, discuss, or confer upon any political question. Such questions the President holds in his own hands, and will submit them to no military conferences or conventions. Meantime you are to press to the utmost your military advantages."[37] In short, unless Johnston was prepared to surrender his army, Grant was to subsume Sherman in command and move toward an immediate military resolution of the war.

After disapproving the terms, the cabinet members issued the following memorandum, which was published in multiple newspapers and detailed the reasons why they had rejected Sherman's deal with Johnston:

> This proceeding of Gen. SHERMAN was unapproved for the following among other reasons:
>
> First -- It was an exercise of authority not vested in Gen. SHERMAN, and on its face shows that both he and JOHNSTON knew that he (Gen. SHERMAN) had no authority to enter into any such arrangement.
>
> Second -- It was a practical acknowledgement of the rebel government.
>
> Third -- It undertook to reestablish the rebel State government, that had been overthrown at the sacrifice of many thousand loyal lives, and an immense treasure and placed arms and munitions of war in the hands of the rebels at their respective capitols, which might be used as soon as the armies of the United States were disbanded, and used to conquer and subdue the loyal States.
>
> Fourth -- By the restoration of the rebel authority in their respective States, they would be enabled to reestablish slavery.
>
> Fifth -- It might furnish a ground of responsibility by the Federal Government to pay the rebel debt, and certainly subjects loyal citizens of the rebel States to the debt consummated by the rebels in the name of the State.

---

37. Ibid.

Sixth -- It put in dispute the existence of loyal State Governments, and the new State of Western Virginia, which had been recognized by every department of the United States Government.

Seventh -- It practically abolishes the confiscation laws, and relieved rebels of every degree, who had slaughtered our people, from all pains and penalties for their crimes.

Eighth -- It gave terms that had been deliberately, repeatedly, and solemnly rejected by President LINCOLN, and better terms than the rebels had ever asked in their most prosperous condition.

Ninth -- It formed no poises of true and lasting peace, but relieved rebels from the pressure of our victories and left them in condition to renew their effort to overthrow the United States Government, and subdue the loyal States, whenever their strength was recruited, and any opportunity should offer.[38]

Unfortunately for Sherman, the unhappy cabinet was determined to publicly embarrass the army commander for trying to end the war.

Grant prepared a letter to Sherman:

HEADQUARTERS ARMIES OF THE UNITED STATES,
Washington, D. C., April 21, 1865.
Maj. Gen. W. T. SHERMAN,
Commanding Military Division of the Mississippi:

GENERAL: The basis of agreement entered into between yourself and General J. E. Johnston for the disbandment of the Southern army and the extension of the authority of the General Government over all the territory belonging to it, sent for the approval of the President, is received. I read it carefully myself before submitting it to the President and Secretary of War and felt satisfied that it could not possibly be approved. My reasons for these views I will give you at another time in a more extended letter. Your agreement touches upon questions of such vital importance that as soon as read I

---

38. "Sherman's Army; Gen. Sherman Negotiating with Gen. Johnston. His Action Repudiated by the President and the Cabinet. Hostilities to Commence at Once. President Lincoln's Instructions to be Carried Out. Lieut.-Gen. Grant Hastens to the Scene of Action. Sherman's Order Suspending Hostilities. Great Dissatisfaction Created by it in the Army," *New York Times*, April 24, 1865.

addressed a note to the Secretary of War notifying him of their receipt and the importance of immediate action by the President, and suggested in view of their importance that the entire cabinet be called together that all might give an expression of their opinions upon the matter. The result was a disapproval by the President of the basis laid down, a disapproval of the negotiations altogether, except for the surrender of the army commanded by General Johnston, and directions to me to notify you of this decision. I cannot do so better than by sending you the inclosed copy of a dispatch (penned by the late President, though signed by the Secretary of War) in answer to me on sending a letter received from General Lee proposing to meet me for the purpose of submitting the question of peace to a convention of officers. Please notify General Johnston immediately on receipt of this of the termination of the truce and resume hostilities against his army at the earliest moment you can, acting in good faith. The rebels know well the terms on which they can have peace and just when negotiations can commence, namely, when they lay down their arms and submit to the laws of the United States. Mr. Lincoln gave the full assurances of what he would do, I believe, in his conference with commissioners met in Hampton Roads.

Very respectfully, your obedient servant,
U. S. GRANT,
Lieutenant-General.[39]

Grant sent his letter, along with the March 3 letter Stanton had forwarded, to Sherman by telegraph.

"I was summoned to Gen. Grant's office at 10 P.M. and before 12 P.M. had accompanied him to the boat," Hitchcock stated. He recognized that if Grant arrived in person carrying President Andrew Johnson's private message to Sherman, then matters of great importance were about to occur in the coming days.[40]

Hitchcock, Grant, and a number of Grant's staff officers sailed down the Potomac River from Washington, D.C., to Fort Monroe,

---

39. *OR* 47, 3:263-264.
40. Howe, *Marching with Sherman*, 304. This was the first time that Hitchcock had met Grant. "Gen. Grant is in almost every respect a very unlike man to Gen. Sherman, in demeanor as well as appearance," Hitchcock wrote. "He is very quiet and taciturn, with none of Sherman's vivacity of appearance or manner, and none of his off-hand, ready, entertaining conversation. That is, I see nothing of that, and though I do not doubt his mind is just now fully occupied with the gravest questions of the day, which would explain unusual thoughtfulness in any man, yet it is evidently also habitual." Ibid.

Virginia, near Hampton Roads. There, they boarded a steamer to Morehead City, North Carolina, and then took a train to Raleigh. At 4:00 p.m. on April 22, Grant wired Stanton, "As soon as dispatches can be got off for General Halleck and General Sheridan I will start from here for Morehead City."[41]

The message to Maj. Gen. Henry Halleck stated: "The truce entered into by Sherman will be ended as soon as I can reach Raleigh. Move Sheridan with his cavalry toward Greensborough, N.C., as soon as possible. I think it will be well to send one corps of infantry also, the whole under Sheridan. The infantry need not go farther than Danville unless they receive orders hereafter to do so." Halleck did as ordered.[42] On the morning of April 23, Grant informed Stanton that he had arrived in Beaufort, North Carolina, and would depart for Raleigh as soon as a train could be located.[43]

Sherman cabled Johnston at 8:00 p.m. that evening. "Major Hitchcock reports his arrival at Morehead City with dispatches from Washington, and will be here in the morning. Please be in readiness to resume negotiations when the contents of dispatches are known," Sherman wrote.[44]

That night, Sherman composed a message to Ellen, which said, "Hitchcock should be back the day after tomorrow and then I will know. I can start in pursuit of Johnston—who is about Greensboro, on short notice; but I would prefer not to follow him back to Georgia. A pursuing army cannot travel as fast as a fleeing one in its own country." He then explained his primary concern: "There is great danger of the Confederate armies breaking up into guerillas, and that is what I most fear. Such men as Wade Hampton, Forrest, Wirt Adams, etc., never will work and nothing is left for them but death or highway robbery. They will not work and their negroes are all gone, their plantations destroyed, etc. I will be glad if I can open a way for them abroad. Davis, Breckenridge, etc., will go abroad or get killed in pursuit. My terms do not embrace them but apply solely to the Confederate armies. All not in regular muster rolls will be outlaws. The people of Raleigh are quiet and submissive enough, and also the North Carolinians are subjugated, but the young men, after they get over the effects of recent disasters and wake up to the realization that nothing is left them but to work, will be sure to stir up trouble, but I hope we can soon fix them off."[45]

41. *OR* 47, 3:276.
42. Ibid., 276-277.
43. Ibid., 286.
44. Ibid., 287.
45. Howe, *Home Letters of General Sherman*, 347-348.

Sherman did not know that Grant had been traveling with Hitchcock. "Of course, I was both surprised and pleased to see the general, soon learned that my terms with Johnston had been disapproved, was instructed by him to give the forty-eight hours' notice required by the terms of the truce, and afterward to attack or follow him," Sherman recalled about the surprise meeting with his friend Grant.[46] Hearing the news of Grant's arrival, a visibly relieved Maj. Gen. Henry W. Slocum declared to Maj. Gen. Carl Schurz, "All will be well. Grant is here. He has come from Washington to set things right."[47]

General Howard remembered that Grant's visit "was a memorable one. His close friendship for Sherman prevented anything that might have been unfavorable to a speedy peace, and allayed all asperities; but he could not remove the deep chagrin Sherman felt, not that his terms had been disapproved, for that was discretionary with the President, but because he had been so publicly and cruelly denounced by the War Department."[48]

Grant advised Sherman that the cabinet had rejected the initial terms. He described the terms that he had given to Lee, telling Sherman he was authorized to offer the same terms to Johnston. "I sent Sherman to do this himself," recalled Grant. "I did not wish the knowledge of my presence to be known to the army generally; so I left it to Sherman to negotiate the terms of the surrender solely by himself, and without the enemy knowing that I was anywhere near the field. As soon as possible, I started to get away, to leave Sherman quite free and untrammelled."[49]

Lt. Gen. Ulysses S. Grant, commander in chief of all Union armies, and Sherman's friend and patron.

(Library of Congress)

46. Sherman, *Memoirs*, 2:358.
47. Schurz, *Reminiscences*, 3:117.
48. Howard, *Autobiography*, 2:157-158. Major General Jacob D. Cox, commander of the 23rd Corps of Maj. Gen. John M. Schofield's Army of the Ohio, recalled, "Grant's since friendship and his freedom from the least desire to exhibit his own power had made him act as a visitor rather than a commander. He appreciated Sherman's perfect readiness to accept the methods dictated by the civil authorities, and saw that his zeal was as ardent as it was at Atlanta or Savannah." Cox, *Military Reminiscences*, 2:493.
49. Grant, *Personal Memoirs*, 2:517.

Referring to Stanton's letter, specifically the enclosed note regarding Lincoln's instructions from March 3, an angry Sherman told the secretary of war, "That was the first and only time I ever saw that telegram, or had one word of instruction on the important matter involved in it; and it does seem strange to me that every bar-room loafer in New York can read in the morning journals official matter that is withheld from a general whose command extends from Kentucky to North Carolina." He also noted, "General Grant had orders from the President, through the Secretary of War, to direct military movements, and I explained to him the exact position of the troops, and he approved of it most emphatically; but he did not relieve me or express a wish to assume command."[50]

While Sherman huddled with Grant, Union officers swarmed around Hitchcock, looking for news from Washington, D.C. A staff officer asked, "Well, Major—do you bring back peace or war?" Hitchcock replied, "I brought back General Grant!"[51] Grant's presence largely spoke for itself.

After leaving Sherman, Grant reported to Stanton. "I reached here this morning, and delivered to General Sherman the reply to his negotiations with Johnston. He was not surprised, but rather expected their rejection. Word was immediately sent to Johnston terminating the truce, and information that civil matters could not be entertained in any convention between army commanders," he wrote. Grant continued, "General Sherman has, been guided in his negotiations with Johnston entirely by what he thought was precedent authorized by the President. He had before him the terms given by me to Lee's army and the call of the rebel legislature of Virginia, authorized by General Weitzel, as he supposed with the sanction of the President and myself. At the time of the agreement General Sherman did not know of the withdrawal of authority for the meeting of that legislature. The moment he learned through the papers that authority for the meeting had been withdrawn he communicated the fact to Johnston as having bearing on the negotiations had."[52]

Sherman immediately notified Johnston that the truce would expire in 48 hours.[53] A few minutes later, he sent a second dispatch: "I have replies from Washington to my communications of April 18. I am

50. *OR* 47, 1:34.
51. Howe, *Marching with Sherman*, 309.
52. Ibid., 3:293.
53. Ibid. Sherman wrote, "You will take notice that the truce or suspension of hostilities agreed to between us will cease in forty-eight hours after this is received at your lines under first of the articles of our agreement."

instructed to limit my operations to your immediate command and not to attempt civil negotiations. I therefore demand the surrender of your army on the same terms as were given General Lee at Appomattox, of April 9, instant, purely and simply."[54] Grant approved both dispatches before they were sent. Sherman then instructed Maj. Gen. James H. Wilson to make arrangements to resume hostilities on April 26. He also drafted orders for his army to prepare to move on Johnston's command as soon as the truce expired.[55]

Maj. Gen. James H. Wilson, commander of an independent cavalry corps operating in Alabama.

(Library of Congress)

Sherman's combined armies passed in review on April 24. "We were considerably surprised to find General Grant sitting by the side of Sherman as we passed the reviewing stand. We wondered why he should be there. We suspected he had come to command further operations against the enemy," a Wisconsin soldier recalled.[56] "In the interval we maintained a truce in the nature of statu quo, and the army was reviewed, and, to put it mildly, never did [Raleigh] witness such a sight before," a soldier of the 104th Ohio proudly declared. "As the troops passed the reviewing stand on Capitol Square where stood Gens. Grant, Sherman, Howard, Logan, Schofield, Cox, Kilpatrick, and others of prominence, with battalion after battalion marching by, one of the citizens, standing near the line of march, remarked, 'The sight is awe-inspiring.' May I add, it showed that the men of the West were invincible."[57] One soldier commented that Grant's presence "had an additional incentive (if such were needed) to acquit ourselves well."[58]

"Grant...was present at my review of the Seventeenth Corps day before yesterday, and yesterday he visited and rode among the camps of my Fifteenth Corps," Howard told his wife on April 26. "The men received him with great enthusiasm."[59]

54. Ibid., 294.
55. Ibid., 294-295.
56. *Story of the Service of Company E*, 430.
57. L. F. Becker, "Campaigning with a Grand Army. Some of the 104th Ohio's Service in the Latter Part of the War," *National Tribune*, November 23, 1899.
58. Jamison, *Recollections*, 328.
59. Howard, *Autobiography*, 2:159.

As the review ended and the men broke ranks to return to their camps, a Wisconsin soldier exclaimed, "We've got to march tomorrow, you see if we haven't! General Grant has come here for the purpose of having us move against Johnston and will himself take command; now you just mark my word!"[60] Another soldier observed, "Air thick with rumors—sick being sent to hospitals—trains loading with supplies and ammunition—every indication of a forward movement."[61]

The Union public opinion strongly differed from Sherman's actions. Still enraged by Lincoln's assassination, the Northerners sought revenge for the fallen president and wanted to show the Confederates no mercy.[62] Stanton took the extraordinary step of allowing Major General Halleck to prepare and issue an order to Maj. Gens. George G. Meade, Philip H. Sheridan, and Horatio G. Wright, who all commanded separate forces operating in Virginia; the order also included Maj. Gens. James H. Wilson, in Georgia, and Edward R. S. Canby, in Alabama. The order advised the generals "to pay no regard to any truce or orders of General Sherman suspending hostilities, on the ground that Sherman's agreements could bind his own command only, and no other. They are directed to push forward, regardless of orders from any one except General Grant, and cut off Johnston's retreat." Halleck's instruction for Meade, Sheridan, and Wright not to obey any of Sherman's orders, not surprisingly, terribly offended Sherman, who never forgave Halleck for issuing such a command.[63]

---

60. *Story of the Service of Company E*, 431.
61. Jamison, *Recollections*, 328.
62. President Johnson received two notes that appear in the *Civil War's official records*:

PHILADELPHIA, April 24, 1865.
(Received 1.50 p. in.)
His Excellency A. JOHNSON, President of the United States:
Almost unanimous against the Sherman armistice. Feeling tremendous. I will be in Washington to-morrow.
J. W. FORNEY.

PROVIDENCE, R. I., April 24, 1865.
(Received 2.35 p. in.)
His Excellency ANDREW JOHNSON, President of the United States:
Loyal men deplore and are outraged by Sherman's arrangement with Johnston. He should be promptly removed.
WILLIAM SPRAGUE,
U.S. Senator.

OR 47, 3:294.
63. Ibid., 311. In fact, Sherman was so offended that he refused to shake Halleck's hand when he saw his former friend in Washington, D.C., in May 1865, when his army arrived for the Grand Review.

Further, New York newspapers, in particular, railed against Sherman. "General Sherman, the distinguished and admirable soldier, has fatally compromised himself, we fear, in entering into the forbidden field of diplomacy as a peacemaker," the *New York Herald* declared. "The astounding dispatches from the War Department which we published yesterday, embracing the armistice and peace programme entered into between himself and General Joe Johnston, place the conqueror of Georgia and South Carolina in a truly unfortunate position."

After elaborating about the reasons why the government rejected Sherman's agreement with Johnston, the editorial concluded with a harsh assessment of the general. "We fear that General Sherman, like General Fremont and General McClellan, has forgotten the soldier in attempting at the same time to play the politician, and that, like them, in anticipating, he has lost the opportunity. We have heard him as a soldier, and justly too, ranked with that great military genius, the Duke of Marlborough. The parallel may now be extended to the blunders of the great Duke as a politician, with this difference: that he never committed such a great political blunder as this peace protocol of General Sherman. From the country at large he has cast his political fortunes into the peace democracy—a poor and contemptible faction. For his own sake, however, we shall be glad to hear that on the receipt of the intelligence of the late appalling calamity at Washington, General Sherman will have realized the extent of his indiscretion, and repair it in the capture or satisfactory surrender of Johnston's army in advance of the arrival of General Grant. This appears now to be the only chance for General Sherman to repair the single but stupendous mistake which so unexpectedly interposes to overshadow his glorious reputation."[64]

---

64. "The Astounding News from General Sherman—His Rash Armistice and the Consequences," *New York Herald*, April 24, 1865. *The New York Times* ran a similar uncomplimentary editorial the next day, which declared, "Every one who chooses to give the matter reflection sees that, even if there had been no serious military blunder involved in the granting of an armistice, and no grave political error in the terms of the compact, there was still the loudest call for remonstrance and rebuke when a military subordinate dared to undertake to set aside, even conditionally, not only the plainest acts of Congress, the most solemn orders of the Executive, but the best considered judgments of the Supreme Court as well...And it is notable that is the oracles that have spoken most favorably in recent times of these peace missionaries that now propose to throw a mantle of charity and tenderness over an arrangement that has opened for the rebel leaders an unobstructed highway to Texas or Mexico, if it has not also furnished them with an escort of thirty odd thousand troops under Johnston's command." See "Sherman's Scheme of Peace and our Great Calamity," *New York Times*, April 25, 1865.

The *New York Times* also criticized the Union general and opined, "Gen. Sherman, we fear, has made a very grave mistake, and been fairly beaten by that cunning traitor, the rebel Secretary of War."[65] Another article from the same edition of the Times repeated a similar theme: "The manner in which Breckinridge brought about the Sherman surrender seems to have been altogether perfect. One of the rebel's best devices was to put our commander entirely off his guard on the question of slavery. 'The discussion of slavery is at an end,' said this arch-traitor. 'The amendment to the Constitution abolishing slavery will be accepted by the people of the South.' Yet the wily outlaw brought the victim to the humiliating point of singing an instrument designed to make the institution of slavery perpetual."[66]

Despite the media firestorm, Grant understood Sherman's anger. "Sherman, from being one of the most popular generals of the land (Congress having even gone so far as to propose a bill providing for a second lieutenant general for the purpose of advancing him to that grade), was denounced by the President and Secretary of War in very bitter terms," he wrote. "Some people went so far as to denounce him as a traitor—a most preposterous term to apply to a man who had rendered so much service as he had, even supposing he had made a mistake in granting such terms as he did to Johnston and his army." Grant declared, "If Sherman had taken authority to send Johnston with his army home, with their arms to be put in the arsenals of their own States, without submitting the question to the authorities at Washington, the suspicious might have some foundation."[67]

Peter Eltinge, a New York soldier serving with Sherman's army, demonstrated that not all of Sherman's men supported his actions. Eltinge wrote to his father, "What do you think of the Sherman-Johnston agreement? I was never more surprised in my life when I read the Agreement that Sherman had made with Johnston and which he even dared to send to Washington for approval. I cannot account for this strange conduct of Gen. Sherman. He has certainly lowered himself much in the opinion of the whole Army and a majority of Loyal citizens. The credit and renown that he had won by his great campaign has nearly all been lost by his attempting to make himself a great Peacemaker."[68]

---

65. "From Gen. Sherman's Army: Sherman's Conference with Johnston. Interesting Particulars of the Interview. Johnston Informs Sherman Where Wilson is Raiding and Wants Him Stopped," *New York Times*, April 27, 1865.
66. "Sherman and Breckinridge," *New York Times*, April 27, 1865.
67. Grant, *Personal Memoirs of U. S. Grant*, 2:515-516.
68. Peter Eltinge to his father, May 5, 1865, Bradley Collection.

The criticism about Sherman did not resonate with the Union high command. Howard told a friend, "I am deeply sorry for the abuse General Sherman is getting at the hands of the press. He meant right, and the reasons for offering generous terms are not rightly set forth by the press. How easy it is to impute wrong motives!"[69]

Schofield also defended Sherman and said, "However unwise Sherman's action may have been, the uproar it created, and the attacks upon his honor and integrity for which it was made the excuse, were utterly inexcusable. They were probably unexampled as an exhibition of the effect of the great and unusual excitement upon the minds of men unaccustomed to such moral and mental strain."[70]

Miffed, Sherman wrote to Stanton:

> **HDQRS. MILITARY DIVISION OF THE MISSISSIPPI,**
> **In the Field, Raleigh, N.C., April 25, 1865.**
> **Hon. E. M. STANTON,**
> **Secretary of War, Washington:**
>
> **DEAR SIR: I have been furnished a copy of your letter of April 21 to General Grant, signifying your disapproval of the terms on which General Johnston proposed to disarm and disperse the insurgents on condition of amnesty, &c. I admit my folly in embracing in a military convention any civil matters, but unfortunately such is the nature of our situation that they seem inextricably united, and I understood from you at Savannah that the financial state of the country demanded military success, and would warrant a little bending to policy. When I had my conference with General Johnston I had the public examples before me of General Grants terms to Lee's army and General Weitzel's invitation to the Virginia Legislature to assemble. I still believe the Government of the United States has made a mistake, but that is none of my business; mine is a different task, and I had flattered myself that by four years patient, unremitting, and successful labor I deserved no reminder such as is contained in the last paragraph of your letter to General Grant. You may assure the President I heed his suggestion.**

---

69. Oliver O. Howard, "General Howard's Address," *Report of the Proceedings of the Society of the Army of the Tennessee at the Twenty-Eighth Meeting, Held at St. Louis, Mo., November 18-19, 1896* (Cincinnati: Press of F. W. Freeman, 1897), 79.
70. Schofield, *Forty-Six Years in the Army*, 349.

I am, truly,
W. T. SHERMAN,
Major-General.[71]

This inappropriate and wrong-headed treatment at the hands of Stanton and Halleck enraged Sherman. Major General Carl Schurz, serving as Slocum's temporary chief of staff, accompanied Slocum to a meeting at Sherman's headquarters in Raleigh. Schurz watched as Sherman "paced up and down the room like a caged lion, and, without addressing anybody in particular, unbusomed himself with an eloquence of furious invective which for a while made us all stare," he recalled. "He lashed the Secretary of War as a mean, scheming, vindictive politician, who made it his business to rob military men of the credit earned by exposing their lives in the service of their country. He berated the people who blamed him for what he had done as a mass of fools, not worth fighting for, who did not know when a thing was well done. He railed at the press, which had altogether too much freedom; which had become an engine of vilification; which should be bridled by severe laws, so that the fellows who wielded too loose a pen might be put behind bars—and so on, and so on."[72]

When Sherman testified before the Joint Committee on the Conduct of the War in May 1865, he said, "It was only after I had fulfilled all this that I learned, for the first time, through the public press, that my conduct had been animadverted upon, not only by the Secretary of War, but by General Halleck and the press of the country at large. I did feel hurt and wronged that Mr. Stanton coupled with the terms of my memorandum, confided to him, a copy of a telegram to General Grant, which he had never sent to me." Sherman continued, "By coupling the note to General Grant with my memorandum he gave the world fairly and clearly to infer that I was in possession of it; now, I was not in possession of it; and I have reason to know that Mr. Stanton knew I was not in possession of it. Next met me General Halleck's telegram, indorsed by Mr. Stanton, in which they publicly avowed an act of perfidy, namely, the violation of my truce, which I had a right to make, and which by the laws of war and by the laws of Congress is punishable by death, and no other punishment."

Sherman was not finished. "Next they ordered an army to pursue my enemy, who was known to be surrendering to me, in the presence of General Grant himself, their superior officer; and, finally, they sent orders to General Wilson and to General Thomas, my subordinates, acting under me on a plan of the most magnificent scale, admirably

---

71. OR 47, 3:301-302.
72. Schurz, *Reminiscences*, 3:116-117.

executed, to defeat my orders and to thwart the interests of the government of the United States." He concluded, "I did feel indignant—I do feel indignant."[73]

Sherman, seething, wrote to Grant after writing to the secretary of war:

> **HDQRS. MILITARY DIVISION OF THE MISSIS-SIPPI,**
> **In the Field, Raleigh, N.C., April 25, 1865.**
> **Lieut. Gen. U.S. GRANT, Present:**
>
> **GENERAL: I had the honor to receive your letter of April 21, with inclosure, yesterday, and was well pleased that you came along, as you must have observed that I held the military control so as to adapt it to any phase the case might assume. It is but just that I should record the fact that I made my terms with General Johnston under the influence of the liberal terms you extended to the army of General Lee at Appomattox Court-House on the 9th, and the seeming policy of our Government, as evidenced by the call of the Virginia Legislature and governor back to Richmond under your and President Lincoln's very eyes. It now appears that this last act was done without consultation with you or any knowledge of Mr. Lincoln, but rather in opposition to a previous policy well considered. I have not the least desire to interfere in the civil policy of our Government, but would shun it as something not to my liking; but occasions do arise when a prompt seizure of results is forced on military commanders not in immediate communication with the proper authority.**
>
> **It is probable that the terms signed by General Johnston and myself were not clear enough on the point well understood between us; that our negotiations did not apply to any parties outside the officers and men of the Confederate armies, which would have been easily remedied. No surrender of an army not actually at the mercy of an antagonist was ever made without terms, and these always define the military status of the surrendered. Thus you stipulated that the officers and men of Lee's army should not be molested at their homes so long as they obeyed the laws at the place of their residence. I do not wish to discuss the points involved in our recognition of the State governments in actual**

---

73. "Sherman-Johnston," 6.

existence, but merely state my conclusions to await the solution of the future.

Such action on our part in no manner recognizes for a moment the so-called Confederate Government, or makes us liable for its debts or acts. The laws and acts done by the several States during the period of rebellion are void because done without the oath prescribed by the Constitution of the United States, which is a condition precedent. We have a right to use any sort of machinery to produce military results, and it is the commonest thing for military commanders to use the civil Government in actual existence as a means to an end. I do believe we could and can use the present State governments lawfully, constitutionally, and as the very best possible means to produce the object desired, viz, entire and complete submission to the lawful authority of the United States.

As to punishment for past crimes, that is for the judiciary, and can in no manner of way be disturbed by our acts, and so far as I can I will use my influence that rebels shall suffer all the personal punishment prescribed by law, as also the civil liabilities arising from their past acts. What we now want is the mere forms of law by which common men may regain the positions of industry so long disturbed by the war.

I now apprehend that the rebel armies will disperse, and instead of dealing with six or seven States we will have to deal with numberless bands of desperadoes, headed by such men as Mosby, Forrest, Red Jackson, and others, who know not and care not for danger and its consequences.

I am, with great respect, your obedient servant,
W. T. SHERMAN,
Major-General.[74]

While Sherman fumed, events on the Confederate side were forcing things to a conclusion.

On the afternoon of April 24, after reading the letters from his remaining cabinet officers encouraging him to accept the terms, Davis informed Johnston that he had approved the terms of the convention with Sherman, writing: "The Secretary of War has delivered to me the copy you handed to him of the basis of an agreement between yourself

74. *OR* 47, 3:302-303.

and General Sherman. Your action is approved. You will so inform General Sherman, and, if the like authority be given by the Government of the United States to complete the arrangement, you will proceed on the basis adopted. Further instructions will be given as to the details of negotiation and the methods of executing the terms of agreement when notified by you of the readiness on the part of the general commanding U.S. forces to proceed with the arrangement."[75] Davis correctly doubted whether the Union government would approve the convention since it declared an amnesty for the civilian authorities of the Confederacy.

However, within an hour of learning of Davis's approval, Johnston received Sherman's messages about ending the truce and demanding his surrender. Johnston immediately reported the contents of the two dispatches to Maj. Gen. John C. Breckinridge by telegraph. He requested instructions and suggested disbanding the army to prevent Union armies from further devastating the countryside.[76]

Breckinridge replied, "Does not your suggestion about disbanding refer to the infantry and most of the artillery? If it be necessary to disband these they might still save their small-arms and find their way to some appointed rendezvous. Can you not bring off the cavalry and all of the men you can mount from transportation and other animals, with some light field pieces? Such a force could march away from Sherman and be strong enough to encounter anything between us and the Southwest. If this course be possible, carry it out and telegraph your intended route."[77]

Johnston remained convinced of the correctness of his approach. After reports that Macon, Georgia, and Mobile, Alabama, had fallen to Wilson and Canby, he answered, "Your dispatch received. We have to save the people, spare the blood of the army, and save the high civil functionaries. Your plan, I think, can only do the last. We ought to prevent invasion, make terms for our troops, and give an escort of cavalry to the President, who ought to move without loss of a moment. Commanders believe the troops will not fight again. We think your plan impracticable."[78]

After discussing matters at length with Gen. P. G. T. Beauregard, who agreed with Johnston's proposed course of action, Johnston concluded that because "the same unaccountable silence was maintained on the part of what was still called the Government of the Confederate States, General Johnston and General Beauregard were

75. *OR* 47, 3:834.
76. Johnston, *Narrative of Military Operations*, 411; OR 47, 3:835.
77. *OR* 47, 3:835.
78. Ibid.

forced to conclude that Mr. Davis was unwilling to assume any further responsibility and wished to transfer its weight to their shoulders. They were undeterred by this consideration," Beauregard's biographer noted.[79] At 1:30 a.m. on April 26, Johnston advised Davis that he had written Sherman to request a meeting to discuss surrendering his command.[80]

Breckinridge responded to Johnston: "Should you think it impracticable to move off the infantry and artillery, allow Lieutenant-General Hampton to receive such of the men of those arms as may desire to join the cavalry service, together with such transportation and other animals as they require."[81] Davis also wrote to Lt. Gen. Wade Hampton, telling the South Carolinian that he should attempt to join Davis's flight to Mexico.[82]

Breckinridge's instructions profoundly troubled Johnston, who later explained his motivations. "I objected, immediately, that this order provided for the performance of but one of the three great duties then devolving upon us—that of securing the safety of the high civil officers of the Confederate Government; but neglected the other two—the safety of the people, and that of the army," Johnston recalled in his post-war memoir. "I also advised the immediate flight of the high civil functionaries under proper escort. The belief that impelled me to urge the civil authorities of the Confederacy to make peace, that it would be a great crime to prolong the war, prompted me to disobey these instructions—the last that I received from the Confederate Government. They would have given the President an escort too heavy for flight, and not strong enough to force a way for him; and would have spread ruin over all the South, by leading the three great invading armies in pursuit." Consequently, Johnston was "determined to do all in my power to bring about a termination of hostilities"—even if that meant disobeying a direct order.[83]

79. Roman, *The Military Operations of General Beauregard*, 404.
80. *OR* 47, 3:836.
81. Ibid., 837.
82. Ibid. The topic of Hampton's refusal to surrender is addressed in Appendix D. General Braxton Bragg, no longer having any field command duties and unwilling to serve under Johnston's command, eventually caught up to Davis and the remnants of his cabinet near Abbeville, South Carolina, on May 1, 1865. He arrived in time to witness the breakup of Davis's party and to distribute the remaining funds from the Confederate treasury. Bragg also used his insight and influence as the senior remaining general officer to get Davis to acknowledge the Confederacy's defeat at the cabinet's final meeting on May 4. He then left Davis and was eventually captured by elements of the 15th Pennsylvania Cavalry. Bragg was paroled and returned to his home, ending his military career. Grady McWhiney and Judith Ann Hallock, *Braxton Bragg and Confederate Defeat*, 2 vols. (Tuscaloosa: University of Alabama Press, 1991), 2:258.
83. Johnston, *Narrative of Military Operations*, 411-412.

That same day, Lt. Gen. A. P. Stewart, a longtime corps commander of the Army of Tennessee, rode to Johnston's headquarters and learned that he had decided to conclude the final surrender terms. Only the army's esteem for Johnston seemed to be holding it together. One of Stewart's staff officers observed that "the eagerness of the men to get to their homes now is beyond picture." Stewart made speeches to three different portions of the remnant of his command, "explaining to them the reason General Johnston refuses the acceptance of the terms, the same being that all over a certain rank will be held for treason." Stewart skewed the truth so that the dwindling Confederate army would stay together long enough for Johnston to arrange a proper surrender in order to protect his soldiers, even if the misstatements raised concerns about the possibility of prosecution.[84]

Lt. Gen. Alexander P. Stewart, commander of the Army of Tennessee.

(Valentine Museum)

While the Confederate drama played out, Sherman turned his attention to preparing the army to move in the morning upon the expiration of the truce. "It is useless to deny that the officers and men of the army were chagrined and disappointed at this result," one of Sherman's adjutants, Maj. George W. Nichols, said, "orders were at once issued to the troops to return to the camps, which had been temporarily abandoned. Orders were also given out to the entire army to hold itself in readiness to march."[85]

"Everyone anticipates, and I think everyone regrets, another march," Major Hitchcock said, "for this time, if the Army does advance, it is necessarily in pursuit not of a single object, as heretofore, or to reach a definite 'objective point,' but to pursue a flying enemy and meanwhile to live on the country." He continued, "As I write, the General—I should say the Generals—are waiting for Johnston's reply to a communication sent out to him yesterday...I cannot but hope even

84. Bromfield Ridley, *Battles and Sketches of the Army of Tennessee* (Mexico, MO: Missouri Printing and Publishing Co., 1906), 464.
85. Nichols, *The Story of the Great March*, 318.

yet, as I do most earnestly, that Johnston's reply may be such as to obviate the necessity of our again 'sallying forth'; but I confess it is rather hope than expectation."[86]

A 92nd Illinois Mounted Infantry soldier, of Brig. Gen. Thomas J. Jordan's brigade of Kilpatrick's division, noted, "The men of the Regiment were very willing to resume hostilities, if it was necessary to do so, and to do, as Grant had written to Sherman, 'press Johnston hard, and end the war at once.' But there was not a soldier in the Regiment but that felt that it would be cruelty to fight another battle. Every man was conscious of the fact that the war was really over; but orders were orders, and they were ready to resume hostilities."[87]

The order to move "was understood, of course, as an order to prepare to advance toward Johnston's army," a New Yorker stated. "The work of preparation was begun with unwonted alacrity and spirit, and with such expressions as the following. 'If we march after Johnston now, and meet him as an enemy, damn him; he will wish he had surrendered decently.'"[88] Such was the mood of Sherman's army, which remained to finish the work and go home.

A member of the 9th Pennsylvania Cavalry wrote in his diary, "We remained in camp and tirned over our unservasable ordinance and preparen for a move." The same trooper also noticed "several flags of truce came in and went out."[89]

However, about 6:00 p.m., a courier reined in carrying a dispatch from Johnston. The dispatch read:

> **HEADQUARTERS ARMY OF TENNESSEE,**
> **In the Field, April 25, 1865. (Received 6.15 p.m.)**
> **Major-General SHERMAN, U. S. Army:**
>
> **Your dispatch of yesterday received. I propose a modification of the terms you offered, such terms for the army as you wrote on the 18th; they also modified according to change of circumstances, and a further armistice to arrange details and meeting for that purpose.**
>
> **JOS. E. JOHNSTON,**
> **General**[90]

86. Howe, *Marching with Sherman*, 309.
87. *Ninety-Second Illinois Volunteers*, 247.
88. Mowris, *History of the One Hundred Seventeenth Regiment*, 212.
89. Quoted in *John W. Rowell, Yankee Cavalrymen: Through the Civil War with the Ninth Pennsylvania Cavalry* (Knoxville: University of Tennessee Press, 1971), 252.
90. *OR* 47, 3:304. Theodore C. Wilson of the *New York Herald* interviewed Lt.

Sherman noted that Johnston did not know that Grant was present in Raleigh. Sherman consulted with Grant who advised him to meet with Johnston and receive his surrender on the same terms as Lee.[91] Sherman responded to Johnston by telling him that they would meet again at the Bennett house at noon on April 26.[92]

Johnston replied that night, although his note did not reach Sherman until early on the morning of April 26. He wrote:

> **IN THE FIELD, April 25, 1865.**
> **(Received 7:03 a. m. 26th.)**
> **Maj. Gen. W. T. SHERMAN,**
> **Commanding U.S. Forces:**
>
> **GENERAL: I have had the honor to receive your dispatch of yesterday, summoning this army to surrender on the terms accepted by General Lee at Appomattox Court-House. I propose instead of such a surrender, terms based on those drawn up by you on the 18th for disbanding this army, and a further armistice and conference to arrange these terms. The disbanding of General Lee's army has afflicted this country with numerous bands having no means of subsistence but robbery, a knowledge of which would, I am sure, induce you to agree to other conditions.**
>
> **Most respectfully, your obedient servant,**
> **J. E. JOHNSTON,**
> **General.**[93]

Johnston shared Sherman's chief concern: he feared his army would disintegrate and form into lawless guerrilla bands. Johnston was as eager to avoid that situation as Sherman. However, Johnston's statement that he was unwilling to accept only the terms offered to Lee created uncertainty about whether the generals' third, and final,

---

Gen. William J. Hardee on April 30. Wilson asked Hardee whether he thought there would be guerrilla warfare, and Hardee responded, "So help me, God, sir, if we do I am willing and ready to fight to put an end to it." When Wilson asked Hardee if he thought other Confederate generals agreed with his sentiments, Hardee said, "I have not the slightest doubt but they will use every means they can command to bring quietness and security again in the land. They will in no wise support those who do not obey the laws." Theodore C. Wilson, "Johnston's Surrender," *New York Herald*, May 9, 1865.
91. Sherman, *Memoirs*, 2:362.
92. *OR* 47, 3:304.
93. Ibid., 305.

meeting would finally bring an end to the brutal conflict between north and south.

CHAPTER SIX

APRIL 26: THE THIRD MEETING

Weary from the delays, the Union soldiers were ready to see the war end. Major General William T. Sherman's adjutant Maj. George W. Nichols recalled, "That there will be a surrender of Johnston's army there can be no doubt, the Rebels are not in a condition to fight a battle. Johnston is as anxious as we to put his army in such a position that they will not break up into predatory bands to maraud and desolate the country; nor do we desire to undertake a pursuit which would involve continued expenditure of means with no compensating results."[1]

Still unhappy with his poor treatment by Secretary of War Edwin Stanton, Maj. Gen. Henry Halleck, and the press, Sherman brusquely boarded a train to Durham's Station on April 26. Major Generals John M. Schofield, John Logan, and Oliver O. Howard accompanied him. Although Sherman had ordered that the troops be ready to move on a moment's notice, he also specified that no movement should be made until he returned to headquarters from the conference.[2] Like the two prior occasions, Sherman and his entourage, including Schofield and Howard, rode the five miles to the Bennett house. This time, however, Gen. Joseph E. Johnston was not awaiting his opponent's arrival. An accident caused his train to be nearly two hours late, and left with no other choice, the Union officers patiently waited for him.[3]

The truce was scheduled to end at noon that day, and the Union cavalry moved out at 12:00 p.m. "During the morning Kilpatrick had received instructions to renew the pursuit, and promptly at 12 m. the bugle sounded 'assembly' through all our corps, soon followed by 'boots and saddles,' when the cavalry formed column and moved out with a cheer while our campfires still burned," a captain of the 10th Ohio Cavalry remembered. "Before the Second and Third Brigades had reached Durham Station the order was countermanded, and we returned to camp and the Second Brigade to Chapel Hill." The men

---

1. Nichols, *The Story of the Great March*, 318-319.
2. *OR* 47, 3:314.
3. Ibid., 312.

Maj. Gen. John M. Schofield, commander of the Army of the Ohio.

(Library of Congress)

realized what this meant—the war was about to end.[4]

Johnston finally arrived about 2:00 p.m. The commanding generals greeted each other warmly. Sherman introduced Schofield and Howard to the Confederate leader. Sherman and Johnston then retired into the Bennett house, closing the door behind them.[5] Sherman told Johnston he could offer the Appomattox terms, but Johnston felt that those terms alone were inadequate and requested additional guarantees for his men's safety. Sherman recognized that additional terms were probably needed, but he feared that the government would reject anything that deviated from the Appomattox terms. Despite discussing these issues, however, the commanders could not reach a resolution.[6]

General Schofield had wanted to accompany Sherman to the meeting on April 18, but Sherman declined, wanting Schofield, who was second-in-command, to remain behind in case something happened to him. However, on April 26, Sherman requested that Schofield accompany him. "At length I was summoned to their presence, and informed in substance that they were unable to arrange the terms of capitulation to their satisfaction," Schofield said. "They seemed discouraged at the failure of the arrangement to which they had attached so much importance, apprehensive that the terms of Grant and Lee, pure and simple, could not be executed, and that if modified at all, they would meet with a second disapproval. I listened to their statements of the difficulties they had encountered, and then stated how I thought they could all be arranged." Schofield suggested preparing two documents: one document would encompass only the Appomattox terms, and the second one would address Johnston's concerns.

After hearing what Schofield had to say, Johnston replied, "I think General Schofield can fix it." Sherman "intimated to me to write, pen and paper being on the table where I was sitting, while the two great antagonists were nervously pacing the floor," Schofield recollected. "I

---

4. "A 10th Ohio Cavalryman," "Through the Carolinas."
5. Schofield, *Forty-Six Years in the Army*, 351.
6. Bradley, *This Astounding Close*, 215.

at once wrote the 'military convention' of April 26, handed it to General Sherman, and he, after reading it, to General Johnston." Schofield explained that, as department commander, once Sherman departed for Washington, D.C., he could do all that might be necessary to remove any obstacles that hindered the consummation of the agreement. The two officers then signed the first document; when he handed it to Sherman, Johnston declared, "I believe that is the best we can do."[7] Johnston later noted, "We believed that [the agreed-upon terms] would produce a general pacification."[8]

"I found General Sherman, as he appeared on our previous conversation, anxious to prevent further bloodshed, so we agreed without difficulty upon terms putting an end to the war within the limits of our commands, which happened to be coextensive," Johnston later recalled.[9] The Virginian had no choice but to trust Sherman's

---

7. Schofield, *Forty-Six Years in the Army*, 351-352. Major General John McAllister Schofield was born in Gerry, New York, on September 29, 1831. When he was 12 years old, his father, a Baptist minister, took him to Freeport, Illinois. At 16, Schofield worked as a surveyor in Wisconsin, and he taught school there the next year. Although he had originally wanted to become a lawyer, he accepted an appointment to West Point in 1849, graduating seventh in the class of 1853. In the years before the Civil War, he served in Florida and as an instructor at West Point. In 1860, he became a physics instructor at Washington University in St. Louis, Missouri, while on a leave of absence from the army. During the early days of the war, he served as mustering officer for the State of Missouri and as major of the 1st Missouri, which he later reorganized as artillery. Later, Schofield became chief of staff to Gen. Nathaniel Lyon at Missouri's Battle of Wilson's Creek, where Lyon was killed. On November 21, 1862, he was commissioned brigadier general of volunteers and given command of all Union militia in Missouri. From October 1862 to April 1863, Schofield commanded the Army of the Frontier in southwest Missouri and northwest Arkansas. He was promoted to major general on November 29, 1862, but the commission expired before the Senate could approve the promotion. On May 13, 1863, he was reappointed and confirmed. Schofield commanded the 14th Corps in Tennessee, and, from May 1863 to January 1864, commanded the Department of the Missouri. During the Atlanta Campaign, he commanded the Army of the Ohio (the 23rd Corps), and when Sherman departed on the March to the Sea, Schofield was left under the command of Maj. Gen. George H. Thomas to defend against Gen. John Bell Hood's invasion of Tennessee. With part of the 23rd Corps and part of the 4th Corps, he soundly defeated Hood's army at Franklin, Tennessee, on November 30, 1864. Two weeks later at the Battle of Nashville, he commanded the 23rd Corps again. As a reward for his services, Schofield was promoted to brigadier general in the Regular Army, to date from the Battle of Franklin. He then was assigned to command the newly-formed Department of North Carolina and participated in the Carolinas Campaign. He received a brevet to major general in the Regular Army as a reward for his service. Schofield served in the Regular Army for 46 years, retiring as a lieutenant general after a stint as superintendent at West Point. Warner, *Generals in Blue*, 425-426.
8. Johnston, "My Negotiations With General Sherman," 194.
9. Johnston, *Narrative of Military Operations*, 412.

assurances that he would make certain that the Confederate soldiers were adequately fed. Johnston believed that maintaining discipline and ensuring that the men were fed was the only way to avoid the army's dispersion into anarchy.[10]

The first document Schofield drafted, which Sherman and Johnston signed, follows:

> Terms of a military convention entered into this 26th day of April, 1865, at Bennett's house, near Durham's Station, N.C., between General Joseph E. Johnston, commanding the Confederate Army, and Maj. Gen. W. T. Sherman, commanding the United States Army in North Carolina.
>
> 1. All acts of war on the part of the troops under General Johnston's command to cease from this date.
>
> 2. All arms and public property to be deposited at Greensborough, and delivered to an ordnance officer of the United States Army.
>
> 3. Rolls of all the officers and men to be made in duplicate, one copy to be retained by the commander of the troops, and the other to be given to an officer to be designated by General Sherman, each officer and man to give his individual obligation in writing not to take up arms against the Government of the United States until properly released from this obligation.
>
> 4. The side-arms of officers and their private horses and baggage to be retained by them.
>
> 5. This being done, all the officers and men will be permitted to return to their homes, not to be disturbed by the United States authorities so long as they observe their obligation and the laws in force where they may reside.
>
> J. E. JOHNSTON,
> General, Commanding C. S. Forces in North Carolina.
>
> W. T. SHERMAN,
> Major-General, Commanding U.S. Forces in North Carolina.
> RALEIGH, N.C., April 26, 1865.
> Approved:
> U. S. GRANT,
> Lieutenant-General.[11]

---

10. Cox, *Reminiscences*, 3:495.
11. *OR* 47, 3:313.

After Johnston and Sherman signed the document, Sherman called for his clerk Pvt. Arthur Granger of the 15th Pennsylvania Cavalry. Granger made two copies, one for Johnston and one for Sherman, who both signed them. "My share of the surrender was the pen and holder and inkstand, which I still possess," Granger remarked years later—Sherman gifted his clerk the items to show his appreciation. "I tried to purchase from Mr. Bennett the table cover on which the writing was done, but the old fellow could not be induced to part with it," the private recalled.[12]

That night, Grant endorsed the terms so no questions would arise about their acceptability.[13] Schofield overheard Grant declare that "the only change he would have made would have been to write General Sherman's name before General Johnston's. So would I if I had thought about it; but I presume an unconscious feeling of courtesy toward a fallen foe dictated the order in which their names were written," Schofield later remembered.[14]

"General Sherman assured me that he would remove from the department all the troops he had brought into it as soon as practicable, after returning to his headquarters," Johnston stated, "leaving only those of General Schofield's command, who were thought necessary for the maintenance of law and order." He also observed that "General Sherman was accompanied on this occasion by several among the most distinguished officers of the United States Army. The impression was made distinctly on my mind that they, and the army generally, desired peace on the conditions of the convention of the 18th, and regretted the rejection of those terms by the President of the United States."[15]

---

12. Granger, "The Fifteenth at General Joe Johnston's Surrender," 595. Two days later, Capt. William H. Day, Maj. Gen. Judson Kilpatrick's provost marshal, sent a detail to persuade James Bennett to sell him the drop-leaf table and cover. They offered him $10 and a good horse but also told Bennett that they had orders to take it if he refused the offer. Left with no choice, Bennett accepted the offer. The next morning, Bennett walked to Durham Station to collect his dues. He was told that the horse was gone but would return shortly. Bennett returned the next day and found that Day was gone. He never got that horse or payment for the table. Five years later, he made a claim for restitution for the table and other stolen goods after learning that the table had sold for $3,000. He never did collect despite repeated attempts to do so. See Bradley, *This Astounding Close*, 219.
13. Sherman, *Memoirs*, 2:363.
14. Schofield, *Forty-Six Years in the Army*, 352. Schofield considered his role an honor in the drafting and execution of the final convention. He wrote, "I was General Sherman's subordinate, and owed him all the help I could give in every way. He may have regarded my services, and perhaps justly, as little more than clerical, after it was all over, even if he thought of the matter at all."
15. Johnston, *Narrative of Military Operations*, 414-415.

After drafting the initial terms, Schofield prepared supplemental terms based on his discussions with Johnston:

> **Military convention of April 26, 1865.**
> **Supplementary terms**
>
> **First. The Confederate troops to retain their transportation.**
>
> **Second. Each brigade or separate body to retain a number of arms equal to one-seventh of its effective total, which, when the troops reach their homes, will be received by the local authorities for public purposes.**
>
> **Third. Officers and men to be released from their obligation at the same time with those of the Army of Virginia.**
>
> **Fourth. Artillery horses to be used for field transportation when necessary.**
>
> **Fifth. The horses and other private property of officers and men to be retained by them.**
>
> **Sixth. Troops from Arkansas and Texas to be transported by water from Mobile or New Orleans to their homes by the United States.**
>
> **Seventh. The obligations of private soldiers to be signed by their company officers.**
>
> **Eighth. Naval officers within the limits of General Johnston's command to have the benefit of the stipulations of this convention.**[16]

Neither Grant nor the civil authorities in Washington, D.C., disputed any of the provisions. Thus, Joe Johnston, convinced that it would be "the greatest of human crimes to continue the war," surrendered nearly 90,000 Confederate soldiers located in North Carolina, South Carolina, Georgia, and Florida, disobeying Confederate President Jefferson Davis's specific orders by doing so. Although some Confederate soldiers remained in the field after the events at Bennett Place, Johnston had arranged the largest surrender of Southern troops.[17]

With their difficult work finally finished, Sherman and Johnston invited James Bennett and their officers to join them for a toast. The

16. *OR* 47, 3:321.
17. Ibid., 321 and 482; Johnston, "My Negotiations with General Sherman,"187.

Maj. Gen. Matthew C. Butler of South Carolina, commander of the division of cavalry from the Army of Northern Virginia.

(USAHEC)

24-year-old Brig. Gen. Thomas M. Logan, who commanded the brigade of South Carolina cavalry assigned to Butler's Division.

(Library of Congress)

two commanders introduced their subordinates. Johnston had brought with him Maj. Gen. Matthew C. Butler, a protégé of Lt. Gen. Wade Hampton and a handsome young lawyer who had lost a foot to a Union artillery shot at the June 9, 1863, Battle of Brandy Station in Virginia. Brigadier General Thomas M. Logan, who commanded Butler's former brigade of South Carolinians, also accompanied Johnston. Logan, only 24 years old, had a boyish appearance, prompting Sherman to suggest that he must have been the youngest general in either army. When Sherman learned that Logan would appreciate a train ride to his South Carolina home, Sherman offered him a seat on his train back to Raleigh. Surprised, Logan thanked the Ohioan but indicated that he was not yet ready to leave. "Very well," Sherman responded. "Just come to Kilpatrick here any time. He will see that you get to me, and I will help you all I can."[18]

After composing the supplemental terms, Schofield arranged for the delivery of 250,000 rations—representing ten day's rations for 25,000 men—to Johnston's army, along with wagons to haul them. Sherman hoped to prevent the newly-surrendered Confederate troops

---

18. *Cincinnati Daily Commercial*, May 5, 1865.

from stealing from their own people. Now that the Confederates were their countrymen once more, the Union high command did all it could to ensure that they were well treated while the Southerners waited to give their paroles; the Union officers also made sure that the soldiers had sufficient weapons to keep the peace and to protect private property.[19]

The enlisted men of both sides mingled freely while the generals worked out the final details of the surrender. "I talked with many of the Yankee soldiers who told me they were glad the war was over, glad we would not have to kill each other any more," a Rebel recalled years after the war. "I do not think Sherman was as mean as he has been pictured, for he gave us our horses and side-arms and every fourth man ammunition and told us to go home...and go to work."[20]

In the meantime, while the Federal armies remained in place pursuant to Sherman's orders, the Confederate army continued its retreat until Gen. P. G. T. Beauregard halted at about 1:30 p.m. However, Johnston's soldiers deserted in droves, determined to go home before receiving their paroles. "May I ever be spared such a sight as I witnessed when the order to move was given," a North Carolinian noted. "Whole regiments remained on [camp]ground, refusing to obey."[21] Stragglers threw away their weapons, prompting orders to be issued that only those with weapons would be provided rations.[22] "We were overpowered but not subdued," the proud Southern soldiers declared.[23]

After he and Johnston parted for the third time, Sherman went to the telegraph office at Durham's Station. He wrote:

TWENTY-EIGHT MILES FROM RALEIGH,
April 26, 1865
3 p.m. (Received 5.30 p.m.)

General GRANT:

General Johnston was detained by an accident to his railroad. We have now agreed substantially to the terms of Lee's army for his at Greensborough, and will sign the terms before parting. Better await my coming this evening.

19. Schofield, *Forty-Six Years in the Army,* 352.
20. Jay S. Hoar, ed., "'General' James Reid Jones: Last Witness to Bennett Place Surrender," *Blue & Gray* Vol. 2, No. 11 (April-May, 1985), 58.
21. Johnson Hagood, *Memoirs of the War of Secession, from the Original Manuscripts of Johnson Hagood* (Columbia, SC: The State Company, 1910), 371.
22. Bradley, *This Astounding Close,* 219-220.
23. "Joe Johnston," *New York Herald,* May 10, 1865.

W. T. SHERMAN
Major-General, Commanding.[24]

A bit later, he sent a second note:

DURHAM'S, April 26, 1865.

General GRANT:

The convention is signed all right. Will be down in a couple of hours.

W. T. SHERMAN,
Major-General.[25]

This was Sherman's moment of triumph, and Grant, knowing that his dear friend deserved to savor that victory, made the wise choice to remain in Raleigh and allow Sherman to receive Johnston's surrender on his own.[26] Sherman and his officers had dinner with Maj. Gen. Judson Kilpatrick and then boarded the train to Raleigh.

"Thus was surrendered to us the second great army of the so-called Confederacy, and though undue importance has been given to the so-called negotiations which preceded it, and a rebuke and public disfavor cast on me wholly unwarranted by the facts," a defiant Sherman wrote for his report about those extraordinary events. "I rejoice in saying it was accomplished without further ruin and devastation to the country, without the loss of a single life to those gallant men who had followed me from the Mississippi to the Atlantic, and without subjecting brave men to the ungracious task of pursuing a fleeing foe that did not want to fight. As for myself, I know my motives, and challenge the instance during the past four years where an armed and defiant foe stood before me that I did not go in for a fight, and I would blush for shame if I had ever insulted or struck a fallen foe."[27]

After approving the terms of the convention between Sherman and Johnston, Grant advised Stanton. "Sherman and Johnston had another interview to-day, and Johnston has surrendered on same terms as Lee accepted," Grant wrote. "I think the great bulk of the army will start for Washington overland in a few days. I will be guided by

24. *OR* 47, 3:312
25. Ibid., 312.
26. "I suspect that had General Grant been like most men, he would have gone and received the surrender of Johnston himself, and would have taken the glory of it to himself," a Wisconsin soldier of the 20th Corps said. "In this here, as everywhere, may be seen the unselfish motives of the man." *Story of the Service of Company E*, 431-432.
27. *OR* 47, 1:34-35.

circumstances in the absence of any instructions from you. I think we will hold on here for some time."[28]

Once the soldiers left the Bennett home, souvenir hunters descended upon it. A Philadelphia newspaper correspondent noted that "the house is being carried off piecemeal. After it the cottage, fence and trees will go, and in due time there will be an excavation to mark the spot where the disappearing Bennett cottage now stands."[29]

The Union soldiers waited impatiently to hear what had happened at the Bennett house. Rumors flew among soldiers with little else to do to pass the time. "Camp full of rumors from Reb troops going home and deserters," Bvt. Maj. Gen. Alpheus S. Williams recorded in his diary. "Wade Hampton killed by Johnston; and Johnston by one of his men."[30] As the train chuffed into the station in Raleigh, the soldiers held their breath, waiting for news. A Northerner said, "The train will stop at Logan's headquarters, two miles down the road. The result of the conference will be made known there, and, if favorable, we shall know, too, for the boys down there will cheer so that we shall hear them."

The soldiers listened carefully. They heard the train slow and then stop. "All was silent. And then—a long and protracted cheer. A few seconds later, cheers broke out a little nearer to us. There were renewed cheers as the tidings flew toward us from regiment to regiment," a Wisconsin man recalled. "We knew well enough what the result of the conference had been, yet we were very anxious to hear it directly." A few minutes later, a lieutenant declared, "Boys, the thing is all settled, and we are to march back to Raleigh in the morning."

With official word of the surrender, the celebration began: "And then—but how can I tell it? If there be any mode of expression of joy that we did not employ on that occasion, it is either one we had not yet learned or some new-fangled affair that has been invented since the war," the same soldier observed. "We built a great big fire that threw our shadow out into the moonlight; we chased one another through the bushes; some of the boys who were in bed when the tidings came, got up and joined the ceremonies in undress uniform; they climbed trees at some risk of scratching their bare shins on the knots; they shook the branches and played squirrel; one of them put on his accouterments and went through the manual of arms...all of these things were done after we had shouted ourselves hoarse. When we had

---

28. Ibid., 3:311.
29. "The Bennett House," *Philadelphia Inquirer,* May 8, 1865.
30. Alpheus S. Williams diary, entry for April 26 and 27, 1865, Alpheus S. Williams Papers, Archives, Detroit Public Library, Detroit, Michigan.

got fairly tired out, we went to bed and dreamed of home."[31] An Illinois soldier remembered, "At dark the train returns and Gen. Blair gives the news that Johnston has surrendered unconditionally his army with the states of Ga. S.C. & N.C. The rejoicing in the 17th Corps is intense for though it was ready to fight to the death it felt that a further effusion of blood would be a useless sacrifice."[32] Another 17th Corps soldier succinctly exclaimed, "Gen. Blair announces the surrender of Johnston and peace in consequence—rockets and cheers!"[33]

Major Henry Hitchcock, who played such an important role during the negotiations, waxed philosophical that night. "It will be a hundred times harder for me now to remain in the service when we were deep in the mud and swamps of South Carolina or in front an enemy near Averysboro and Bentonville," he told his wife. "There was something like a definite object there; for the sort of occupation or want of occupation I look forward to now I confess I have no relish, especially the loafing part of it. However, the war is over now, thank God, in its breadth and strength."[34] Major Thomas Osborn, who commanded the artillery battalion assigned to the 20th Corps, nonchalantly observed, "Gen. Howard's army has nothing to do. We are through with our work."[35]

As the reality of Johnston's long-sought surrender sank in, thoughts rapidly turned toward home and hearth. "We were two hundred and forty miles from Richmond," a soldier of the 52nd Ohio remarked, "and expected to reach that place in twenty days." From there, it was only a matter of time until the men mustered out and returned to their families.[36]

While all were excited that the war was finally over, not everyone agreed about the outcome. "The protracted parley between those two representative commanders at that stage of the war, was felt by the army, as a humiliating event," an unhappy New Yorker commented. "The proceeding contrasted significantly with those attending the surrender of Vicksburg."[37]

---

31. *The Story of the Service of Company E*, 432-433.
32. Andersen, *The Civil War Diary of Allen Morgan Geer*, 217.
33. Jamison, *Recollection of Pioneer and Army Life*, 328. Part of the celebration included signal rockets launching from the dome of the North Carolina State Capitol building in Raleigh. See Bradley, *This Astounding Close*, 221-222.
34. Howe, *Marching with Sherman*, 316.
35. Harwell and Racine, *The Fiery Trail*, 217.
36. Stewart, *Dan McCook's Regiment*, 170.
37. Mowris, *History of the One Hundred Seventeenth Regiment*, 213.

That night, Major General Halleck sent a dispatch to Secretary of War Stanton indicating that the orders that had angered Sherman remained in place.

> RICHMOND, VA., April 26, 1865 9.30 p.m.
> (Received 10.45 p.m.)
>
> Hon. E. M. STANTON,
> Washington:
>
> **Generals Meade, Sheridan, and Wright are acting under orders to pay no regard to any truce or orders of General Sherman suspending hostilities, on the ground that Sherman's agreements could bind his own command only, and no other. They are directed to push forward, regardless of orders from any one except General Grant, and cut off Johnston's retreat. Beauregard has telegraphed to Danville that a new arrangement had been made with Sherman, and that the advance of the Sixth Corps was to be suspended till further orders. I have telegraphed back to obey no orders of General Sherman, but to push forward as rapidly as possible. The bankers here have information to-day that Jeff. Davis specie is moving south from Goldsborough in wagons as fast as possible. I suggest that orders be telegraphed through General Thomas that Wilson obey no orders of Sherman, and notifying him and General Canby and all commanders on the Mississippi River to take measures to intercept the rebel chiefs and their plunder. The specie taken with them is estimated here at from six to thirteen millions.**
>
> H. W. HALLECK,
> **Major-General Commanding.**[38]

When Grant learned of the situation, he acted quickly to correct it. At 10:00 p.m. that night, Grant advised Halleck, "General Johnston surrendered the forces under his command, embracing all from here to the Chattahoochee, to General Sherman, on the basis agreed upon between General Lee and myself for the Army of Virginia. Please order Sheridan back to Petersburg at once. If you think proper a sufficient force may go on to Danville to take possession of all munitions of war that may be stored there. Send copy of this to the Secretary of War."[39]

---

38. *OR* 47, 3:311-312.
39. Ibid., 312.

Sherman continued to stew over his treatment by the high command. He defended his actions when he drafted his report on May 9. "I still adhere to my then opinions, that by a few general concessions, glittering generalities, all of which in the end must and will be conceded to the organized States of the South, that this day there would not be an armed battalion opposed to us within the broad area of the dominions of the United States," he wrote. "Robbers and assassins must in any event result from the disbandment of large armies, but even these should be and could be taken care of by the local civil authorities without being made a charge on the national treasury."[40]

Davis realized that Johnston was going to disobey orders and surrender to Sherman, so he decided to flee from Charlotte, North Carolina. Davis hoped to find his wife in South Carolina and then head for the Trans-Mississippi, where he wanted to continue the war. Davis convened the final meeting of his cabinet and announced his plan. Unwilling to accompany Davis on his flight to Mexico, Attorney General George Davis and Adj. Gen. Samuel Cooper both resigned that day.[41] The remaining cabinet officers fled with Davis. His cavalry

---

40. Ibid., 1:35
41. Jefferson Davis wrote to George Davis:

Charlotte, N.C., 25th April, 1865.
Hon. Geo. Davis, C. S. Attorney General.

My Dear Sir: — I have no hesitation in expressing to you my opinion that there is no obligation of honor which requires you, under existing circumstances, to retain your present office. It is gratifying to me to be assured that you are willing, at any personal sacrifice, to share my fortunes when they are least promising, and that you only desire to know whether you can aid me in this perilous hour to overcome surrounding difficulties. It is due to such generous friendship that I should candidly say to you that it is not probable for some time to come your services will be needful.

It is with sincere regret that I look forward to being separated from you. Your advice has been to me both useful and cheering. The Christian spirit which has ever pervaded your suggestions, not less than the patriotism which has marked your conduct, will be remembered by me when in future trials I may have need for both.

Should you decide (my condition having become rather that of a soldier than a civil magistrate) to retire from my Cabinet, my sincere wishes for your welfare and happiness will follow you; and I trust a merciful Providence may have better days in store for the Confederacy, and that we may hereafter meet, when, our country's independence being secured, it will be sweet to remember how we have suffered together in the time of her sorest trial.

Very respectfully and truly your friend,

Jefferson Davis.

George Davis resigned the next day; Jefferson Davis accepted the resignation gracefully.

The final Confederate Attorney General, George Davis.

(North Carolina Museum of History)

escort wreaked havoc on the civilians of Charlotte, looting as they went. Seeing these depredations, Davis's aide John Taylor Wood sighed, "So we are falling to pieces."[42]

Johnston and Beauregard resented how Davis had treated them. "The fact is patent that the Confederate Government (or those who formerly constituted it) abandoned Generals Johnston and Beauregard, and the forces under them, in their extremity, without advice or instructions, and without any information whatever concerning its whereabouts or its intended movements," Beauregard's nephew, Col. Alfred Roman, stated. "The truth is that at the time we speak of Generals Johnston and Beauregard represented the only Confederate organization then in existence in the East. They fully realized the fact, and knew that nothing could be gained by hesitation or delay with an adversary as conversant as

---

Charlotte, N.C., April 26, 1865.

Hon. Geo. Davis, C.S. Attorney General.

My Dear Sir: — Your letter dated yesterday, tendering your resignation, has been received. While I regret the causes which compel you to this course, I am well assured that your conduct now, as heretofore, is governed by the highest and most honorable motives. In accepting your resignation, as I feel constrained to do, allow me to thank you for the important assistance you have rendered in the administration of the government, and for the patriotic zeal and acknowledged ability with which you have discharged your trust.

Accept my thanks, also, for your expressions of personal regard and esteem, and the assurance that those feelings are warmly reciprocated by me.

With the hope that the blessings of heaven may attend you and yours,

I am most cordially your friend,
Jefferson Davis.

James Sprunt, *Chronicles of the Cape Fear River 1660-1916* (Raleigh: Edwards & Broughton, 1916), 567-568.

42. Davis, *Rise and Fall of the Confederate Government*, 2:689; Mrs. James A. Fore, "Last Meeting of Confederate Cabinet Held in Charlotte," *Raleigh State Journal*, March 2, 1917; John Taylor Wood diary, entries for April 24-25, 1865 John Taylor Wood Papers, Southern Historical Collections, Perkins Library, University of North Carolina, Chapel Hill, North Carolina.

General Sherman was with the exact condition of affairs in his front. Hence General Johnston's determined action."[43]

As Major Nichols said, "The evidence goes to show that Johnston has been induced to surrender quite as much by the discontent and threats of his own soldiers as by the Federal force in his rear. The Rebel troops see the utter folly of farther resistance, and refuse to fight longer. Johnston has pursued the only wise course left open to him."[44]

Not knowing whether the surrender would occur, Johnston's troops moved out on the morning of April 26, only to have the order countermanded. "May I ever be spared such a sight as I witnessed when the order to move was given," Capt. W. E. Stoney recounted. "Whole regiments remained on the ground, refusing to obey. In the last ten days desertion had reduced Kirkland's brigade from 1,600 to 300 men; Clingman's and the brigade of [North Carolina Junior Reserves of Hoke's Division] had suffered, but not so much. Now not more than forty men in each brigade followed Kirkland and Clingman from the ground." Chaos reigned. "All the sensational reports which have so loosened the bands of discipline originate at their headquarters, and many of them are playing first hands in the shameless appropriation of public property that is going on. This last remark applies principally to General Hardee's headquarters, and much feeling is elicited among the troops by the appropriation there of supplies intended for and much needed by them."[45]

Colonel William Stokes commanded the 4th South Carolina Cavalry, which was part of Maj. Gen. Matthew C. Butler's division. "Hearing on the evening of the 26th of April that the surrender would take place the following day, and not desiring to go through the formality of surrendering the Regiment which I commanded, I ordered the camp struck at 8:30 p.m. and march toward Asheboro, N.C.," Stokes recorded. "Reached Asheboro at 8:30 p.m. April 27th. At this place I disbanded the Regiment and sent it home." Paroles would await these South Carolina horse soldiers.[46]

When Johnston finally made it to his headquarters in Greensboro, he composed a telegraph to the governors of the various states of the Confederacy explaining the reasons for acting as he did. Johnston wrote:

43. Roman, *The Military Operations of General Beauregard*, 2:406.
44. Nichols, *The Story of the Great March*, 320.
45. Brooks, *Memoirs of Secession*, 371.
46. Lloyd Halliburton, ed., *Saddle Soldiers: The Civil War Correspondence of General William Stokes of the 4th South Carolina Cavalry* (Orangeburg, SC: Sandlapper Publishing Co., 1993), 199.

> The disaster in Virginia, the capture by the enemy of all our workshops for the preparation of ammunition and repairing of arms, the impossibility of recruiting our little army opposed to more than ten times its number, or of supplying it except by robbing our own citizens, destroyed all hope of successful war, I have made, therefore, a military convention with Major-General Sherman, to terminate hostilities in North and South Carolina, Georgia, and Florida. I made this convention to spare the blood of this gallant little army, to prevent further sufferings of our people by the devastation and ruin inevitable from the marches of invading armies, and to avoid the crime of waging a hopeless war.[47]

With that, and with his conscience clear, Joe Johnston set about making certain that his army had adequate food and supplies so that his men could be paroled and sent home to their families. Johnston was confident that he had done the right thing for his men and for his country. He was right.

---

47. Johnston, *Military Narrative*, 415; Johnston, "My Negotiations with General Sherman," 195.

CONCLUSION

On April 27, the two army commanders announced the result of their negotiations to their respective commands. Major General William T. Sherman published his announcement to the Union army:

HDQRS. MIL. DIV. OF THE MISSISSIPPI,
In the Field, Raleigh, N.C., April 27, 1865.

The general commanding announces a further suspension of hostilities and a final agreement with General Johnston which terminates the war as to the armies under his command and the country east of the Chattahoochee. Copies of the terms of the convention will be furnished Major-Generals Schofield, Gillmore, and Wilson, who are specially charged with the execution of its details in the Department of North Carolina, Department of the South, and at Macon and Western Georgia. Captain Myers, Ordnance Department, U.S. Army, is hereby designated to receive the arms, &c., at Greensborough, and any commanding officer of a post may receive the arms of any detachment and see that they are properly stored and accounted for. General Schofield will procure at once the necessary blanks, and supply the other army commanders, that uniformity may prevail; and great care must be taken that all the terms and stipulations on our parts be fulfilled with the most scrupulous fidelity, whilst those imposed on our hitherto enemies be received in a spirit becoming a brave and generous army. Army commanders may at once loan to the inhabitants such of the captured mules, horses, wagons, and vehicles as can be spared from immediate use, and the commanding generals of armies may issue provisions, animals, or any public supplies that can be spared, to relieve present wants and to encourage the inhabitants to renew their peaceful pursuits and to restore the relations of friendship among our fellow-citizens and countrymen. Foraging will forthwith cease, and when necessity or long marches compel the taking of forage, provisions, or any kind of private property, compensation will be made on the spot, or, when the disbursing officers are not provided with funds, vouchers will be given in proper form, payable at the nearest military depot.

By order of Maj. Gen. W. T. Sherman:

L. M. DAYTON,
Assistant Adjutant-General[1]

With hostilities over, Sherman intended to treat the people of the South, particularly the former soldiers of the Confederacy, kindly.

Sherman sent a copy of his order to his adversary Gen. Joseph E. Johnston. The Union commander's letter is warm and conciliatory.

HDQRS. MILITARY DIVISION OF THE MISSISSIPPI,
In the Field, Raleigh, N.C., April 27, 1865.

General JOHNSTON,
Commanding Confederate Armies, &c., Greensborough:

GENERAL: I herewith inclose you copies of my Field Orders, Nos. 65 and 66, which give General Schofield full and ample power to carry into effect our convention, and I hope at your personal interview with General Schofield you satisfied your mind of his ability and kind disposition toward the inhabitants of North Carolina. In addition to the points made at our interview of yesterday, I have further instructed General Schofield to facilitate what you and I and all good men desire, the return to their homes of the officers and men composing your army, to let you have of his stores ten days rations for 25,000 men. We have abundance of provisions at Morehead City, and if you send trains here they may go down with our trains and return to Greensborough with the rations specified. Colonel Wright did intend to send his construction train up to-day, but did not get up his carpenters in time. The train with square timber and carpenters will go up in the morning, and I think by the morning of the 29th your trains can run down on the road and fall in with ours of the 30th. I can hardly estimate how many animals fit for farm purposes will be loaned to the farmers, but enough, I hope, to insure a crop. I can hardly commit myself how far commerce will be free, but I think the cotton still in the country and the crude turpentine will make money with which to procure supplies. General Schofield in a

---

1. *OR* 47, 3:322.

few days will be able to arrange all such matters. I wish you would send the enclosed parcel for General Wilson, as it contains the orders 65 and 66, and instructions to release all his prisoners on the conditions of our convention. Now that war is over, I am as willing to risk my person and reputation as heretofore to heal the wounds made by the last war, and I think my feeling is shared by the whole army. I also think a similar feeling actuates the mass of your army, but there are some unthinking young men, who have no sense or experience, that unless controlled may embroil their neighbors. If we are forced to deal with them, it must be with severity, but I hope they will be managed by the people of the South.

I am, with respect, your obedient servant,

W. T. SHERMAN,
Major-General, U.S. Army.[2]

With that, Sherman bade farewell to his former opponent.

Johnston's order announcing the surrender stated:

GENERAL ORDERS, No. 18
HEADQUARTERS ARMY OF TENNESSEE,
Near Greensborough, N.C., April 27, 1863.

By the terms of a military convention made on the 26th instant, by Maj. Gen. W. T. Sherman, U.S. Army, and General J. E. Johnston, C.S. Army, the officers and men of this army are to bind themselves not to take up arms against the United States until properly relieved from that obligation, and shall receive guarantees from the U.S. officers against molestation by the U.S. authorities so long as they observe that obligation and the laws in force where they reside. For these objects duplicate muster-rolls will be made immediately, and after the distribution of the necessary papers the troops will march under their officers to their respective States, and there be disbanded, all retaining personal property. The object of this convention is pacification to the extent of the authority of the commanders who made it.

Events in Virginia, which broke every hope of success by war, imposed on its general the duty of sparing the blood of this gallant army and saving our country from further devastation and our people from ruin.

---

2. Ibid., 320-321.

J. E. JOHNSTON,
General.[3]

Johnston's greatest concerns remained preventing the fragmentation of his army from forming into guerrilla bands and maintaining peace and security.

Also on April 28, Sherman discovered how badly Secretary of War Edwin Stanton had treated him and how the press had excoriated him. Seething again, he addressed his concerns in a letter to Gen. Ulysses S. Grant:

HDQRS. MILITARY DIVISION OF THE MISSISSIPPI,
In the Field, Raleigh, N.C., April 28, 1865.

Lieut. Gen. U. S. GRANT,
General-in-Chief, Washington, D.C.:

GENERAL: Since you left me yesterday I have seen the *New York Times* of the 24th, containing a budget of military news authenticated by the signature of the Secretary of War, which is grouped in such a way as to give very erroneous impressions. It embraces a copy of the basis of agreement between myself and General Johnston of April 18, with commentaries which it will be time enough to discuss two or three years hence, after the Government has experimented a little more in the machinery by which power reaches the scattered people of the vast area of country known as the South; but in the meantime I do think that my rank, if not past services, entitled me at least to the respect of keeping secret what was known to none but the cabinet until further inquiry could have been made, instead of giving publicity to documents I never saw and drawing inferences wide of the truth.

I never saw or had furnished me a copy of President Lincoln's dispatch to you of the 3d of March until after the agreement, nor did Mr. Stanton, or a human being, ever convey to me its substance or anything like it. But, on the contrary, I had seen General Weitzel's invitation to the Virginia legislature, made in Mr. Lincoln's very presence, and had failed to discover any other official hint of a plan of reconstruction, or any ideas calculated to allay the fears of the people of the South, after the

3. Ibid., 833-834.

destruction of their armies and civil authorities would leave them without any government at all. We should not drive a people into anarchy, and it is simply impossible for our military power to reach all the recesses of their unhappy country. I confess I did not wish to break General Johnston's army into bands of armed men, roving about without purpose and capable only of infinite mischief. But you saw on your arrival that I had my army so disposed that his escape was only possible in a disorganized shape, and, as you did not choose to direct military operations in this quarter, I infer you were satisfied with the military situation. At all events, the instant I learned what was proper enough, the disapproval of the President, I acted in such a manner as to compel the surrender of General Johnston's whole army on the same terms you prescribed to General Lee's army when you had it surrounded and in your absolute power.

Mr. Stanton, in stating that my orders to General Stoneman were likely to result in the escape of Mr. Davis to Mexico or Europe, is in deep error. Stoneman was not at Salisbury then, but had gone back to Statesville. Davis was supposed to be between us, and therefore Stoneman was beyond him. By turning toward me he was approaching Davis, and had he joined me as ordered I would have had a mounted force, greatly needed for that and other purposes.

But even now, I don't know that Mr. Stanton wants Davis caught, and as my official papers, deemed sacred, are hastily published to the world it will be imprudent for me to state what has been done in that respect. As the editor of the *Times* has (it may be) logically and fairly drawn from this singular document the conclusion that I am insubordinate, I can only deny the intention. I have never in my life questioned or disobeyed an order, though many and many a time have I risked my life, my health, and reputation in obeying orders, or even hints, to execute plans and purposes not to my liking. It is not fair to withhold from me plans and policy, if any there be, and expect me to guess at them, for facts and events appear quite different from different standpoints. For four years I have been in camp dealing with soldiers, and I can assure you that the conclusion at which the cabinet arrived, with such singular unanimity, differs from mine. I conferred freely with the best officers in this army as to the points involved in this controversy, and strange to say they were singularly unanimous in the other conclusion, and they will learn with pain and amazement that I am deemed insubordinate and wanting in common sense; that

I, who, in the complications of last year, worked day and night, summer and winter, for the cause and the Administration, and who have brought an army of 70,000 men in magnificent condition across a country deemed impassable, and placed it just where it was wanted almost on the day appointed, have brought discredit on our Government. I do not wish to boast of this, but I do say that it entitled me to the courtesy of being consulted before publishing to the world a proposition rightfully submitted to higher authority for proper adjudication, and then accompanied by other statements which invited the press to be let loose upon me. It is true that non-combatants, men who sleep in comfort and security whilst we watch on the distant lines, are better able to judge than we poor soldiers, who rarely see a newspaper, hardly can hear from our families, or stop long enough to get our pay. I envy not the task of reconstruction, and am delighted that the Secretary has relieved me of it. As you did not undertake to assume the management of the affairs of this army, I infer that on personal inspection your mind arrived at a different conclusion from that of the Secretary of War. I will therefore go on and execute your orders to their conclusion, and when done, will with intense satisfaction leave to the civil authorities the execution of the task of which they seem to me so jealous. But as an honest man and soldier, I invite them to follow my path, for they may see some things and hear some things that may disturb their philosophy.

With sincere respect,
W. T. SHERMAN,
Major-General, Commanding.

P.S. As Mr. Stanton's singular paper has been published I demand that this also be made public, though I am in no manner responsible to the press, but to the law and my proper superiors.

W. T. SHERMAN,
Major-General, Commanding[4]

4. Ibid., 334-335.

The next day, April 29, Sherman summoned his lieutenants to his headquarters. Major Generals John M. Schofield, Alfred Terry, and Judson Kilpatrick were to remain on duty in North Carolina, while the rest of Sherman's army was ordered to march north at a leisurely pace to Richmond, Virginia, and then on to Washington, D.C., for a grand review to be held in May.[5]

That night, Sherman wrote to his wife, Ellen, "The mass of the people south will never trouble us again. They have suffered terrifically, and I now feel disposed to befriend them—of course not the leaders and lawyers, but the armies who have fought and manifested their sincerity though misled by risking their persons. But the rascals who by falsehood and misrepresentation kept up the war, they are infamous." He continued, "It will be difficult for anyone to tread a straight path amid these new complications, but I will do my best. I perceive the politicians are determined to drive the Confederates into guerilla bands, a thing more to be feared than open organized war. They may fight it out. I won't." Concluding, Sherman said, "We could settle the war in three weeks by giving shape to the present disordered dements, but they may play out their game."[6]

On the night of April 27, the remaining Confederate soldiers confronted the reality of their plight. "Some raved and swore that they would never submit to it," Lt. Edwin H. Rennolds of the 3rd Tennessee Consolidated recalled.[7] Captain Bromfield Ridley served on Army of the Tennessee corps commander Lt. Gen. A. P. Stewart's staff for much of the war. "All is confusion and unrest," Ridley penned, "and the stern realization that we are subdued and ruined is upon us." He pondered, "Oh! how is it in the Yankee camps tonight? Rejoicing, triumphing and reveling in the idea of glory. Think of it, the big dog has simply got the little dog down."[8]

A captain of a Texas regiment noted in his diary that his comrades stayed up all night lamenting their plight, and "if crying would have done any good, we could have cried all night." The next day, those Rebel soldiers signed a parole document and were issued one dollar in silver. Another Texan jotted in his diary, "Men [Granbury's brigade] are beginning to realize the situation; and are talking about going home to Texas. Our guns have all been turned in, to our Ordnance

5. Sherman, *Memoirs*, 2:368.
6. Howe, *Home Letters of General Sherman*, 349-350.
7. Edwin H. Rennolds, *A History of Henry County Commands Which Served in the Confederate States Army, Including Rosters of the Various Companies Enlisted in Henry County, Tenn.* (Jacksonville, FL: Sun Publishing Co., 1904), 116.
8. Ridley, *Battles and Sketches*, 465-466.

officers. And we suppose to save us from further humiliation there has not been a Yank in sight of us yet."[9]

Later that day, the officers of the late Brig. Gen. Hiram S. Granbury's Texas Brigade composed a touching note to Johnston: "We...respectfully desire to assure Gen. Johnston of our undiminished confidence and esteem and fully sympathizing with him in the present unfortunate state of our affairs do most cordially tender him the hospitality of our State and our homes such as the future may provide for us." Eighteen officers signed the emotional message, in which they requested that Johnston visit them before leaving—no one knows whether Johnston obliged.[10]

The officers of the 8th Texas Cavalry of Maj. Gen. Joseph Wheeler's Corps called on Lt. Gen. William J. Hardee's headquarters at Greensboro. Hardee told them all that he knew that the men did not want to surrender. He advised 23-year-old Capt. "Doc" Mathews, the commander of the 8th Texas, that he should take the remnant of his regiment—about 120 men—to Mobile, Alabama, and join Lt. Gen. Richard Taylor's army. "I don't want to see your regiment surrendered to the enemy," Hardee said.

Mathews returned to camp that night and had the bugler sound assembly so that he could address his men. He repeated Hardee's advice and said, "I am too young a man to assume the responsibility of such an undertaking, but I now offer my resignation as commander of the regiment." The captain asked each company commander to take charge of his respective company and stated, "Hold a council to determine your course and each company decide and act for itself regardless of what others may do." Company F voted to join Taylor, and 15 to 18 of its remaining troopers left for Alabama. Most of them never surrendered.[11]

"Our regiment at first notice of the surrender, decided to make their way out and not take parole, but General Wheeler came down and made them a talk, stating the terms of the surrender to be that the cavalry would be permitted to retain their horse and sidearms and go home unmolested if they could show a parole," Capt. Henry W. Graber of the 8th Texas Cavalry recollected, "but if not they would be

9. Brown, *One of Cleburne's Command*, 171.
10. *OR* 47, 3:848-849.
11. J. K. P. Blackburn, "Reminiscences of the Terry Rangers," included in Thomas W. Cutrer, ed., *Terry Texas Ranger Trilogy* (Austin, TX: State House Press, 1996), 173-174. Taylor surrendered his army before Company F's men reached Mobile. When the soldiers learned this, they forged paroles and made their way home without ever surrendering.

treated and shot as Guerrillas. Under this condition General Wheeler advised them to surrender, which they decided to do."[12] Captain Tom Weston, who commanded Company H of the 8th Texas, later told trooper J. K. P. Blackburn that he had the honor of surrendering the 8th Texas at Greensboro and that there were only 90 men present in the ranks to receive paroles. At one time, the 8th Texas numbered nearly 1,200 men.[13]

Colonel C. Irvine Walker, commander of the 10th South Carolina Infantry, told his wife, "Johnston's army has at last had to relinquish the cause it has so nobly defended, and all the country east of the Mississippi is at the mercy of the enemy. God protect us in our hour of adversity." He continued, "I had no hopes of carrying on a guerrilla warfare for a cause and in a country which was abandoned by the Government, which was surrounded by a mob of thieves and plunderers." Walker concluded, "We are not subdued, but rather than push matters to the bitter end we yield the struggle until our country is able to renew it with greater chance of success. We are overpowered, but our spirit and determination that the South shall yet be independent is unconquered."[14]

On April 28, Johnston wrote to Sherman to advise him that he had halted the movement of Maj. Gen. Matthew C. Butler's cavalry, but some troopers were beyond his reach who could not be notified.[15] Later that day, he responded to Sherman's letter from April 27, displaying the deep respect that had developed between the two men.

> **Greensborough, April 28, 1865.**
> **HEADQUARTERS, Maj. Gen. W. T. SHERMAN,**
> **Commanding U.S. Forces:**
>
> **GENERAL: Your dispatches to Major-Generals Stoneman and Wilson, received to-day, have been forwarded. I have also had the honor to receive your letter of yesterday and your Order 65. The enlarged patriotism manifested in these papers reconciles me to what I had previously regarded as the misfortune of my life that of having had you to encounter in the field. The enlightened and humane policy you have adopted will certainly be successful. It is fortunate for the people of North**

12. Thomas W. Cutrer, ed., *A Terry Texas Ranger: The Life Record of H. W. Graber* (Austin, TX: State House Press, 1987), 244-245.
13. Blackburn, "Reminiscences of the Terry Rangers," 174.
14. William Lee White and Charles Denny Runion, eds., *Great Things Are Expected of Us: The Letters of Colonel C. Irvine Walker, 10th South Carolina Infantry, C.S.A.* (Knoxville: University of Tennessee Press, 2009), 175.
15. *OR* 47, 3:336.

Carolina that your views are to be carried out by one so capable of appreciating them. I hope that you are as well represented in the other departments of your command; if so, an early and complete pacification in it may be expected. I very gladly accept your generous offer of food for the troops here, and have directed the trains, which are to bring it up, to go down loaded with Government cotton, which is here. One of the cavalry brigades reported to have moved westward from the Yadkin has returned. Some 3,000 cavalry was collected near Charlotte and on the Catawba, including two brigades from East Tennessee. The commanding officer expressed his readiness to obey the terms of the convention, but has since left Charlotte, and I have not yet learned where his troops are. I hope and believe that there will be occasion for severities to none but members of bands of robbers now existing in many parts of the country. It is said that most of the North Carolinians have returned to their homes from anxiety to begin their former work, and believe that they require no guaranty for personal safety. The disposition you express to heal the wounds made by the past war has been evident to me in all our interviews. You are right in supposing that similar feelings are entertained by the mass of the army. I am sure that all the leading men in it will exert their influence for that object. My copy of the convention has been unaccountably lost. I therefore beg of you the kindness to give me another.

I am, general, &c.,
J. E. JOHNSTON.[16]

The mutual respect the commanders had built for each other became the foundation for a long, warm friendship that lasted until their deaths, only a month apart, in 1891.

Sherman arrived at Morehead City, North Carolina, on May 4. Upon arrival, he learned that U.S. Supreme Court Chief Justice Salmon P. Chase and Chase's daughter Nettie were also there after traveling aboard the U.S.R.C. Wayanda to conduct a tour of the vanquished South.[17] Sherman made his way to the Wayanda to visit Chase. "To say that I was merely angry at the tone and substance of

16. Ibid., 336-337.
17. David Donald, ed., *Inside Lincoln's Cabinet: The Civil War Diaries of Salmon P. Chase* (New York: Longmans, Green & Co., 1954), 271; Sherman, *Memoirs*, 2:369.

these published bulletins of the War Department, would hardly express the state of my feelings. I was outraged beyond measure, and was resolved to resent the insult, cost what it might." Sherman showed the documents to Chase, an Ohioan who was one of Sherman's political patrons and a leader of the Radical Republicans, and had a long, frank discussion with the Chief Justice. Chase "explained to me the confusion caused in Washington by the assassination of Mr. Lincoln, the sudden accession to power of Mr. Johnson, who was then supposed to be bitter and vindictive in his feelings toward the South, and the wild pressure of every class of politicians to enforce on the new President their pet schemes."

Chief Justice of the United States Supreme Court Salmon P. Chase of Ohio, one of Sherman's political patrons.

(Library of Congress)

Chase showed Sherman a letter he had written to President Abraham Lincoln that was published in two different newspapers, urging Lincoln to recognize the freed slaves as equal to the white population in all respects. "He was the first man, of any authority or station, who ever informed me that the Government of the United States would insist on extending to the former slaves of the South the elective franchise, and he gave as a reason the fact that the slaves, grateful for their freedom, for which they were indebted to the armies and Government of the North, would, by their votes, offset the disaffected and rebel element of the white population of the South," Sherman recalled.[18]

---

18. Sherman, *Memoirs*, 2:372-374. Despite Grant's efforts to heal the rift between Sherman and Halleck, it never happened. Halleck wrote to Sherman, "You have not had during this war, nor have you now, a warmer friend and admirer than myself. If, in carrying out what I knew to be the wishes of the War Department in regard to your armistice, I used language which has given you offence, it was unintentional and I deeply regret it. If fully aware of the circumstances under which I acted, I am certain you would not attribute to me any improper motive. It is my wish to continue to regard and receive you as a personal friend. With this statement I leave the matter in your hands." *OR* 47, 3:454. Sherman declined the proffered olive branch. "I cannot consent to the renewal of a friendship I had prized so highly till I can see deeper into the diabolical plot than I now do," the general said. Ibid. Their friendship was never truly restored—Halleck died in January 1872 before any rapprochement occurred.

The discussion with Chase calmed Sherman's anger as he impatiently waited passage to the nation's capital. A storm kept Sherman and Chase in port in Morehead City until May 7. Once the skies cleared, Sherman boarded a ship to carry him to Washington, D.C.

"At last the long struggle is over—a temporary disappointment is closely followed by the intimation that our services as soldiers have been crowned with the greatest possible success and already a part of the army has commenced its march towards the polar star—to us the pilot to home and freedom," 22nd Wisconsin soldier Harvey Reid, who served on the staff of a 20th Corps brigade, wrote. "Three days ago, however, our spirits were at almost their lowest ebb. Our hopes had been so strongly excited when the arrangement between Sherman and Johnston was first consummated, not only from the fact that hostilities were actually suspended, but because General Sherman himself and our other commanders seemed so confident that their proceedings would be ratified." Grant appeared at the review of the 17th Corps, which Reid took as an "ominous" sign. The general's presence set off a frenzy of rumors that President Andrew Johnson had rejected the agreement. When orders to march arrived, "the curses were 'not loud but deep.'" Reid's brigade had started moving in the direction of Holly Springs, 15 miles south of Raleigh, when word arrived that Johnston had surrendered to Sherman, countermanding the orders to march. "It is surprising how the road had shortened in three days," Reid quipped, eagerly anticipating the march home.[19]

On May 5, Kilpatrick's cavalry division was sent to find Wheeler's troopers and see to their surrender. They found the Confederate cavalry about 25 miles from Greensboro camped in a strip of woods along the road. The Union soldiers had dismounted and were unsaddling their horses when they spotted a large cavalry force marching straight toward them. A quick glance through field glasses confirmed the troopers were Confederates. The Federals quickly mounted and moved out with skirmishers forward. The rest of the regiment deployed in a line of battle across the road, awaiting a charge, when the skirmishers spotted a white flag of truce and called out for the column to halt. They soon learned that Wheeler and his command were on their way to Greensboro to surrender. Someone escorted Wheeler to Kilpatrick's headquarters, while the rest of his command followed. "As the head of the column came up the officers exchanged salutes, while we all joined in three hearty cheers, which was returned by the rank and file; but the officers looked downcast and sullen,

---

19. Frank L. Byrne, ed., *The View from Headquarters: Civil War Letters of Harvey Reid* (Madison: Wisconsin Historical Society, 1965), 244-245.

evidently not enjoying the situation as we did," an Ohioan remarked. "To us it meant joy and hope; in a word, the war was over, and that meant home."

The Confederates were familiar foes—the two commands had "met face to face a hundred times on the scout, on picket, on the skirmish-line, on the battlefield, by night and by day, Summer and Winter, from Murfreesboro, Tenn., to Chattanooga, Ringgold, Tunnel Hill, Resaca, Marietta, Atlanta, Lovejoy's Station, Jonesboro, thence on the march to the sea, Bear Creek, Macon, Milledgeville, Waynesboro, Savannah, Blackville, Barnwell, Aiken, Averysboro, Bentonville, Wadesboro, New Gilead, Lancaster, Fayetteville, Olive Grove, Raleigh, Chapel Hill, etc." The Federals watched as the weary Rebel veterans passed by. "We could see it in their brown, scarred faces. A wiry-looking set; poorly clad; some wearing caps, others hats; their carbines slung over their backs; part with sabers clanking against the stirrups; their battle flags in rags, with scarcely a vestige left but the staff; with a battery or so and a few wagons in the rear," the Ohio captain observed. "One would say, 'Yank, you have got my horse,' and another, 'There is my horse,' while our boys recognized a horse here and there in the column they once rode. We stood it as long as we could, and finally asked them to halt, dismount, and have something to eat and drink; which they finally did, as Wheeler had reached Kilpatrick's quarters, and the column halted."

While Kilpatrick and Wheeler met, the men of both sides "mingled with officers and men, and exchanged congratulations at the prospects of peace. The soldiers seemed to enjoy a friendly chat over their cup of coffee, exchanging captured horses, and I doubt if we had been friends for years we would have parted with better feeling. As the column passed on, the sun only a few feet above the tops of the trees, we could see their glistening arms as they receded over the dusty road, when, passing to the rear of our division, they bivouacked for the night, and the next morning started for Greensboro."[20]

The 104th Ohio Volunteer Infantry drew the task of serving as provost marshals for the stacking of arms and paroling of Johnston's army in Greensboro. The Buckeyes arrived in Greensboro on May 2. "Here we found over 20,000 of the Johnnies," a veteran noted. "The 104th being the first Union regiment in the place, a detail was at once made, and guards placed around the captured property; the rest of the brigade followed us, and as fast as possible a wagon train with rations, etc., came on, so we could continue sharing rations with our no-longer foes, while the work of paroling and sending the Confederates to their

20. "A 10th Ohio Cavalryman," "Campaign Through the Carolinas."

Brig. Gen. and Admiral Raphael Semmes, the first Confederate officer paroled at Greensboro.

(American Civil War Museum)

homes proceeded with ere the middle of the month was finished." On May 16, the Buckeyes were relieved from duty and began their trek home.[21]

The first to sign his parole was Raphael Semmes, who simultaneously held the ranks of Rear Admiral and Brigadier General after his sailors were transferred to the army shortly before the fall of Richmond. Semmes and the few remaining Rebel naval cadets served as part of Confederate President Jefferson Davis's escort until their surrender.[22] About 16,000 men remained with Johnston's army when the paroles began on May 1. The missing soldiers had already deserted and gone home without obtaining their paroles. "After four long years of bloody conflict, we lay down our arms, horn blowing and drum beating cease," Confederate soldier Hezekiah M. Corkle recorded in his diary. "Our foes show to us a more liberal disposition than the most sanguine expected." Indeed, reconciliation became the theme of the day.[23]

Johnston's paroled soldiers received about one dollar in silver from a cache of money that the general had been hoarding, prompting one officer to recall that it was the only pay he had received in more than a year.[24] "The brigade was paid today one dollar and a quarter in silver per man, the last, I suppose, of the Confederate treasury," Capt. W. E. Stoney proudly said. "I shall have mine made into a medal to keep and value as received from the dying hands of my government. It is the greatest earthly satisfaction and my only consolation now, that I entered her service on the day of the inauguration of this war; was never absent from my command except by authority or from wounds, and continued in the field until the last day."[25]

21. Becker, "Campaigning with a Grand Army."
22. Bradley, *This Astounding Close*, 236. Semmes was later arrested for violating his status as a prisoner of the U.S. Navy by escaping from the sinking CSS Alabama. His parole protected him, however, and Semmes was released from custody in 1866.
23. Hezekiah M. Corkle diary, entry for April 30, 1865, Southern Historical Collection, Wilson Library, University of North Carolina, Chapel Hill, North Carolina.
24. Bradley, *This Astounding Close*, 226.
25. Brooks, *Memoirs of the War of Secession*, 372.

The soldiers experienced a mix of emotions at their paroles, including embarrassment. "I never felt so mortified in my life as this morning when I went into the presence of the Yankee Officers to sign my parole," Colonel Walker lamented. "I was introduced to the gentlemen, but only saluted very formally, trying to look as dignified as possible. Some officers took their hands upon being presented, but I would have been shot before I would have done it. They have forced me to yield to the U.S. Gov., but have not changed my feelings towards it in the slightest degree. I feel and will always feel the same hatred to them, however events may compel me to hide it. I shall I believe live to see the Independence of the C.S. yet." Walker, undoubtedly, spoke for many of Johnston's soldiers.[26]

"The day we surrendered our regiment it was a pitiful sight to behold," Pvt. Sam Watkins of the 1st Tennessee Infantry remembered, referring to the attrition in his regiment's ranks during four years of war. "If I remember correctly, there were just sixty-five men in all, including officers, that were paroled that day." The 1st Tennessee originally numbered 1,200 officers and men. "It was indeed a sad sight to look at, the old First Tennessee Regiment. A mere squad of noble and brave men, gathered around the tattered flag that they had followed in every battle through that long war. It was so bullet-riddled and torn that it was just a few blue and red shreds that hung drooping while it, too, was stacked with our guns forever."[27]

"A few more days and Johnston's army would have starved out," Col. J. Fred Waring, of the Jeff Davis Legion Cavalry of Butler's division, resignedly noted on May 1. "It was perhaps wise, but it was certainly hard to give up after having struggled manfully for four years. The blue uniforms in Greensboro are certainly unpleasant to look at."[28]

Before it was all said and done on May 2, about 32,000 Confederate soldiers had given their paroles. The men stacked their arms in a

---

26. White and Runion, *Great Things Are Expected of Us*, 176. After the surrender, Colonel Walker noticed that the regimental colors were missing. As his troops moved out of camp, one of his officers handed Walker a parcel and told him not to open it until he reached home. On arriving home, Walker opened the package and found the 10th South Carolina's tattered battle flag, which had been saved after the regiment was cut off on the final day of the Battle of Bentonville in North Carolina. Walker treasured the gift. Ibid., 177. Today, the flag can be found in the collection of the Confederate Relic Room, Columbia, South Carolina.
27. Sam R. Watkins, *"Co. Aytch," Maury Grays, First Tennessee Regiment; or, A Side Show of the Big Show* (Chattanooga, TN: Times Printing Co., 1900), 219-220.
28. Waring diary, entry for May 1, 1865.

REBEL SMALL-ARMS TURNED OVER BY JOHNSTON'S ARMY TO LIEUTENANT LYSTER, CHIEF OF
ORDNANCE, DEPARTMENT NORTH CAROLINA, GREENSBOROUGH, MAY 3, 1865.

Small arms surrendered by Johnston's army at Greensboro.
(Harper's Weekly)

formal ceremony and then started for home, with many facing long, arduous walks.[29]

However, despite these travails, the war was over. "After turning in our guns and getting our paroles, we felt relieved. No more picket duty, no more guard duty, no more fighting, no more war," Capt. Samuel Foster of the 18th Texas Dismounted Cavalry said. "It is all over, and we are going home. Home after an absence of four years from our families and our friends."[30] On May 1, a Northern newspaper accurately published, "With this surrender the formidable military organization of the rebellion is extinguished and truly indeed may we regard the final end of the war as rapidly approaching."[31]

"We separated about the first day of May 1865, and marched to our homes with the full consciousness of duty well performed," Maj. Gen.

29. For a detailed monograph devoted to the surrender ceremonies at Greensboro, see Robert M. Dunkerly, *The Confederate Surrender at Greensboro: The Final Days of the Army of Tennessee, April 1865* (Jefferson, NC: McFarland, 2013).
30. Brown, *One of Cleburne's Command*, 173.
31. "From North Carolina. The Surrender of Johnston," *Evening Star*, May 1, 1865.

ACCOUTREMENTS OF JOHNSTON'S ARMY TURNED OVER TO J. S. CLINGMAN, ORDNANCE OFFICER, DEPARTMENT NORTH CAROLINA, MAY 2, 1865.—[SKETCHED BY DAVIS.]

Ordnance surrendered by Johnston's army at Greensboro
(Harper's Weekly)

Matthew C. Butler recalled, years later. "We made no apologies, and have made none since. The only regret felt or expressed were that we had not triumphed in our cause and won the final victory, after so much hard fighting and so many sacrifices...A few years more and there will be nothing left except the sacred memories of their lives and the lofty example of their unselfish patriotism."[32]

The rest of Sherman's Union soldiers departed Raleigh and headed for Richmond about May 1. Major General Henry W. Slocum, who commanded the Army of Georgia, remembered, "On the evening before we left Raleigh the mails from the North arrived, and with them a large number of New York papers. On the following day, while we were about five miles from the city, my attention was called to a group of soldiers standing around a cart under which they had built a fire. The cart and its contents were being burned, while a young man in citizen's dress, with the mule that had been taken from the cart, was looking on." Slocum sent a staff officer to find out what was going on.

The leader of the group told the staff officer, "Tell General Slocum that cart is loaded with New York papers for sale to soldiers. These

---

32. Brooks, *Butler and His Cavalry*, 33.

papers are filled with the vilest abuse of General Sherman. We have followed Sherman through a score of battles and through nearly two thousand miles of the enemy's country, and we do not intend to allow these vile slanders against him to be circulated among his men." Slocum wryly commented, "This was the last property that I saw destroyed by Sherman's army, and I witnessed the scene with keener satisfaction than I had felt over the destruction of any property since the day we left Atlanta."[33]

"The day broke in the most delightful manner. The sun shone forth after the heavy rain of the previous night in all his splendor, and gave to the cool morning air his brightest and most cheery glances," a Northern correspondent, who marched north with the troops, reported. "So opened the day on which the left wing of the grand army commenced its joyful march toward home—sweet home. When at daylight their tents were struck, and the bugle gaily sounded the 'forward,' of all that host who proudly marched beneath the 'bonnie blue which bears a single star,' there was not one whose bosom did not swell with pride and exultation as though he was marching north, crowned with victory."

Furthermore, the same correspondent wrote: "Joy beamed from every eye when home was in the mind, and every looked joyful only to be dimmed as the melancholy tragedy at Washington was recalled by the over working brain. Yet as hope and joy are the ruling passions of the successful, the moments of grief, though poignant, were few. Joyfully then the Twentieth Corps, which led the advance of the Army of Georgia, marched from their camps on a march which cannot but be barren of the usual topics of interest which spring from the movements of an army, and yet will be fruitful in others more novel and as entertaining." He continued, "How the troops are received on the route, what are the sentiments of the inhabitants upon the great social problem of re-union which now perplexes the profoundest minds, when the army will arrive at the principal towns on its way, when it will finally reach its destination at Alexandria, and a thousand other items which cannot be anticipated, will fill the place in the public mind which has been during four years occupied by war and rumors of war."[34]

Sherman's troops enjoyed a leisurely march north. "Very striking is the difference between this march and all other previous," an Illinois soldier observed. "The people remain contentedly at home, men are plenty, a safety guard is at each house, and our soldiers make no effort

33. Slocum, "Final Operations of Sherman's Army," 757.
34. Hatcher, *The Last Four Weeks of the War*, 310-311.

to forage or destroy."[35] Another Federal remarked, "We'd never had such a march before. There was no enemy to watch or care for, and no foraging was done. The fires that had followed us on all our marches had gone out, and they were not rekindled. At night we put out only camp guards; no more picket duty to do. Everything about the march seemed strange—almost unreal. We could hardly take in the fact that we were homeward bound."[36]

It took four to five days to reach Richmond. Some of the 20th Corps soldiers had been close enough to Richmond in 1862 to recognize the city's spires, and they looked on with great satisfaction. The men rested there for a few days before continuing their journey to Alexandria, Virginia. Once in Alexandria, they established camps and prepared for the Grand Review of the Armies, scheduled for May 23 and 24, 1865, when the combined armies of the Union passed in review for the final time. The Army of the Potomac marched on May 23, while the western armies marched on May 24.

When Sherman arrived in the nation's capital he called on Grant and President Andrew Johnson, as well as several cabinet members. Each told Sherman that they were unaware of what Stanton had done and expressed their disapproval regarding the secretary of war's actions. "As Mr. Stanton made no friendly advances, and offered no word of explanation or apology, I declined General Grant's friendly offices for a reconciliation, but, on the contrary, resolved to resent what I considered an insult, as publicly as it was made. My brother, Senator [John] Sherman, who was Mr. Stanton's neighbor, always insisted that Mr. Stanton had been frightened by the intended assassination of himself, and had become embittered thereby. At all events, I found strong military guards around his house, as well as all the houses occupied by the cabinet and by the principal officers of Government; and a sense of insecurity pervaded Washington, for which no reason existed." Sherman never forgave Stanton for the insults he inflicted upon him after the first two meetings with Johnston.[37]

On May 22, Sherman appeared before the Joint Committee on the Conduct of the War, a Congressional body dominated by the Radical Republicans in Congress who were supposed to investigate war policy but meddled in military matters instead. Now that the war was over, the Joint Committee welcomed Sherman's views regarding the final days of the conflict, including the fate of the Confederate treasury.[38]

---

35. Andersen, *The Civil War Diary of Allen Morgan Geer*, 217.
36. *Story of the Service of Company E*, 434.
37. Sherman, *Memoirs*, 2:376.
38. Obviously, a detailed discussion of the Joint Committee on the Conduct of the War strays far from the scope of this project. For a detailed consideration

Sherman stated, "General Halleck's measures to capture General Johnston's army, actually surrendered to me at the time, at Greensboro, on the 26th of April, simply excited my contempt for a judgment such as he was supposed to possess." Sherman did not believe Halleck's claim about the amount of treasure that was recovered—"such a train would have been composed of from fifteen to thirty-two six-mule teams to have hauled this specie, even if it all were in gold. I suppose the exact amount of treasure which Davis had with him is now known to a cent; some of it was paid to his escort, when it disbanded at and near Washington, Georgia, and at the time of his capture he had a small parcel of gold and silver coin, not to exceed ten thousand dollars, which is now retained in the United States Treasury-vault at Washington, and shown to the curious."

On May 24, 1865, a couple days after Sherman testified before the Joint Committee, his armies marched in the Grand Review of the Armies in Washington, D.C., where the men passed in review one last time before President Johnson, the cabinet, Grant, Meade, many dignitaries, and tens of thousands of grateful citizens who turned out to cheer them on.[39] Sherman described the grandiose event:

> Punctually at 9 a. m. the signal-gun was fired, when in person, attended by General Howard and all my staff, I rode slowly down Pennsylvania Avenue, the crowds of men, women, and children, densely lining the sidewalks, and almost obstructing the way. We were followed close by General Logan and the head of the Fifteenth Corps. When I reached the Treasury-building, and looked back, the sight was simply magnificent. The column was compact, and the glittering muskets looked like a solid mass of steel, moving with the regularity of a pendulum. We passed the Treasury-building, in front of which and of the White House was an immense throng of people, for whom extensive stands had been prepared on both sides of the avenue. As I neared the brick-house opposite the lower corner of Lafayette Square, some one asked me to notice Mr. Seward, who, still feeble and bandaged for his wounds, had been removed there that he might behold the troops. I moved in that direction and took off my hat to Mr. Seward, who sat at an upper window. He recognized the salute, returned it, and then we rode on

of its activities, see Bruce Tap, *Over Lincoln's Shoulder: The Committee on the Conduct of the War* (Lawrence: University Press of Kansas, 1998)

39. "From Washington: The Grand Review of the Armies (Official). Details of the Great Review. Revision of Our Revenue System. Deserved Promotion," *New York Times*, May 18, 1865.

steadily past the President, saluting with our swords. All on his stand arose and acknowledged the salute. Then, turning into the gate of the presidential grounds, we left our horses with orderlies, and went upon the stand, where I found Mrs. Sherman, with her father and son. Passing them, I shook hands with the President, General Grant, and each member of the cabinet. As I approached Mr. Stanton, he offered me his hand, but I declined it publicly, and the fact was universally noticed. I then took my post on the left of the President, and for six hours and a half stood, while the army passed in the order of the Fifteenth, Seventeenth, Twentieth, and Fourteenth Corps.

It was, in my judgment, the most magnificent army in existence—sixty-five thousand men, in splendid physique, who had just completed a march of nearly two thousand miles in a hostile country, in good drill, and who realized that they were being closely scrutinized by thousands of their fellow-countrymen and by foreigners. Division after division passed, each commander of an army corps or division coming on the stand during the passage of his command, to be presented to the President, cabinet, and spectators. The steadiness and firmness of the tread, the careful dress on the guides, the uniform intervals between the companies, all eyes directly to the front, and the tattered and bullet-riven flags, festooned with flowers, all attracted universal notice. Many good people, up to that time, had looked upon our "Western army" as a sort of mob; but the world then saw, and recognized the fact, that it was an army in the proper sense, well organized, well commanded and disciplined; and there was no wonder that it had swept through the South like a tornado. For six hours and a half that strong tread of the Army of the West resounded along Pennsylvania Avenue; not a soul of that vast crowd of spectators left his place; and, when the rear of the column had passed by, thousands of the spectators still lingered to express their sense of confidence in the strength of a Government which could claim such an army.[40]

Sherman correctly assessed that his snub of Stanton did not go unnoticed. "Unless all the reports that reach us from Washington are false, Gen. Sherman in deliberately and ostentatiously making a

40. Sherman, *Memoirs*, 2:377-378.

personal issue with the Secretary of War (Mr. Stanton) for an official act," a New York newspaper sniffed. "He took the occasion of a grand review, ordered and held largely in his honor, and in the presence of a vast multitude assembled to rejoice in the return of peace, to refuse of Mr. Stanton when tendered to him in friendly greeting."[41]

At the end of the Grand Review, the armies returned to camp, awaiting orders to muster out and return to their homes. Sherman's veterans, once again, became farmers, clerks, and factory workers, just as they had been before the war.

Sherman composed a farewell order to his beloved army:

> **Headquarters Military Division of the Mississippi,**
> **In the Field, Washington, D. C., May 30, 1865.**
>
> **The general commanding announces to the Armies of the Tennessee and Georgia that the time has come for us to part. Our work is done, and armed enemies no longer defy us. Some of you will go to your homes, and others will be retained in military service till further orders. And now that we are all about to separate, to mingle with the civil world, it becomes a pleasing duty to recall to mind the situation of national affairs when, but little more than a year ago, we were gathered about the cliffs of Lookout Mountain, and all the future was wrapped in doubt and uncertainty.**
>
> **Three armies had come together from distant fields, with separate histories, yet bound by one common cause—the union of our country, and the perpetuation of the Government of our inheritance. There is no need to recall to your memories Tunnel Hill, with Rocky-Face Mountain and Buzzard-Roost Gap, and the ugly forts of Dalton behind.**
>
> **We were in earnest, and paused not for danger and difficulty, but dashed through Snake-Creek Gap and fell on Resaca; then on to the Etowah, to Dallas, Kennesaw; and the heats of summer found us on the banks of the Chattahoochee, far from home, and dependent on a single road for supplies.**
>
> **Again we were not to be held back by any obstacle, and crossed over and fought four hard battles for the possession of the citadel of Atlanta. That was the crisis of our history. A doubt still clouded our future, but we solved the problem, destroyed Atlanta, struck boldly**

---

41. Quoted in *Charlotte Western Democrat*, June 6, 1865.

across the State of Georgia, severed all the main arteries of life to our enemy, and Christmas found us at Savannah.

Waiting there only long enough to fill our wagons, we again began a march which, for peril, labor, and results, will compare with any ever made by an organized army. The floods of the Savannah, the swamps of the Combahee and Edisto, the "high hills" and rocks of the Santee, the flat quagmires of the Pedee and Cape Fear Rivers, were all passed in mid-winter, with its floods and rains, in the face of an accumulating enemy; and, after the battles of Averysboro and Bentonville, we once more came out of the wilderness, to meet our friends at Goldsboro. Even then we paused only long enough to get new clothing, to reload our wagons, again pushed on to Raleigh and beyond, until we met our enemy suing for peace, instead of war, and offering to submit to the injured laws of his and our country. As long as that enemy was defiant, nor mountains nor rivers, nor swamps, nor hunger, nor cold, had checked us; but when he, who had fought us hard and persistently, offered submission, your general thought it wrong to pursue him farther, and negotiations followed, which resulted, as you all know, in his surrender.

How far the operations of this army contributed to the final overthrow of the Confederacy and the peace which now dawns upon us, must be judged by others, not by us; but that you have done all that men could do has been admitted by those in authority, and we have a right to join in the universal joy that fills our land because the war is over, and our Government stands vindicated before the world by the joint action of the volunteer armies and navy of the United States. To such as remain in the service, your general need only remind you that success in the past was due to hard work and discipline, and that the same work and discipline are equally important in the future. To such as go home, he will only say that our favored country is so grand, so extensive, so diversified in climate, soil, and productions, that every man may find a home and occupation suited to his taste; none should yield to the natural impatience sure to result from our past life of excitement and adventure. You will be invited to seek new adventures abroad; do not yield to the temptation, for it will lead only to death and disappointment.

Your general now bids you farewell, with the full belief that, as in war you have been good soldiers, so in peace you will make good citizens; and if, unfortunately, new war should arise in our country, Sherman's army will be the first to buckle on its old armor, and come forth to defend and maintain the Government of our inheritance.

By order of Major-General W. T. Sherman,
L. M. Dayton, Assistant Adjutant-General.[42]

And with a fond, emotional farewell, Sherman began a peacetime career, leading to his promotion of full general.

On May 4, with the task of paroling his troops finally completed, Johnston disbanded his headquarters and thanked his staff, bidding them well in their future endeavors. "The scene was an affecting one," newspaper correspondent Theodore C. Wilson reported, "and all who witnessed it regarded it in that light."[43]

Like Sherman, Johnston also offered a warm goodbye to his troops:

General Orders No. 53.

Comrades: In terminating our official relations, I earnestly exhort you to observe faithfully the terms of pacification agreed upon; and to discharge the obligations of good and peaceful citizens, as well as you have performed the duties of thorough soldiers in the field. By such a course, you will best secure the comfort of your families and kindred, and restore tranquility to our country.

You will return to your homes with the admiration of our people, won by the courage and noble devotion you have displayed in this long war. I shall always remember with pride the loyal support and generous confidence you have given me.

I now part with you with deep regret—and bid you farewell with feelings of cordial friendship; and with earnest wishes that you may have hereafter all the prosperity and happiness to be found in the world.

J. E. Johnston, General.
Official: Archer Anderson, A. A. G.[44]

42. Sherman, *Memoirs*, 2:379-380.
43. "Mr. Theodore C. Wilson's Dispatch," *New York Herald*, May 10, 1865.
44. Johnston, *Military Narrative*, 418-419.

And just like that, according to Wilson, "the headquarters of the rebel Army of Tennessee ceased to have an existence—commencing its journey to history and posterity."[45] Like the men of his command, Joe Johnston headed home to Charlotte to try to resume a life that, for the first time since his youth, did not include military service.

* * *

"War is not merely an act of policy but a true political instrument, a continuation of political intercourse, carried on with other means," Carl von Clausewitz famously wrote in his study about the early nineteenth-century Napoleonic Wars. "What remains peculiar to war is simply the peculiar nature of its means. War in general, and the commander in any specific instance, is entitled to require that the trend and designs of policy shall not be inconsistent with those means. That, of course, is no small demand; but however much it may affect political aims in a given case, it will never do more than modify them. The political object is the goal, war is the means of reaching it, and, in so far as their violent nature will admit, it will have a continuous influence on them."[46]

In a democratic republic such as the United States, where the military is subservient to the civilian authority, Clausewitz's analysis is even more apropos. In the Civil War's case, the political goal was to suppress the rebellion and to reconstruct the Union—no other solution would be acceptable. The armies of the North were the instrumentality for accomplishing the political policy goal.

No event casted a longer shadow over Sherman's and Johnston's efforts to make peace than did the tragic, untimely assassination of President Abraham Lincoln. Johnston realized that the surrender of Gen. Robert E. Lee's army meant the end of the Confederacy, and he was determined to make peace on the best terms possible. The Confederate commander had little leverage, other than one important factor: unlike Lee's army, Johnston's army was not surrounded, and Sherman knew it would be extremely difficult to compel him to surrender.

"The dispersion of Lee's army and the surrender of the remnant which remained with him destroyed the hopes I entertained when we parted," Jefferson Davis, the Confederacy's president, wrote on April 23. Davis's statement demonstrates that he did not understand the dire circumstances or the remaining Confederate armies' state of morale. "Had that army held together, I am now confident that we...would

---

45. "Mr. Theodore C. Wilson's Dispatch."
46. Carl von Clausewitz, *On War, Michael Howard and Peter Paret, trans.* (Princeton, NJ: Princeton University Press, 1976), 87.

have been today on the high road to independence. Even after that disaster, if the men who straggled, say thirty or forty thousand in number, had come back with their arms and disposition to fight, we might have repaired the damage; but all was sadly the reverse of that," Davis complained. "They threw away theirs, and were uncontrollably resolved to go home."

Bitterly, Davis continued, "J. E. Johnston and Beauregard were hopeless as to recruiting their forces from the dispersed men of Lee's army, and equally so as to their ability to check Sherman with the forces they had. Their only idea was to retreat, of the power to do so they were doubtful, and subsequent desertions from their troops have materially diminished their strength and, I learn, still more weakened their confidence." He concluded, "The loss of arms has been so great that, should the spirit of the people rise to the occasion, it would not at this time be possible adequately to supply them with the weapons of war."[47]

When he penned his memoirs years later, Davis wrote, "Johnston's line of retreat was open, and supplies had been placed upon it. His cavalry was superior to that of the enemy, as had been proved in every conflict between them. Maury and Forrest and Tyler still had armies in the field—not large, but strong enough to have collected around them the men who had left Johnston's army and gone to their homes to escape a surrender, as well as those who under similar circumstances had left Lee. The show of continued resistance, I then believed, as I still do, would have overcome the depression which was spreading like a starless night over the country, and that the exhibition of a determination not to leave our political future at the mercy of an enemy which had for four years been striving to subjugate the States would have led the United States authorities to do, as Mr. Lincoln had indicated—give any terms which might be found necessary speedily to terminate the existing war."[48]

Davis also declared, "General Lee was compelled to surrender; General Johnston consented to surrender." However, with the benefit of hindsight, one of Maj. Gen. Joseph Wheeler's troopers said, "The compulsion of Lee by Grant, on April 9th, preceded and actually added to the compulsion of Johnston by Sherman, April 26th. The privilege of consent was never allowed by the enemy to either, nor was there ground to charge against the two Confederate generals that one,

47. "The Final Collapse. Confederate Papers Captured at the End of the War,"
   The Sun, February 14, 1886.
48. Davis, *The Rise and Fall of the Confederate Government*, 2:692-693.

more than the other, would have consented in advance of the extremity of compulsion."[49]

Johnston understood that since his army was not surrounded, Sherman could not force him to surrender without a final battle. "But I saw that we must come up somewhere," Johnston commented a few days later. "We would certainly have had to stop at the Mississippi, so I negotiated as I did with General Sherman, believing it criminal to prolong a hopeless war another day," he told *New York Herald* correspondent Theodore C. Davis on April 30. "The fate of the Confederacy was decided in Virginia. When Lee surrendered there was an end to it. Had I marched my army away, as I could have done, it was only dragging Sherman after me. He would have foraged on the country, and I would have been compelled to do the same. The country would have been devastated, and we would have had to come to some terms at last."[50]

Johnston deserves a great deal of credit for recognizing the reality of the Confederacy's situation and for taking steps to end the war. Lieutenant Colonel A. R. Chisholm, a Confederate staff officer, stated, "Johnston and Beauregard decided to settle matters as best they could for the benefit of the Army and the Southern States, as for their own personal safety they did not seem to have a thought.[51]

Sherman had similar sentiments about the matter. Johnston "could not have resisted my army an hour if I could have got hold of him; but he could have escaped from me by breaking up into small parties, or by taking the country roads, travelling faster than any army with trains could have pursued," he told the Joint Committee on the Conduct of the War on May 22, 1865. "There was no question as to the result of a battle, and I knew it; every soldier knew it; every man in North Carolina knew it. Johnston said in the first five minutes of our conversation that any further resistance on his part would be an act of folly, and all he wanted was to keep his army from dispersing."[52]

Sherman's adjutant Maj. George Nichols shared Sherman's opinion. "The evidence goes to show that Johnston has been induced to surrender quite as much by the discontent of his own soldiers as by the Federal force in his rear," he wrote. "The Rebel troops see the utter folly of farther resistance, and refuse to fight longer. Johnston has pursued the only wise course left open to him."[53] Again, Johnston

---

49. Quoted in DuBose, *General Joseph Wheeler and the Army of Tennessee*, 466.
50. Davis, "Johnston's Surrender."
51. "Notes Personal of Lt. Col. Alex Robt. Chisholm," 89.
52. "Sherman-Johnston," 15.
53. Nichols, *The Great March*, 320.

deserves recognition for handling the circumstances so well and for doing the right thing, even though that meant defying Davis's direct order.

Johnston further detailed his decision-making process to an unknown recipient in a May 6, 1865, letter that was published in the Official Records of the Civil War:

CHARLOTTE, May 6, 1865.

Having made a convention with Major-General Sherman to terminate hostilities in North and South Carolina, Georgia, and Florida, it seems to me proper to put before the people of those States the condition of military affairs which rendered the measure absolutely necessary. On the 26th of April, the day of the convention, by the returns of the three lieutenant-generals of the Army of Tennessee, that under my command, the number of infantry and artillery present and absent was 70,510. The total present, 18,578; the effective total or fighting force, 14,179. On the 7th of April, the date of the last return I can find, the effective total of the cavalry was 5,440. But between the 7th and 26th of April it was greatly reduced by events in Virginia and apprehensions of surrender. In South Carolina we had Young's division of cavalry, less than 1,000, besides reserves and State troops, together much inferior to the Federal force in that State. In Florida we were as weak. In Georgia our inadequate force had been captured at Macon. In Lieutenant-General Taylor's department there were no means of opposing the formidable army under General Canby, which had taken Mobile, nor the cavalry under General Wilson, which had captured every other place of military importance west of Augusta. The latter had been stopped at Macon by the armistice as we had been at Greensborough, but its distance from Augusta being less than half of ours, that place was in its power. To carry on the war therefore, we had to depend on the Army of Tennessee alone. The United States could have brought against it twelve or fifteen times its number in the armies of Generals Grant, Sherman, and Canby, and with such odds against us, and without the means of procuring ammunition or repairing arms, without money or credit to provide food, it was impossible to continue the war, except as robbers. The consequences of prolonging the struggle would only have been the destruction or dispersion of our bravest men, and great suffering of women and children by the desolation and ruin inevitable from the marching of 200,000 men through the country. Having failed in an attempt to obtain terms giving security to citizens as well as soldiers, I had to choose between wantonly bringing the evils of war upon those I had been chosen to defend, and averting those calamities with the confession that hopes were dead, which every thinking Southern man had already lost. I therefore stipulated with General Sherman for the security of the brave and true men committed to me on terms which also terminate hostilities in all the country over which our commands extended and announced it to your governors by telegraph as follows.

J. E. JOHNSTON.[54]

Colonel John Logan Black commanded the Confederate 1st South Carolina Cavalry for most of the war, serving under Lt. Gen. Wade Hampton for much of it. "I have sometimes since the war been disposed to censure some of Gen'l Johnston's acts about the time of the surrender, yet it is hard to do this as no one can realize the situation he occupied," Black wrote, years after war. "It is true he might have made some move that would have prolonged the struggle for a few months but in this time the misery and bloodshed would have been awful & Johnston had the sagacity to see it." Everyone but Jefferson Davis agreed that there was no reason to prolong the bloodshed.[55]

Major General John M. Schofield, who drafted the two documents Sherman and Johnston signed on April 26, left behind an especially insightful analysis the ramifications of their actions about those events, which is worth repeating in its entirety.

> The question of the abstract wisdom of the terms of the Sherman-Johnston "memorandum" has little to do with that of Sherman in agreeing to it. Any person at all acquainted with the politics of the dominant party at that time would have known that it was at least unwise to introduce political questions at all. Besides, he had the example of his superior, the general-in-chief, who had just accepted the surrender of the principal Confederate army from the Confederate generalissimo without any

54. *OR* 47, 3:872-873.
55. Eleanor D. McSwain, ed., *Crumbling Defenses or Memoirs and Reminiscences of John Logan Black, Colonel C.S.A.* (Macon, GA: The J. W. Burke Co., 1960), 110.

political conditions; and the knowledge of President Lincoln's assassination, which must have made the country unwilling to consent to more liberal terms than had before been granted. Yet, however unwise Sherman's action may have been, the uproar it created, and the attacks upon his honor and integrity for which it was made the excuse, were utterly inexcusable. They were probably unexampled as an exhibition of the effect of great and unusual excitement upon the minds of men unaccustomed to such moral and mental strain.

The most charitable view of this matter seems also to be the most just namely, that the high officers of government were completely unnerved and lost their heads under the terrible strain produced by President Lincoln's assassination, increased somewhat, perhaps, by a natural apprehension of what might come next. The contrast between this state of excitement in Washington and the marked calm that prevailed throughout the army was very instructive, and it was difficult for any soldier to understand at that time the state of mind in Washington. No part of the people could have felt more deeply or with greater indignation the loss the country had suffered, and the infamous crime by which it had been accomplished. Yet not a ripple of excitement could be seen anywhere in the army. The profound calm which pervades the atmosphere surrounding a great, disciplined, self-confident army is one of the most sublime exhibitions of human nature.

That Sherman felt "outraged beyond measure," was natural and indeed inevitable. He had committed an error of judgment arising from political inexperience and a failure to appreciate the difference between Mr. Lincoln's humane purposes toward individual Confederates and his political policy. But the error was of the least possible practical consequence, and there was not the slightest excuse for making it public at the time, in violation of all rules of official courtesy. All that it was necessary or right to do was to tell Sherman to correct his error.

While the effect of these ferocious bulletins received some time later was such as General Sherman fully describes, the first effect of the simple disapproval of the convention, both upon Sherman and Johnston, not referred to by either in their published narratives, may be interesting to the readers of history. General Sherman was manifestly much disappointed and mortified at the rejection of his terms, although he had been prepared somewhat by expressions of opinion from others in the interval, and both he and Johnston at their last meeting seemed sad and dejected.

To understand this, it must be remembered that Johnston's army was not surrounded, and its surrender could not have been compelled. Unless the terms of capitulation could be made such as the troops themselves would be willing to accept, they would, it was apprehended, break up into guerrilla bands of greater or less strength and carry on the war in that way indefinitely. So strongly was I impressed at the time with General Johnston's apprehension, that I was often thereafter haunted in my dreams with the difficulties I was actually encountering in the prosecution of military operations against those remnants of the Confederate armies, in marshy and mountainous countries, through summer heats and winter storms. It was several years after the war that I became fully satisfied, at night, that it was really over.[56]

Schofield concluded:

It may not be possible to judge how wise or unwise Sherman's first "memorandum" might have proved if it had been ratified. It is always difficult to tell how things that have not been tried would have worked if they had been. We now know only this much that the imagination of man could hardly picture worse results than those wrought out by the plan that was finally adopted namely, to destroy everything that existed in the way of government, and then build from the bottom on the foundation of ignorance and rascality.

The de facto State governments existing at the time of the surrender would have been of infinite service in restoring order and material prosperity, if they had been recognized by the military authority of the United States and kept under military control similar to that exercised by the district commanders under the "reconstruction acts." And such recognition would in no manner have interfered with any action Congress might have thought it wise to take looking to the organization of permanent governments and the admission of senators and

56. Schofield, *Forty-Six Years in the Army*, 348-350.

representatives in Congress. After two years of "reconstruction" under President Johnson's "policy," the Southern State governments were no better than those he had destroyed. Then Congress took the matter in hand, and after years of labor brought forth State governments far worse than either of those that had been torn down.

Party ambition on the one hand, and timidity on the other, were the parents of these great follies. The presidential succession was the mainspring of the first movement and of the opposition thereto, while that and party majority in Congress were the motives of the later "reconstruction." Both ingloriously failed, as they deserved to do. How much stronger the Republican party would have been if it had relied upon the loyal States which had sustained it through the war, instead of timidly distrusting them and trying to bolster itself up by the aid of the negro and "carpet-bag" governments in the South!

Political reconstruction ought not to have been thought of at the close of the war. What was then needed was local civil government under such military control as might be necessary, restoration of order, industry, and material prosperity, leading to a gradual reorganization of the society which had been completely broken up by the war. After this had been done, and Congress had decided upon the conditions of full restoration, it would have been time enough to inaugurate political reconstruction. This was clear enough at the time to those who had studied the subject and knew by personal observation the real condition and feeling of the Southern people. But the leading politicians of either party do not appear to have had the wisdom and moral courage to advocate such a policy. Both were impatient to see their party represented on the floors of Congress by members from the South.

It was something of the kind above suggested which was aimed at by Generals Sherman and Johnston, and which was deemed wise by the leading generals both North and South. There were several conditions in the memorandum that were clearly inadmissible, though easy of correction without changing the essential features of the document. This was to be expected from a hasty effort to solve a great political problem by a man without political education or experience. Sherman's failure was not unlike that of great politicians who undertake to command armies. Their general ideas may be very good, but they have no knowledge of details, and hence make mistakes resulting in failure.

As now seen, projected upon the dark background of the political history of the Southern States during the twelve years from 1865 to 1877, and compared with the plans of political doctrinaires in 1865, under the light of experience and reason, the Sherman-Johnston memorandum and Sherman's letters of that period seem self-luminous with political wisdom. Sherman needed only the aid of competent military advisers in whom he had confidence to have made him one of the greatest generals of any age, and he would have needed only the aid of competent political advisers to have made him a great statesman. But he looked almost with contempt upon a "staff," and would doubtless have thought little better of a "cabinet."[57]

In essence, the tragic assassination of Abraham Lincoln merely two days before the initial meeting between Sherman and Johnston poisoned the possibility of the generals' attempts to find a political solution. The understandable rage unleashed by the news of Lincoln's assassination triggered a wave of vindictiveness among Northern politicians, particularly among the Radical Republicans in control of Johnson's administration. Joe Johnston recognized as much when he lamented that with Lincoln's death, the South had lost its best friend. It was unfeasible that these two simple, honest soldiers could bring about a political solution on their own after years of hard war or have any realistic hope that the government would approve their efforts. The commanders did their best under some extremely adverse circumstances, and Sherman overstepped his boundaries in the process.

Sherman and Johnston had nothing but the best of intentions. After four years of brutal, bloody war, both knew that the Confederacy had been vanquished. Had Lincoln not been assassinated, Sherman's political solution might have been accepted. However, the Union general had no chance without Lincoln. But that does not detract from Johnston's courage to disobey a direct order from Davis, or Sherman's decision to make peace, or the remarkable efforts of two remarkable men to bring about the dawn of a new day.

For that, we all owe William T. Sherman and Joseph E. Johnston a debt of gratitude.

---

57. Ibid., 353-356.

EPILOGUE

BENNETT PLACE TODAY

A fter the armies and the destruction they brought left the Raleigh area in May 1865, calm returned to the 350-acre farm of James and Nancy Bennett. The Bennetts remained at the farm for the rest of their lives—James died in 1878, followed by Nancy in 1884.[1] The challenges of Reconstruction hurt the family's formerly prosperous farming operation. By the 1870s, the Bennetts made most of their money from growing and selling apples, potatoes, and seed corn, as well as from selling off sections of their farm.[2]

Eliza Anne, James's and Nancy's daughter, married Robert Duke, the brother of tobacco magnate Washington Duke and resided on her parents' farm after they died. James's and Nancy's granddaughter Roberta and her husband, J. M. Shields, acquired the property from Eliza Duke. In 1889, they sold the property to Brodie Duke, son of Washington Duke, and moved to Raleigh. However, the house stood vacant.[3]

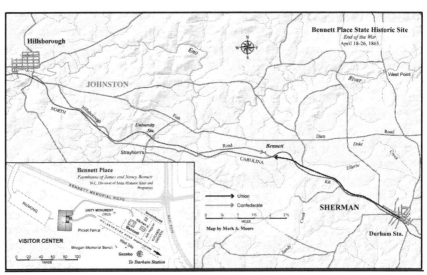

1. Arthur C. Menius, III, "James Bennitt: Portrait of an Antebellum Yeoman," *North Carolina Historical Review* 58 (October 1981), 324.
2. Ibid., 325.
3. Arthur C. Menius, III, "The Bennett Place," 1979 unpublished manuscript, 3-5. Copy in files, Bennett Place State Historic Site, Durham, North Carolina.

Bennett Place as it appeared in 1904. Note the poor condition of the house.

(Library of Congress)

In 1890, Brodie Duke recognized that the then-abandoned Bennett farm had historical significance. He offered it for sale at the 1893 World's Columbian Exposition in Chicago. When he found no takers, Duke sold the remaining 35 acres to Samuel Morgan, who came from a local Durham County farming family. Morgan intended to develop the Bennett farm into a historical attraction. However, he died before doing so, and the property fell into disrepair. "By 1905, the dwelling had almost collapsed," the authors of a 1980 archaeological report stated. "The grounds were littered with debris from the falling structures and any glimmer of its once historic past was all but gone."[4] And then tragedy struck in 1921 when the original Bennett house burned to the ground.

Fortunately, though, the idea of turning the property into a historic site had already caught on. A local attorney named R. O. Everett and a state legislator named Frank L. Fuller began the process to transform the Bennett farm into an attraction. They requested that the state of North Carolina maintain the site and contribute toward the erection of an appropriate monument if the Morgan family would donate the land. All agreed, and the 35 acres were deeded to the Bennett Place Memorial Commission. The Unity Monument—a

---

4. Sacchi and Erlandson, "An Intensive Archaeological Survey," 10.

marker consisting of two granite columns, representing the North and the South, and topped by a lintel inscribed with the word "Unity"—was dedicated in November 1923, despite objections of from the local chapter of the United Daughters of the Confederacy who were opposed to any monument commemorating the Confederacy's defeat.

Local dignitaries and surviving veterans attended. Julian Shakespeare Carr, a partner in the world-famous Bull Durham tobacco company and local philanthropist, was a veteran of the 3rd North Carolina Cavalry of the Civil War. Carr was also the former commander of North Carolina's United Confederate Veterans and carried the honorific title of "General Carr," even though he mustered out at Appomattox, Virginia, as a private.[5] He presided over the dedication ceremony for the handsome Unity Monument.[6]

In the 1930s, the commission erected a stone wall around the property and a stone bench across from the house. Unfortunately, enthusiasm for developing the site dwindled, and only general maintenance was performed for the following two decades. In 1958, a benefactor, Mrs. Magruder Dent, donated $8,000 to restore the surrender site, which would help memorialize her grandfather who was part of Gen. Joseph E. Johnston's army. The Unity Monument was the only structure on the site until 1959. With the centennial of the Civil War approaching, the commission deeded the property to the North Carolina Department of Archives and History, which made plans to redevelop the property as a significant attraction in time for the 100th anniversary of the surrender of Johnston's army.[7]

Using old photographs and sketches and descriptive statements, the long-destroyed farm buildings were reconstructed and restored "exactly like they were...when General Johnston and General Sherman met for their historic conferences."[8] Two early twentieth-century structures that resembled the Bennett house were moved to the site and altered to match the original structures. A smoke house was constructed from leftover wood.[9]

On April 29, 1962, the 97th anniversary of Johnston's surrender, the "Day of Unity" arrived. More than 500 people attended the

5. Carr has an interesting story. For a full-length biography, see Mena Webb, *Jule Carr: General Without an Army* (Chapel Hill: University of North Carolina Press, 1987).
6. *Durham Herald*, November 23, 1923.
7. Sacchi and Erlandson, "An Intensive Archaeological Survey," 12.
8. W. S. Tarleton, "Report on the Bennett House Restoration," unpublished research report, North Carolina Department of Archives and History, August 27, 1959, copy in files at Bennett Place State Historic Site, 3.
9. Sacchi and Erlandson, "An Intensive Archaeological Survey," 12.

Bennett Place as it appears today.

(Author's Collection, photography by Melissa Fox Jones)

dedication ceremonies, and more than 10,000 people toured the site during the first year of its operation. In 1965, Vice President Hubert H. Humphrey delivered the keynote address commemorating the centennial of the Sherman-Johnston agreement. His words highlighted the importance of the site. "We should always remember this lesson from the past," Humphrey declared. "We must never permit the spirit of radicalism to poison the minds and the hearts of the American people. This is the real lesson we can learn from Bennett Place."[10]

In 1975, a trailer was placed on the property to serve as a temporary visitor center while plans were made to construct a permanent one. After an extensive archaeological survey, a location was chosen for the new permanent visitor center, and construction commenced.[11] The main site is approximately four acres in size.

Today, "the Visitor Center contains a museum gallery of three rooms of exhibits telling the story of the Bennett Family and the events encompassing the largest surrender of the American Civil War," according to the Bennett Place website. "Military weaponry, farm

10. "Address of Vice-President Hubert H. Humphrey, Bennett Place Commemoration, Durham, North Carolina," April 25, 1965, James Bennitt Papers, Manuscripts Division, Perkins Library, Duke University, Durham, North Carolina.
11. Sacchi and Erlandson, "An Intensive Archaeological Survey," 12.

The Unity Monument on the grounds of Bennett Place.

(Author's Collection, photography by Melissa Fox Jones)

tools, and other Civil War artifacts are part of the collection on display. In addition, the Everett-Thissen Research Library contains more than 1,000 books, periodicals, and documents relating to the Civil War and the Bennett Family story. The theater shows the short orientation film, 'Dawn of Peace' during operating hours."[12] The visitor center also features a gift shop. There are outdoor exhibits and a small bandstand, as well as picnic tables and nature trails. A re-enactment of the surrender events takes place annually, along with other occasional special events that occur throughout the year.

In 2014, the Bennett Place Support Fund, Inc., a local advocacy group, raised sufficient money to purchase a 1.98-acre portion of the original farm that was in imminent danger of being commercially developed, increasing the park's holdings to 38 acres. This wooded parcel not only serves as a buffer between the tranquil Bennett Place and a heavily developed commercial area, but it also preserves another portion of the original farm for posterity and helps maintain its pristine state.

While thousands visit the Bennett Place State Historic Site each year, the volume of visitors lags far behind that of the National Park Service's Appomattox Court House site in Appomattox, Virginia. There, the federal government acquired the entire town and recreated its buildings. The park features 1,325 acres, including the location where fighting occurred on the morning of April 9, 1865. The surrender ceremony site is one of the primary focuses of the Appomattox village.

Appomattox Court House National Historical Park stands in stark contrast to the small Bennett Place State Historic Site, even though the events that occurred at Bennett Place were more momentous and

---

12. "Bennett Place: Facilities,"
    http://www.nchistoricsites.org/bennett/facilities.htm (accessed on February 26, 2017). Dan Nance's original oil painting of "The First Meeting," which appears on the cover of this book, hangs in the visitor center's museum.

The Visitor Center at Bennett Place.
(Author's Collection, photography by Melissa Fox Jones)

officially ended the Civil War. Johnston's surrender at Bennett Place has long been overshadowed by the events that occurred at Appomattox Court House village. Hopefully, this book will bring well-deserved and long-overdue attention to the efforts of William T. Sherman and Joseph E. Johnston.

APPENDIX A

ORGANIZATION OF THE FORCES IN NORTH CAROLINA AS OF APRIL 26, 1865[1]

UNION FORCES
MAJ. GEN. WILLIAM T. SHERMAN

Headquarters Guard

7th Company Ohio Sharpshooters (Lt. James Cox)

Engineers and Mechanics

1st Michigan (Col. John B. Yates)
1st Missouri (five companies) (Lt. Col. William Tweeddale)

Artillery (Bvt. Maj. Gen. William F. Barry)

RIGHT WING
ARMY OF THE TENNESSEE
MAJ. GEN. OLIVER O. HOWARD

Escort:
5th Illinois Cavalry (Co. K) (Capt. William Duncan)
4th Company Ohio Cavalry (Capt. John L. King)
Pontoon Train Guard
14th Wisconsin (Co. E) (Capt. William I. Henry)

Fifteenth Army Corps (Maj. Gen. John A. Logan)

First Division (Bvt. Maj. Gen. Charles R. Woods)

First Brigade (Bvt. Brig. Gen. William B. Woods)

126th Indiana (Col. Reuben Williams)
26th Iowa (Maj. John Lubbers)
27th Missouri (Col. Thomas Curly)
31st/32nd Missouri (six companies) (Lt. Col. Abraham J. Seay)

---

1. This order of battle is adapted from the one included in Mark L. Bradley, *This Astounding Close: The Road to Bennett Place* (Chapel Hill: University of North Carolina Press, 2000), 275-301. The author is grateful for this outstanding work.

76th Ohio (Lt. Col. Edward Briggs)

Second Brigade (Col. Robert F. Catterson)

26th Illinois (Lt. Col. Ira J. Bloomfield)
40th Illinois (Lt. Col. Hiram W. Hall)
103rd Illinois (Lt. Col. George W. Wright)
97th Indiana (Lt. Col. Aden G. Cavins)
100th Indiana (Maj. Ruel M. Johnson, Capt. John W. Headington)
6th Iowa (Lt. Col. William H. Clune)
46th Ohio (Lt. Col. Edward N. Upton)

Third Brigade (Col George A. Stone)

4th Iowa (Maj. Albert R. Anderson)
9th Iowa (Maj. Alonzo Abernethy)
25th Iowa (Lt. Col. David J. Palmer)
30th Iowa (Lt. Col. Aurelius Roberts)
31st Iowa (Lt. Col. Jeremiah W. Jenkins)

Second Division (Maj. Gen. William B. Hazen)

First Brigade (Col. Theodore Jones)

55th Illinois (Capt. Charles A. Andress)
116th Illinois (Lt. Col. John E. Maddux, Capt. Necolas Geschwind)
127th Illinois (Lt. Col. Frank S. Curtiss)
6th Missouri (Lt. Col. Delos Van Deusen)
30th Ohio (Lt. Col. Emerson P. Brooks)
57th Ohio (Lt. Col. Samuel R. Mott)

Second Brigade (Col. Wells S. Jones)

111th Illinois (Col. James S. Martin)
83rd Indiana (Capt. Charles W. White, Capt. William N. Craw)
37th Ohio (Lt. Col. Louis von Blessingh)
47th Ohio (Col. Augustus C. Parry)
53rd Ohio (Maj. Preston R. Galloway)
54th Ohio (Lt. Col. Israel T. Moore)

Third Brigade (Brig. Gen. John M. Oliver)

48th Illinois (Lt. Col. Thomas L. B. Weems)
90th Illinois (Lt. Col. Owen Stuart)
99th Indiana (Capt. Josiah Farrar)
15th Michigan (Lt. Col. Frederick S. Hutchinson)
70th Ohio (Lt. Col. Henry L. Philips)

Third Division (Bvt. Maj. Gen. John E. Smith)

First Brigade (Brig. Gen. William Clark)

63rd Illinois (Col. Joseph B. McCown, Capt. Joseph R. Stanford)
93rd Illinois (Lt. Col. Nicholas C. Buswell)
48th Indiana (Capt. Newton Bingham)
59th Indiana (Lt. Col. Jefferson K. Scott, Maj. Thomas A. McNaught)
4th Minnesota (Col. John E. Tourtellotte, Capt Leverett R. Wellman)
18th Wisconsin (Lt. Col. Charles H. Jackson)

Second Brigade (Col. Clark R. Wever, Col. John E. Tourtellotte)

56th Illinois (Lt. Col. John P. Hall)
10th Iowa (Lt. Col. William H. Silsby)
17th Iowa (one company) (Capt. William Horner)
10th/26th Missouri (two companies) (Lt. Theron M. Rice)
80th Ohio (Lt. Col. Pren Metham, Maj. Thomas C. Morris)

Fourth Division (Bvt. Maj. Gen. John M. Corse)

First Brigade (Brig. Gen. Elliott W. Rice)

52nd Illinois (Lt. Col. Jerome D. Davis)
66th Indiana (Lt. Col. Roger Martin)
2nd Iowa (Col. Noel B. Howard)
7th Iowa (Lt. Col. James C. Parrott)

Second Brigade (Col. Robert N. Adams)

12th Illinois (Lt. Col. Hector Perrin)
66th Illinois (Lt. Col. Andrew K. Campbell)
81st Ohio (Maj. William C. Henry)

Third Brigade (Col. Frederick J. Hurlbut)

7th Illinois (Lt. Col. Hector Perrin)
50th Illinois (Lt. Col. William Hanna)
57th Illinois (Maj. Frederick A. Battey)
39th Iowa (Lt. Col. Joseph M. Griffiths)

Unassigned

29th Missouri Mounted Infantry (Col. Joseph S. Gage)
110th U.S. Colored Troops (Maj. William C. Hawley, Capt. Thomas Kennedy, Capt. Zachariah C. Wilson, Capt. Jacob Kemnitzer)

Artillery (Lt. Col. William H. Ross)

> 1st Illinois, Battery H (Capt. Francis DeGress,
> Lt.Robert S. Gray)
> 1st Michigan, Battery B (Lt. Edward B. Wright)
> 1st Missouri, Battery H (Capt. Charles M. Callahan)
> 12th Wisconsin Battery (Capt. William Zickerick)

Seventeenth Army Corps (Maj. Gen. Frank P. Blair Jr)

> 11th Illinois Cavalry (Co. G) (Capt. Stephen S. Tripp)

First Division (Maj. Gen. Joseph W. Mower, Brig. Gen. Manning F. Force)

First Brigade (Brig. Gen. John W. Fuller)

> 64th Illinois (Maj. Joseph S. Reynolds)
> 18th Missouri (Col. Charles S. Sheldon, Lt. Col.
> William H. Minter, Maj. William M. Edgar)
> 27th Ohio (Maj. Isaac N. Gilruth)
> 39th Ohio (Lt. Col. Daniel Weber)

Second Brigade (Brig. Gen. John W. Sprague)

> 35th New Jersey (Col. John J. Cladek)
> 43rd Ohio (Maj. Horace Park)
> 63rd Ohio (Maj. Oscar L. Jackson)
> 25th Wisconsin (Lt. Col. Jeremiah M. Rusk)

Third Brigade (Col. Charles H. DeGroat, Bvt. Brig. Gen. John Tilson)

> 10th Illinois (Lt. Col. David Gillespie)
> 25th Indiana (Lt. Col. James S. Wright)
> 32nd Wisconsin (Lt. Col. Joseph H. Carleton, Maj.
> William H. Burrows)

Third Division (Bvt. Maj. Gen. Mortimer D. Leggett)

First Brigade (Brig. Gen. Charles Ewing)

> 20th Illinois (Capt. Henry King)
> 30th Illinois (Lt. Col. William C. Rhoades, Capt. John
> P. Davis)
> 31st Illinois (Lt. Col. Robert N. Pearson)
> 45th Illinois (Maj. John O. Duer)
> 12th Wisconsin (Col. James K. Proudfit)
> 16th Wisconsin (Col. Cassius Fairchild)

Second Brigade (Brig. Gen. Robert K. Scott)

> 20th Ohio (Lt. Col. Harrison Wilson)
> 68th Ohio (Lt. Col. George E. Welles)

78th Ohio (Col. Greenberry Wiles, Lt. Col. Gilbert D. Munson)
17th Wisconsin (Col. Adam G. Malloy)

Fourth Division (Bvt. Maj. Gen. Giles A. Smith)

First Brigade (Brig. Gen. Benjamin F. Potts)

14th/15th Illinois Battalion (Col. George C. Rogers)
53rd Illinois (Col. John W. McClanahan)
32nd Ohio (Lt. Col. Jefferson J. Hibbets)

Third Brigade (Brig. Gen. William W. Belknap)

32nd Illinois (Capt. John J. Rider)
11th Iowa (Lt. Col. Benjamin Beach)
13th Iowa (Lt. Col. Justin C. Kennedy)
15th Iowa (Maj. George Pomutz)
16th Iowa (Maj. John H. Smith)

Unassigned

9th Illinois Mounted Infantry (Lt. Col. Samuel T. Hughes)

Artillery (Maj. Frederick Welker)

1st Michigan, Battery C (Lt. William W. Hyzer)
1st Minnesota Battery (Capt. William Z. Clayton)
15th Ohio Battery (Capt. James Burdick)

LEFT WING
ARMY OF GEORGIA
MAJ. GEN. HENRY W. SLOCUM

Pontoniers

58th Indiana (Lt. Col. Joseph Moore)

Fourteenth Army Corps (Bvt. Gen. Jefferson C. Davis)

Provost Guard (Lt. Col. E. Hibbard Topping)

110th Illinois (nine companies)
24th Illinois, Co. A

First Division (Brig. Gen. Charles C. Walcutt)

First Brigade (Bvt. Brig. Gen. Harrison C. Hobart)

104th Illinois (Maj. John H. Widmer)
42nd Indiana (Maj. Gideon R. Kellams)
88th Indiana (Maj. Lewis J. Blair)
33rd Ohio (Capt. Joseph Hinson)
94th Ohio (Maj. William H. Snider)

21st Wisconsin (Lt. Col. Michael H. Fitch)

Second Brigade (Bvt. Brig. Gen. George P. Buell)

13th Michigan (Capt. Silas A. Yerkes)
21st Michigan (Lt. Col. Loomis K. Bishop)
69th Ohio (Lt. Col. Joseph H. Brigham)

Third Brigade (Col. Henry A. Hambright)

38th Indiana (Capt. David H. Patton)
21st Ohio (Lt. Col. Arnold McMahan)
74th Ohio (Maj. Robert P. Findley)
79th Pennsylvania (Capt. John S. McBride)

Second Division (Bvt. Maj. Gen. James D. Morgan)

Provost Guard

110th Illinois (Co. B) (Capt. William R. Hester)

First Brigade (Brig. Gen. William Vandever)

16th Illinois (Capt. Herman Lund)
60th Illinois (Maj. James H. McDonald)
10th Michigan (Capt. William H. Dunphy)
14th Michigan (Lt. Col. George W. Grummond)
17th New York (Maj. Alexander S. Marshall)

Second Brigade (Brig. Gen. John G. Mitchell)

24th Illinois (Lt. Col. Peter Ege)
78th Illinois (Lt. Col. Maris R. Vernon)
98th Ohio (Maj. David E. Roatch)
108th Ohio (Lt. Col. Joseph Good)
113th Ohio (Capt. Otway Watson)
121st Ohio (Maj. Aaron B. Robinson)

Third Brigade (Lt. Col. James W. Langley)

85th Illinois (Capt. James R. Griffith)
86th Illinois (Lt. Col. Allen L. Fahnestock)
125th Illinois (Capt. George W. Cook)
22nd Indiana (Capt. William H. Snodgrass)
37th Indiana (one company) (Lt. Socrates Carver)
52nd Ohio (Maj. James T. Holmes)

Third Division (Bvt. Maj. Gen. Absalom Baird)

First Brigade (Col. Morton C. Hunter)

82nd Indiana (Lt. Col. John M. Matheny)
23rd Missouri (four companies) (Maj. John H. Jolley)
11th Ohio (detachment) (Capt. Francis H. Loring)
17th Ohio (Lt. Col. Benjamin H. Showers)

31st Ohio (Capt. Michael Stone, Capt. Eli Wilkin)
89th Ohio (Lt. Col. William H. Glenn)
92nd Ohio (Lt. Col. John C. Morrow)

Second Brigade (Col. Newell Gleason)

75th Indiana (Lt. Col. William O'Brien)
87th Indiana (Lt. Col. Edwin P. Hammond)
101st Indiana (Lt. Col. Thomas Doan)
2nd Minnesota (Lt. Col. Judson W. Bishop)
105th Ohio (Lt. Col. George T. Perkins)

Third Brigade (Lt. Col. Hubbard K. Milward, Brig. Gen. George S. Greene)

74th Indiana (Lt. Col. Thomas Morgan)
18th Kentucky (Maj. John J. Hall, Lt. Col. Hubbard K. Milward)
14th Ohio (Lt. Col. Albert Moore)
38th Ohio (Capt. Charles M. Gilbert)

Artillery (Maj. Charles Houghtaling)

1st Illinois, Battery C (Lt. Palmer F. Scovel)
2nd Illinois, Battery I (Lt. Judson Rich)
19th Indiana Battery (Lt. Clinton Keeler)
5th Wisconsin Battery (Capt. Joseph McKnight, Lt. Elijah Booth Jr.)

Twentieth Army Corps (Bvt. Maj. Gen. Alpheus S. Williams, Maj. Gen. Joseph A. Mower)

First Division (Brig. Gen. Nathaniel J. Jackson, Bvt. Maj. Gen. Alpheus S. Williams)

First Brigade (Bvt. Brig. Gen. James L. Selfrige)

5th Connecticut (Lt. Col. Henry W. Daboll)
123rd New York (Col. James C. Rogers)
141st New York (Lt. Col. Andrew J. McNett)
46th Pennsylvania (Maj. Patrick Griffith)

Second Brigade (Bvt. Brig. Gen. William Hawley)

2nd Massachusetts (Capt. Edward A. Phalen)
13th New Jersey (Lt. Col. Frederick H. Harris)
107th New York (Col. Nirom M. Crane)
150th New York (Col. Alfred B. Smith)
3rd Wisconsin (Lt. Col. George W. Stevenson)

Third Brigade (Brig. Gen. James S. Robinson)

82nd Illinois (Lt. Col. Edward S. Salomon)
101st Illinois (Lt. Col. John B. LeSage)

143rd New York (Col. Horace Boughton)

82nd Ohio (comprising 61st and 82nd Ohio) (Maj. James S. Crall)

31st Wisconsin (Col. Francis H. West)

Second Division (Bvt. Maj. Gen. John W. Geary)

First Brigade (Col. George W. Mindil, Bvt. Brig. Gen. Ario Pardee Jr.)

5th Ohio (Lt. Col. Robert Kirkup)

29th Ohio (Lt. Col. Jonas Schoonover)

66th Ohio (Lt. Col. Eugene Powell, Capt. Theodoric G. Keller)

28th Pennsylvania (Lt. Col. James Fitzpatrick)

147th Pennsylvania (Lt. Col. John Craig)

Second Brigade (Col. Patrick H. Jones)

33rd New Jersey (Lt. Col. Enos Fourat, Maj. Nathaniel K. Bray)

119th New York (Col. John T. Lockman)

134th New York (Lt. Col. Allan H. Jackson)

154th New York (Lt. Col. Lewis D. Warner)

73rd Pennsylvania (Maj. Christian H. Goebel)

Third Brigade (Bvt. Brig. Gen. Henry A. Barnum)

60th New York (Lt. Col. Lester S. Wilson)

102nd New York (Maj. Oscar J. Spaulding)

137th New York (Lt. Col. Koert S. Van Voorhees)

149th New York (Maj. Nicholas Grumbach)

29th Pennsylvania (Col. Samuel M. Zulich)

111th Pennsylvania (comprising 109th and 111th Pennsylvania)(Col. Thomas M. Walker)

Third Division (Bvt. Maj. Gen. William T. Ward)

First Brigade (Col. Henry Case, Bvt. Brig. Gen. Benjamin Harrison)

102nd Illinois (Col. Franklin C. Smith)

105th Illinois (Lt. Col. Everell F. Dutton)

129th Illinois (Lt. Col. Thomas H. Flynn, Col. Henry Case)

70th Indiana (Lt. Col. Samuel Merrill)

79th Ohio (Lt. Col. Azariah W. Doan)

Second Brigade (Bvt. Brig. Gen. Daniel Dustin)

33rd Indiana (Lt. Col. James E. Burton)

85th Indiana (Lt. Col. Alexander B. Crane)

19th Michigan (Maj. David Anderson)

22nd Wisconsin (Lt. Col. Edward Bloodgood)

Third Brigade (Bvt. Brig. Gen. William Cogswell)

20th Connecticut (Lt. Col. Philo B. Buckingham)
33rd Massachusetts (Lt. Col. Elisha Doane)
136th New York (Col. James Wood Jr.)
5th Ohio (Maj. Charles P. Wickham)
73rd Ohio (Maj. Thomas W. Higgins)
26th Wisconsin (Maj. Francis Lackner)

Artillery (Maj. John A. Reynolds, Capt. Charles E. Winegar)

1st New York, Battery I (Capt. Charles E. Winegar, Lt. Warren L. Scott)
1st New York, Battery M (Capt. Edward P. Newkirk)
1st Ohio, Battery C (Lt. Jerome B. Stephens)
Pennsylvania Light, Battery E (Capt. Thomas S. Sloan)

CENTER
ARMY OF THE OHIO
MAJ. GEN. JOHN M. SCHOFIELD

Escort
7th Ohio Cavalry (Co. G) (Capt. John A. Ashbury)
Signal Corps (Capt. Edmund H. Russell)

Engineers
15th New York (three companies) (Maj. Henry V. Slosson)
Artillery (Lt. Col. Terance J. Kennedy)

Tenth Army Corps (Maj. Gen. Alfred H. Terry)

Escort
20th New York Cavalry (Co. I) (Capt. John J. Carroll)

First Division (Bvt. Maj. Gen. Henry W. Birge)

First Brigade at Morehead City and Second Brigade at Wilmington.

Third Brigade (Col. Nicholas W. Day)

24th Iowa (Lt. Col. Edward Wright)
38th Massachusetts (Lt. Col. James P. Richardson)
128th New York (Capt. Henry H. Sincerbox)
156th New York (Capt. Alfred Cooley)
175th New York (five companies) (Capt. Charles McCarthey)
176th New York (Maj. Charles Lewis)

Artillery

22nd Indiana Battery (Lt. George W. Alexander)

Second Division (Bvt. Maj. Gen. Adelbert Ames)

First Brigade (Col. Rufus Daggett)

3rd New York (Lt. Col. Alfred Dunham)
112th New York (Col. Ephraim A. Ludwick)
117th New York (Capt. Edward Downer)
142nd New York (Col. Albert M. Barney)

Second Brigade (Col. William B. Coan, Col. John S. Littell)

47th New York (Col. Christopher R. MacDonald)
48th New York (Capt. Van Rensselaer K. Hilliard, Col.
William B. Coan)
76th Pennsylvania (Maj. Charles Knerr)
97th Pennsylvania (Lt. Col. John Wainwright)
203rd Pennsylvania (Lt. Col. Amos W. Bachman)

Third Brigade (Col. G. Frederick Granger)

13th Indiana (Lt. Col. Samuel M. Zent)
9th Maine (Lt. Col. Joseph Noble)
4th New Hampshire (Capt. John H. Roberts)
115th New York (Lt. Col. Nathan J. Johnson)
169th New York (Col. James A. Colvin)

Artillery

16th New York Battery (Capt. Richard H. Lee)

Third Division (Brig. Gen. Charles J. Paine)

First Brigade (Bvt. Brig. Gen. Delevan Bates)

1st U.S. Colored Troops (Lt. Col. Giles H. Rich)
30th U.S. Colored Troops (Lt. Col. Hiram A. Oakman)
107th U.S. Colored Troops (Col. William H. Revere Jr.)

Second Brigade (Bvt. Brig. Gen. Samuel A. Duncan)

4th U.S. Colored Troops (Lt. Col. George Rogers)
5th U.S. Colored Troops (Col. Giles W. Shurtleff)
39th U.S. Colored Troops (Col. Ozora P. Stearns)

Third Brigade (Col. John H. Holman, Bvt. Brig. General
Albert M. Blackman)

6th U.S. Colored Troops (Col. John W. Ames)
27th U. S. Colored Troops (Lt. Col. John W.
Donnellan)
37th U.S. Colored Troops (Col. Nathan Goff Jr.)

Unattached

3rd U.S. Artillery, Battery E (Lt. John R. Myrick)

Twenty-Third Army Corps (Maj. Gen. Jacob D. Cox)

Engineer Battalion (Capt. Oliver S. McClure)

Provost Guard
9th New Jersey (Co. H)(Capt. Edward S. Pullen)

Artillery (Lt. Col. George W. Schofield, Capt. Giles J. Cockerill)

First Division (Bvt. Maj. Gen. Thomas H. Ruger)

  First Brigade (Bvt. Brig. Gen. Israel N. Stiles)

    120th Indiana (Col. Allen W. Prather)
    124th Indiana (Col. John M. Orr)
    128th Indiana (Lt. Col. Jasper Packard)
    180th Indiana (Col. Willard Warner)

  Second Brigade (Col John C. McQuiston)

    123rd Indiana (Lt. Col. Dewitt C. Walters)
    129th Indiana (Col. Charles A. Zollinger)
    130th Indiana (Col. Charles S. Parrish)
    28th Michigan (Col. William W. Wheeler)

  Third Brigade (Col. Minor T. Thomas)

    25th Massachusetts (Lt. Col. James Tucker)
    8th Minnesota (Maj. George A. Camp)
    174th Ohio (Col. John S. Jones)
    178th Ohio (Col. Joab A. Stafford)

Artillery

    Elgin Battery (Illinois) (Capt. Andrew M. Wood)

Second Division (Maj. Gen. Darius N. Couch, Brig Gen. Joseph A. Cooper)

  First Brigade (Col. Orlando H. Moore, Brig. Gen. Joseph A. Cooper)

    26th Kentucky (Col. Thomas B. Farleigh)
    25th Michigan (Lt. Col. Benjamin F. Orcutt)
    132nd New York (with detachment of 99th New
      York)(Col. Peter J. Claassen)
    52nd Pennsylvania (Lt. Col. John B. Conyngham)

  Second Brigade (Col. John Mehringer)

    107th Illinois (Maj. Thomas J. Milholland)
    80th Indiana (Lt. Col. Alfred D. Owen)
    23rd Michigan (Col. Oliver L. Spaulding)
    111th Ohio (Lt. Col. Isaac R. Sherwood)
    118th Ohio (Lt. Col. Edgar Sowers)

Third Brigade (Col. Silas A. Strickland)

91st Indiana (Lt. Col. Charles H. Butterfield)
50th Ohio (Capt. John S. Conahan)
181st Ohio (Lt. Col. John E. Hudson, Col. John O'Dowd)
183rd Ohio (Col. George W. Hoge)

Artillery

109th Ohio Battery (Capt. Frank Wilson)

Third Division (Brig. Gen. James W. Reilly, Brig. Gen. Samuel P. Carter)

Provost Guard

100th Ohio (Co. F) (Lt. John P. Denny)

First Brigade (Col. Oscar W. Sterl)

12th Kentucky (Lt. Col. Laurence H. Rousseau)
16th Kentucky (Lt. Col. John S. White)
100th Ohio (Capt. Frank Rundell)
104th Ohio (Lt. Col. William J. Jordan)
8th Tennessee (Capt. James W. Berry)

Second Brigade (Bvt. Brig. Gen. John S. Casement)

65th Illinois (Lt. Col. William S. Stewart)
65th Indiana (Lt. Col. John W. Hammond)
9th New Jersey (Col. James Stewart Jr.)
103rd Ohio (Capt. Henry S. Pickands)
177th Ohio (Lt. Col. William H. Zimmerman)

Third Brigade (Bvt. Brig. Gen. Thomas J. Henderson)

112th Illinois (Lt. Col. Emery S. Bond)
63rd Indiana (Lt. Col. Daniel Morris, Maj. Frank Wilcox)
140th Indiana (Col Thomas J. Brady)
17th Massachusetts (Lt. Col. Henry Splaine)

Artillery

1st Ohio, Battery D (Capt. Giles J. Cockerill, Lt. Cecil C. Reed)

Third Cavalry Division (Bvt. Major Gen. Judson Kilpatrick)

First Brigade (Bvt. Brig. Gen. Thomas J. Jordan)

8th Indiana (with battalion of 3rd Indiana) (Lt. Col. Fielder A. Jones)
2nd Kentucky (Maj. Owen Star)
3rd Kentucky (Lt. Col. Robert H. King)

9th Pennsylvania (Lt. Col. David H. Kimmel)

Second Brigade (Bvt. Brig. Gen. Smith D. Atkins)

92nd Illinois Mounted Infantry (Lt. Col. Matthew Van Buskirk)
9th Michigan (Col. George S. Acker)
9th Ohio (Col. William D. Hamilton)
10th Ohio (Col. Thomas W. Sanderson)
McLaughlin's (Ohio) Squadron (Capt. John Dalzell)

Third Brigade (Col. Michael Kerwin, Bvt. Brig. Gen. Thomas T. Heath)

1st Alabama (Maj. Sanford Tramel)
5th Ohio (Maj. George H. Rader)
13th Pennsylvania (Maj. George F. McCabe, Col. Michael Kerwin)

Artillery

23rd New York Battery (Capt. Samuel Kittinger)

CONFEDERATE FORCES

Abbreviations used for the unit stations:

BH= Bush Hill

BLOOM= Bloomington

CHAR= Charlotte

CHES= Chester, South Carolina

CONC= Concord

GRN= Greensboro

HP= High Point

HILLS= Hillsborough

JAMES= Jamestown

LEX= Lexington

SAL= Salisbury

TC= Trinity College

ARMY OF TENNESSEE
GEN. JOSEPH E. JOHNSTON (GRN)

Escort
Holloway's Cavalry Company (Alabama) (Capt. E. M. Holloway)

Second-In-Command
Gen. P.G.T. Beauregard GRN
Escort
Jeff Davis Legion, Co. A (Mississippi) (Lt. R. E. Conner)

Provost Marshal-General
Detachment of Lewis's Brigade and other units (Col. Martin H. Cofer)
Signal Corps (Lt. Eli Duvall)

Hardee's Corps (Lt. Gen. William J. Hardee TC)

Escort and Scouts
Raum's Cavalry Company (Mississippi) (Capt. William C. Raum)
Stono Scouts Company (South Carolina) (Capt. John B. L. Walpole, Lt. Paul T. Gervais)

Brown's Division (Lt. Gen. William J. Hardee)

Smith's Brigade (Brig. Gen. James A. Smith)

1st Florida Consolidated (comprising 1st, 3rd, 4th, 6th, and 7th Florida Infantry and 1st Florida Cavalry [Dismounted]) (Lt. Col. Elisha Mashburn)
1st Georgia Consolidated (comprising 1st, 57th, and 63rd Georgia Infantry) (Col. Charles H. Olmstead)
54th Georgia Consolidated (comprising 37th and 54th Georgia and 4th Battalion Georgia Sharpshooters) (Col. Theodore D. Caswell)

Govan's Brigade (Brig. Gen. Daniel C. Govan (10))

1st Arkansas Consolidated (comprising 1st, 2nd, 5th, 6th, 7th, 8th, 13th, 15th, 19th, and 24th Arkansas and 3rd Confederate) (Col. E. A. Howell)
1st Texas Consolidated (comprising 6th, 7th, 10th, and 15th Texas Infantry and 17th, 18th 24th, and 25th Texas Cavalry [Dismounted]) (Lt. Col. William A. Ryan)

Hoke's Division (Maj. Gen. Robert F. Hoke)

Clingman's Brigade—HP (Brig. Gen. Thomas L. Clingman)

8th North Carolina (Lt. Col. Rufus A. Barrier)
31st North Carolina (Lt. Col. Charles W. Knight)
36th/40th North Carolina (Consolidated) (Lt. Selby
Hardenburgh)
51st North Carolina (Capt. James W. Lippitt)
61st North Carolina (Capt. A. D. Lippitt , Col. William
L. Devane)

Colquitt's Brigade—BLOOM (Brig. Gen. Alfred H.
Colquitt)

6th Georgia (Maj. James M. Culpepper)
19th Georgia (Maj. William Hamilton)
23rd Georgia (Col. Marcus R. Ballenger)
27th Georgia (Col. Charles T. Zachry)
28th Georgia (Lt. Col. W. P. Crawford)

Hagood's Brigade—HP (Lt. Col. James H. Rion , Col.
Robert F. Graham)

11th South Carolina (Capt. B. F. Wyman)
21st South Carolina (Col. Robert F. Graham, Capt.
J.A.W. Thomas)
25th South Carolina (Capt. E.R. Lesesne)
27th South Carolina (Capt. Thomas Y. Simons)
7th South Carolina Battalion (Capt. William Clyburn,
Lt. Col. James H. Rion)

Kirkland's Brigade—BH (Brig. Gen. William W. Kirkland)

17th North Carolina (Capt. Stuart L. Johnston)
42nd North Carolina (Col. John E. Brown)
50th North Carolina (Col. George Wortham)
66th North Carolina/10th North Carolina Battalion
(Consolidated)(Col. John H. Nethercutt)

First Brigade Junior Reserves—HP (Col. Frank S.
Armistead)

1st North Carolina Reserves (Lt. Col. Charles W.
Broadfoot)
2nd North Carolina Reserves (Col. John H. Anderson)
3rd North Carolina Reserves (Col. John W. Hinsdale)
1st (Millard's) North Carolina Reserves Battalion (Capt.
J.L. Eaves)

Cheatham's Division (Maj. Gen. Benjamin F. Cheatham, Maj. Gen. William B. Bate)

Palmer's Brigade—HP (Brig. Gen. Joseph B. Palmer)

1st Tennessee Consolidated (comprising 1st, 6th, 8th, 9th, 16th, 27th, 28th, and 34th Tennessee and 24th Tennessee Battalion)(Lt Col. Oliver A. Bradshaw)
2nd Tennessee Consolidated (comprising 11th, 12th, 13th, 29th, 47th, 50th, 51st, 52nd, and 154th Tennessee)(Lt. Col. George W. Pease)
3rd Tennessee Consolidated (Comprising 4th, 5th, 19th, 24th, 31st, 33rd, 35th, 38th, and 41st Tennessee) (Col. James D. Tillman)
4th Tennessee Consolidated (comprising 2nd, 3rd, 10th, 15th, 18th, 20th, 26th, 30th, 32nd, 37th, and 45th Tennessee and 23rd Tennessee Battalion) (Col. Anderson Searcy)

Gist's Brigade—HP (Col. William G. Foster)

46th Georgia (Lt. Col. Abe Miles)
65th Georgia Consolidated (65th Georgia and 2nd and 8th Georgia Battalions) (Lt. Col. Zachariah L. Watters)
16th/24th South Carolina Consolidated (Maj. B. Burgh Smith)

Artillery (Col. Ambrosio J. Gonzales)

Artillery Battalion—BH (Maj. Basil C. Manly)

Bridges' Battery (Louisiana) (Capt. William M, Bridges)
Atkins's Battery (North Carolina) (Capt. George B. Atkins)
Walter's Battery (South Carolina) (Capt. George H. Walter)
Zimmerman's Battery (South Carolina) (Capt. William E. Zimmerman)
Paris's Battery (Virginia) (Lt. Thomas M. Tucker)

Reserve Artillery Battalion—Bloom (Lt. Col. Del. Kemper)

(Bachman's, Barnwell's, Gaillard's, and Maxwell's Batteries, all of which were part of the Reserve Battalion as of April 10, were either transferred to South Carolina or consolidated with the batteries listed below)
Guerard's Battery (Georgia) (Capt. John M. Guerard)

Lumpkin's Battery (Georgia) (Capt. Edward P. Lumpkin)

1st Missouri Battery (Capt. A. W. Harris)

Charles's Battery (South Carolina) (Capt William E. Charles)

DePass's Battery (South Carolina) (Capt. Charles E. Kanapaux, Lt. Thomas J. Sistrunk)

Schulz's Battery (Palmetto Light Artillery, Co. F., South Carolina (Capt Frederick C Schulz)

Wagener's Battery (German Artillery, Cos. A and C, South Carolina)(Capt. F. W. Wagener)

Huggins's Battery (Tennessee) (Capt. Almaria L. Huggins)

Stewart's Corps—GRN (Lt. Gen. Alexander P. Stewart)

Loring's Division (Maj. Gen. William W. Loring)

Featherston's Brigade—JAMES (Brig. Gen. Winfield S. Featherson)

1st Arkansas Mounted Rifles Consolidated (comprising 1st and 2nd Arkansas Mounted Rifles [Dismounted], and 4th, 9th, and 25th Arkansas Infantry)(Col. Henry G. Bunn)

3rd Mississippi Consolidated (comprising 3rd, 31st, and 40th Mississippi)(Col. James M. Stigler)

22nd Mississippi Consolidated (comprising 1st, 22nd, and 33rd Mississippi and 1st Mississippi Battalion) (Col. Martin A. Oatis)

37th Mississippi Battalion (Maj. Q.C. Heidelberg)

Lowry's Brigade—GRN (Brig. Gen. Robert Lowry)

29th Alabama (Maj. Henry B. Turner)

12th Louisiana (Lt. Col. E. M. Graham)

14th Mississippi Consolidated (comprising 5th, 14th, and 43rd Mississippi) (Col. Robert J. Lawrence)

15th Mississippi Consolidated (comprising 6th, 15th, 20th, and 23rd Mississippi) (Lt. Col. Thomas B. Graham)

Shelley's Brigade—GRN (Brig. Gen. Charles M. Shelley)

1st Alabama Consolidated (comprising 1st, 16th, 26th, 33rd, and eight companies of 45th Alabama (Col. Robert H. Abercrombie)

27th Alabama Consolidated (comprising 27th, 35th, 49th, 55th, and 57th Alabama) (Col. Edward McAlexander)

45th Alabama (Cos. C and H) (Lt. G. P. Bledsoe)—LEX

Anderson's Division (Maj. Gen. Patton Anderson)

Elliot's Brigade—GRN (Lt. Col. J. Welsman Brown)

22nd Georgia Battalion (Maj. Mark J. McMullen)
27th Georgia Battalion (Maj. Alfred L. Hartridge)
2nd South Carolina Artillery (Maj. F. F. Warley)
Manigualt's Battalion (South Carolina) (Capt. Theodore G. Boag)

Rhett's Brigade—GRN (Col. William Butler)

1st South Carolina (Regulars) (Lt. Col. Warren Adams)
1st South Carolina Artillery (Regulars) (Lt. Col. Joseph A. Yates)
15th South Carolina Battalion (Lucas's Battalion) (Capt. Theodore B. Hayne)

Walthall's Division (Maj. Gen. Edward C. Walthall)

Harrison's Brigade—GRN (Col. George P. Harrison)

1st Georgia Regulars (Col. Richard A. Wayne)
5th Georgia (Col. Charles P. Daniel)
32nd Georgia (Lt. Col. E. H. Bacon Jr)

Kennedy's Brigade—GRN (Brig. Gen. John D. Kennedy)

2nd South Carolina Consolidated (comprising 2nd and 20th South Carolina and detachment of Blanchard's Reserves) (Col. William Wallace)
3rd South Carolina Consolidated (comprising 3rd and 8th South Carolina and detachment of Blanchard's Reserves) (Col. Eli. T Stackhouse)
7th South Carolina Consolidated (comprising 7th and 15th South Carolina and detachment of Blanchard's Reserves) (Col. John B. Davis)

Artillery Battalion—GRN (Maj. Gen. Burnet Rhett)

Brooks Battery (Georgia) (Capt. John W. Brooks)
LeGardeur's Battery (Louisiana)(Capt. Gustave LeGardeur Jr)
Parker's Battery (Marion Light Artillery, South Carolina)(Capt. Edward L. Parker)
Stuart's Battery (Beaufort Light Artillery, South Carolina) (Capt. Henry M. Stuart)

Wheaton's Battery (Chatham Light Artillery, Georgia) (Capt. John F. Wheaton)

Lee's Corps—JAMES (Lt. Gen. Stephen D. Lee)

Escort

Ragland's Cavalry Company (Georgia) JAMES (Capt. George G. Ragland)

Hill's Division (Maj. Gen. D. H. Hill)

Sharp's Brigade—HP/JAMES (Brig. Gen. Jacob H. Sharp)

24th Alabama Consolidated (comprising 24th, 28th, and 34th Alabama) (Col. John C. Carter)

8th Mississippi Consolidated Battalion (comprising 5th, 8th, and 32nd Mississippi and 3rd Mississippi Battalion) (Lt. Col. J.R. Moore)

9th Mississippi Consolidated (comprising the 7th, 9th, 10th, 41st, and 44th Mississippi and 9th Mississippi Battalion Sharpshooters)(Lt. Col. William C. Richards)

19th South Carolina Battalion (Consolidated) (comprising 10th and 19th South Carolina)(Lt. Col. C. Irvine Walker)

Brantly's Brigade—GRN (Brig. Gen. William F. Brantly)

22nd Alabama Consolidated (comprising 22nd, 25th, 39th, and 50th Alabama) (Col. Harry T. Toulmin)

37th Alabama Consolidated (comprising 37th, 42nd, and 54th Alabama) (Col. John A. Minter)

24th Mississippi Consolidated (comprising 24th, 27th 29th, 30th, and 34th Mississippi) (Col. R. W. Williamson)

58th North Carolina (Consolidated) (comprising 58th and 60th North Carolina) (Lt. Col. Thaddeus Coleman)

Detachment, Army of Northern Virginia—JAMES (Lt. Col. A.C. McAlister)

Contingent from Lane's Brigade

7th North Carolina (Maj. James S. Harris)

Contingent from Cooke's and Grimes's Brigades

15th North Carolina (Cos. B, F, and I)
27th North Carolina (Cos. C, F, and G)
32nd North Carolina (Cos. E and K)
43rd North Carolina (Co. F)

45th North Carolina (Co. I)
46th North Carolina (Cos. B, D, G, and I)
48th North Carolina (Cos. A and B)
55th North Carolina (Cos. A. and K)

Stevenson's Division (Maj. Gen. Carter L. Stevenson)

Henderson's Brigade—HP (Brig. Gen. Robert J. Henderson)

1st Confederate (Georgia) Consolidated Battalion
(comprising 1st Confederate, 25th, 29th, 30th, and
66th Georgia, and 1st Battalion Georgia
Sharpshooters)(Capt. W. J. Whitsitt)
39th Georgia Consolidated (comprising 34th and 39th
Georgia and detachments of 52nd and 56th Georgia)
(Col. Charles H. Phinizy)
42nd Georgia Consolidated (comprising 36th and 42nd
Georgia and detachments of 34th and 56th Georgia)
(Lt. Col. L. P. Thomas)
40th Georgia Consolidated Battalion (comprising 40th,
41st, and 43rd Georgia) (Lt. Col. S.D. Clements)

Pettus' Brigade—SAL (Brig. Gen. Edmund W. Pettus)

19th Alabama (Col. M. L. Woods)
20th Alabama (Lt. Col. James K. Elliot)
23rd Alabama (Lt. Col Osceola Kyle)
27th Alabama (Co. B) (Lt. Robert G. Hampton)
54th Virginia (Consolidated) Battalion (comprising 54th
and 63rd Virginia) (Lt. Col. Connally H. Lynch)

Artillery—JAMES

J.T. Kanapaux's Battery (South Carolina) (Capt. J.T.
Kanapaux)

Independent Naval Contingent

Naval Regiment—GRN
Flag Off. French Forrest

Naval Brigade—GRN (Rear Adm. And Brig. Gen. Raphael
Semmes)

1st Regiment
2nd Regiment

Unattached Artillery

Artillery Battalion—GRN (Maj. Joseph Palmer)

Havis's Battery (14th Battalion, Co. A., Georgia Light
Artillery) (Capt. M. W. Havis)

Anderson's Battery (14th Battalion, Co. D, Georgia
Light Artillery)(Capt. Ruel Wooten Anderson)
Yates's Battery (Mississippi)(Capt. James H. Yates)
Moseley's Battery (Sampson Artillery, North Carolina)
(Capt. Abner A. Moseley)

Independent Batteries

Abell's Light Artillery (Florida)(Capt Henry F. Abell)
GRN
Swett's Battery (Mississippi) (Lt. H. Shannon) GRN

Artillery (Lt. Col. Joseph B. Starr)

10th North Carolina (1st Artillery) GRN
Darden's Battery (Co. C) (Lt. Alfred M. Darden)
Southerland's Battery (Co. I) (Capt. Thomas L.
Southerland)

3rd North Carolina Battalion GRN (Maj. John W. Moore)

Ellis's Battery (Co. A) (Capt. A. J. Ellis)
Badham's Battery (Co. B) (Capt. William Badham)
Sutton's Battery (Co. C) (Capt. John M. Sutton)
13th North Carolina Battalion GRN
Cumming's Battery (Co. C) (Capt. James D. Cumming)

Dickson's Battery (Co. E.) (Capt. Henry Dickson)
CHES
Kelly's Battery (Chesterfield Artillery, South Carolina)
(Capt. James I. Kelly) GRN

CAVALRY CORPS—GRN

Lt. Gen. Wade Hampton

Maj. Gen. Mathew C. Butler

Butler's Division (Brig. Gen. Evander M. Law, Maj. Gen.
Matthew C. Butler)

Logan's Brigade—GRN (Brig. Gen. Thomas M. Logan)

1st South Carolina Cavalry (Lt. J.A. Ratchford)
4th South Carolina Cavalry (Capt. O. Barber)
5th South Carolina Cavalry (Capt. George Tupper)
6th South Carolina Cavalry (Lt. J.A. Tagart)
19th South Carolina Cavalry Battalion (Lt. W. Ha.
Pagett)

Young's Brigade—GRN (Col. Gilbert J. Wright)

Cobb's Legion Cavalry (Georgia) (Capt. R. Bill Roberts)

Phillips Legion Cavalry (Georgia) (Maj. Wesley W. Thomas)

10th Georgia Cavalry (Capt. Edwin W. Moise)

Jeff Davis Legion (Mississippi) (Col. J. Fred. Waring)

Horse Artillery

Earle's Battery (South Carolina) (Capt. William E. Earle) HP

Halsey's Battery (South Carolina) (Capt. E. Lindsey Halsey) GRN

Wheeler's Cavalry Contingent—CONC

(Formerly Wheeler's Cavalry Corps, Army of Tennessee)

Maj. Gen. Joseph Wheeler

Brig. Gen. William W. Allen

Escort

1st Alabama Cavalry, Co. G (Lt. James M. Smith)

Scout Company

Shannon's Special Scouts (Maj. A. M. Shannon) GRN

Engineer Troop CONC (Lt. L.C. Anderson)

Allen's Division--HILLS (Brig. Gen. William W. Allen, Col. Charles C. Crews)

Anderson's Brigade—HILLS (Brig. Gen. Robert H. Anderson)

3rd Confederate Cavalry (Georgia) (Col. P. H. Rice)

8th Confederate Cavalry (Georgia) (Lt. Col. John S. Prather)

10th Confederate Cavalry (Georgia) (Capt. W. H. Brazier)

5th Georgia Cavalry (Col. Edward Bird)

Crew's Brigade—SAL (Col. Charles C. Crews, Col. John R. Hart)

1st Georgia Cavalry (Lt. Col. George T. Watts)

2nd Georgia Cavalry (Lt. Col. F. M. Ison)

3rd Georgia Cavalry (Lt. Col. J.T. Thornton)

6th Georgia Cavalry (Col. John R. Hart)

12th Georgia Cavalry (Capt. James H. Graham)

Hagan's Brigade—CONC (Col. David T. Blakely)

    1st Alabama Cavalry (Lt. Col. Augustus H. Johnson)
    3rd Alabama Cavalry (Capt. A.P. Forney)
    9th Alabama Cavalry (Lt. Asl. Blansit)
    12th Alabama Cavalry (Capt. A.D. Bennett)
    51st Alabama Cavalry (Col. M. L. Kirkpatrick)

Humes's Division—CHAR (Col. Henry M. Ashby)

    Ashby's Brigade—CHAR (Col. James T. Wheeler)

        1st (or 6th) Tennessee Cavalry (Lt. Col. James H. Lewis)

        2nd Tennessee Cavalry (Lt. Col. John H. Kuhn)
        5th Tennessee Cavalry (Col. George W. McKenzie)
        9th Tennessee Cavalry Battalion (Maj. James H. Akin)

    Harrison's Brigade—CHAR (Col. Baxter Smith)

        3rd Arkansas Cavalry (Maj. William H. Blackwell)
        4th Tennessee Cavalry (Smith's)
        8th Texas Cavalry
        11th Texas Cavalry

Dibrell's Division (Brig Gen. George C. Dibrell)
(Served with Wheeler's cavalry until April 15, 1865 when it was
   detached for special service as President Jefferson Davis's
   escort. Dibrell's Division therefore is not included in the tally
   for Wheeler's cavalry)

    Breckenridge's Brigade (Col. William C. P. Breckenridge)

        1st (or 3rd) Kentucky Cavalry
        2nd Kentucky Cavalry
        9th Kentucky Cavalry

    McLemore's Brigade (Col. William S. McLemore)
        4th (or 8th) Tennessee Cavalry (McLemore's)
        13th Tennessee Cavalry
        Shaw's Battalion (Tennessee)

Post of Greensboro
Brig. Gen. Alfred Iverson
Brig. Gen. John D. Kennedy

> Detachment of Lewis's Brigade (2nd, 4th, 5th, 6th, and 9th Kentucky Mounted Infantry) (Lt. J.M. McGuire)
> > Buckner Guards (2nd Kentucky Cavalry Battalion, Co. B, and 4th Tennessee Cavalry, Co. C) (Lt. Isaiah Yokum)
> > Tucker's Regiment Confederate Infantry (Pioneer Troops) (Col. Julius G. Tucker)

Invalid Corps (North Carolina)
Col. Frank Parker

Troops from various commands

> Maj. Gen. Lunsford L. Lomax and staff and unattached officers and men of the Army of Northern Virginia
> All others (including Brig. Gen. John Echols and staff)

Post of Salisbury
Brig. Gen. Bradley T. Johnson

Detachments, 2nd Maryland Infantry and 1st Maryland Cavalry
Freeman's Battalion (North Carolina)
Salisbury Prison Guard (Co. A) (Capt. C.D. Freeman)
Salisbury Prison Guard (Co. B)(Capt. H. P. Allen)
Salisbury Prison Guard (Co. C) (Sgt. W.J. Whitaker)
1st Regiment Detailed Men (North Carolina)
All others (excluding hospital personnel, hospitalized troops, and units already listed elsewhere)

Post of Charlotte
Col. William J. Hoke

APPENDIX B

THE BASIS FOR SHERMAN'S BELIEF THAT ABRAHAM LINCOLN WOULD HAVE SUPPORTED HIS ACTIONS AT BENNETT PLACE ON APRIL 17, 1865

As we have seen, Maj. Gen. William T. Sherman was convinced that the terms he offered to Gen. Joseph E. Johnston at the April 17, 1865, meeting at Bennett Place were consistent with President Abraham Lincoln's wishes. Instead, vindictive Secretary of War Edwin M. Stanton, determined to avenge Lincoln's assassination, rejected the generals' terms, publicly insulted and humiliated Sherman, and forced Sherman to return to the negotiating table with Johnston. Appendix B examines why Sherman believed he was honoring Lincoln's desires regarding the end of the war.

Once Sherman's army arrived at Goldsboro, North Carolina, on March 25, 1865, Sherman "deemed it of great importance that [he] should have a personal interview" with Lt. Gen. Ulysses S. Grant at Grant's headquarters in City Point, Virginia. Consequently, Sherman was "determined to go in person to City Point as soon as the repairs of the railroad...would permit." The repairs were completed that evening, and Sherman took a train to New Bern, North Carolina, where he spent the night. The next morning he continued to Morehead City, North Carolina, where he boarded the Russia steamer traveling to Fort Monroe, Virginia. After Sherman arrived on March 27, he telegraphed his brother Senator Thomas Sherman at Fort Monroe, and the Russia then sailed up the James River to City Point.[1]

Grant greeted his friend Sherman, and after Sherman visited with the general-in-chief and his family, Grant told Sherman that Lincoln was aboard the nearby River Queen and wanted to see Sherman. Sherman met with Lincoln on March 27 and again on March 28 when Grant, Sherman, Rear Admiral David Dixon Porter, and Lincoln spent

---

1. Sherman, *Memoirs*, 2:324.

"The Peacemakers", by George P. A. Healy. In this depiction of the March 28, 1865 meeting aboard the river steamer River Queen, Sherman, Grant, Lincoln and Porter are seen discussing the fate of the Confederacy.
(Library of Congress)

90 minutes discussing and developing a strategy for handling the surrender of the Confederate armies, which appeared imminent.[2]

Below is Sherman's account about these two important meetings:

> After I had been with him an hour or so, he remarked that the President, Mr. Lincoln, was then on board the steamer River Queen, lying at the wharf, and he proposed that we should call and see him. We walked down to the wharf, went on board, and found Mr. Lincoln alone, in the after-cabin. He remembered me perfectly, and at once engaged in a most interesting conversation. He was full of curiosity about the many incidents of our great march, which had reached him officially and through the newspapers, and seemed to enjoy very much the more

2. The best, most complete account of these events, including Lincoln's two-week stay at City Point, is Noah Andre Trudeau's award-winning *Lincoln's Greatest Journey: Sixteen Days that Changed a Presidency, March 24–April 8, 1865* (El Dorado Hills, CA: Savas-Beatie, 2016). When he returned to Washington, D.C., on April 8, Lincoln had only a week to live.

ludicrous parts—about the "bummers," and their devices
to collect food and forage when the outside world
supposed us to be starving; but at the same time he
expressed a good deal of anxiety lest some accident
might happen to the army in North Carolina during my
absence. I explained to him that that army was snug and
comfortable, in good camps, at Goldsboro; that it would
require some days to collect forage and food for another
march; and that General Schofield was fully competent to
command it in my absence. Having made a good, long,
social visit, we took our leave and returned to General
Grant's quarters, where Mrs. Grant had provided tea.
While at the table, Mrs. Grant inquired if we had seen
Mrs. Lincoln. "No," said the general, "I did not ask for
her;" and I added that I did not even know that she was
on board. Mrs. Grant then exclaimed, "Well, you are a
pretty pair!" and added that our neglect was
unpardonable; when the general said we would call again
the next day, and make amends for the unintended slight.

Early the next day, March 28th, all the principal officers
of the army and navy called to see me, Generals [George
G.] Meade, [Edward O. C.] Ord, [Rufus] Ingalls, etc.,
and Admiral Porter. At this time the River Queen was at
anchor out in the river, abreast of the wharf, and we again
started to visit Mr. and Mrs. Lincoln. Admiral Porter
accompanied us. We took a small tug at the wharf, which
conveyed us on board, where we were again received
most courteously by the President, who conducted us to
the after-cabin. After the general compliments, General
Grant inquired after Mrs. Lincoln, when the President
went to her state-room, returned, and begged us to
excuse her, as she was not well. We then again entered
upon a general conversation, during which General Grant
explained to the President that at that very instant of
time General Sheridan was crossing James River from the
north, by a pontoon-bridge below City Point; that he had
a large, well-appointed force of cavalry, with which he
proposed to strike the Southside and Danville Railroads,
by which alone General Lee, in Richmond, supplied his
army; and that, in his judgment, matters were drawing to
a crisis, his only apprehension being that General Lee
would not wait long enough. I also explained that my
army at Goldsboro was strong enough to fight Lee's army
and Johnston's combined, provided that General Grant
could come up within a day or so; that if Lee would only

remain in Richmond another fortnight, I could march up to Burkesville, when Lee would have to starve inside of his lines, or come out from his intrenchments and fight us on equal terms.

Both General Grant and myself supposed that one or the other of us would have to fight one more bloody battle, and that it would be the last, Mr. Lincoln exclaimed, more than once, that there had been blood enough shed, and asked us if another battle could not be avoided. I remember well to have said that we could not control that event; that this necessarily rested with our enemy; and I inferred that both Jeff. Davis and General Lee would be forced to fight one more desperate and bloody battle. I rather supposed it would fall on me, somewhere near Raleigh; and General Grant added that, if Lee would only wait a few more days, he would have his army so disposed that if the enemy should abandon Richmond, and attempt to make junction with General Jos. Johnston in North Carolina, he (General Grant) would be on his heels. Mr. Lincoln more than once expressed uneasiness that I was not with my army at Goldsboro, when I again assured him that General Schofield was fully competent to command in my absence; that I was going to start back that very day, and that Admiral Porter had kindly provided for me the steamer Bat, which he said was much swifter than my own vessel, the Russia. During this interview I inquired of the President if he was all ready for the end of the war. What was to be done with the rebel armies when defeated? And what should be done with the political leaders, such as Jeff. Davis, etc.? Should we allow them to escape, etc.? He said he was all ready; all he wanted of us was to defeat the opposing armies, and to get the men composing the Confederate armies back to their homes, at work on their farms and in their shops. As to Jeff. Davis, he was hardly at liberty to speak his mind fully, but intimated that he ought to dear out, "escape the country," only it would not do for him to say so openly. As usual, he illustrated his meaning by a story: "A man once had taken the total-abstinence pledge. When visiting a friend, he was invited to take a drink, but declined, on the score of his pledge; when his friend suggested lemonade, which was accepted. In preparing the lemonade, the friend pointed to the brandy-bottle, and said the lemonade would be more palatable if he were to pour in a little brandy; when his guest said, if he could do so 'unbeknown' to him, he would not object." From which illustration I inferred that Mr. Lincoln wanted Davis to escape, "unbeknown" to him.

I made no notes of this conversation at the time, but Admiral Porter, who was present, did, and in 1866 he furnished me an account thereof, which I insert below, but the admiral describes the first visit, of the 27th, whereas my memory puts Admiral Porter's presence on the following day. Still he may be right, and he may have been with us the day before, as I write this chiefly from memory. There were two distinct interviews; the first was late in the afternoon of March 27th, and the other about noon of the 28th, both in the after-cabin of the steamer River Queen; on both occasions Mr. Lincoln was full and frank in his conversation, assuring me that in his mind he was all ready for the civil reorganization of affairs at the South as soon as the war was over; and he distinctly authorized me to assure Governor Vance and the people of North Carolina that, as soon as the rebel armies laid down their arms, and resumed their civil pursuits, they would at once be guaranteed all their rights as citizens of a common country; and that to avoid anarchy the State governments then in existence, with their civil functionaries, would be recognized by him as the government die facto till Congress could provide others.

I know, when I left him, that I was more than ever impressed by his kindly nature, his deep and earnest sympathy with the auctions of the whole people, resulting from the war and by the march of hostile armies through the South; and that his earnest desire seemed to be to end the war speedily, without more bloodshed or devastation, and to restore all the men of both sections to their homes. In the language of his second inaugural address, he seemed to have "charity for all, malice toward none," and, above all, an absolute faith in the courage, manliness, and integrity of the armies in the field. When at rest or listening, his legs and arms seemed to hang almost lifeless, and his face was care-worn and haggard; but, the moment he began to talk, his face lightened up, his tall form, as it were, unfolded, and he was the very impersonation of good-humor and fellowship. The last words I recall as addressed to me were that he would feel better when I was back at Goldsboro. We parted at the gangway of the River Queen, about noon of March 28th, and I never saw him again. Of all the men I ever met, he seemed to possess more of the elements of greatness, combined with goodness, than any other.[3]

Rear Admiral David Dixon Porter commanded the naval force that captured Fort Fisher at Wilmington, North Carolina, in February 1865. President Lincoln stayed on Porter's ship during his stay at City Point, and Porter was Lincoln's constant companion. In 1866, Porter wrote the following account about the March 28 meeting. Sherman included it in his memoirs verbatim:

ADMIRAL PORTER'S ACCOUNT OF THE INTERVIEW WITH MR. LINCOLN.

The day of General Sherman's arrival at City Point (I think the 27th of March, 1865), I accompanied him and General Grant on board the President's flagship, the Queen, where the President received us in the upper saloon, no one but ourselves being present.

Admiral David Dixon Porter, who participated in the City Point conference with Sherman, Grant, and Lincoln.

(Library of Congress)

The President was in an exceedingly pleasant mood, and delighted to meet General Sherman, whom he cordially greeted.

It seems that this was the first time he had met Sherman, to remember him, since the beginning of the war, and did not remember when he had seen him before, until the general reminded him of the circumstances of their first meeting.

This was rather singular on the part of Mr. Lincoln, who was, I think, remarkable for remembering people, having that kingly quality in an eminent degree. Indeed, such was the power of his memory, that he seemed never to forget the most minute circumstance.

The conversation soon turned on the events of Sherman's

3. Sherman, *Memoirs*, 2:324-328. There are no known accounts by Grant describing the meetings. In fact, Grant's memoirs do not even mention that they occurred.

campaign through the South, with every movement of which the President seemed familiar.

He laughed over some of the stories Sherman told of his "bummers," and told others in return, which illustrated in a striking manner the ideas he wanted to convey. For example, he would often express his wishes by telling an apt story, which was quite a habit with him, and one that I think he adopted to prevent his committing himself seriously.

The interview between the two generals and the President lasted about an hour and a half, and, as it was a remarkable one, I jotted down what I remembered of the conversation, as I have made a practice of doing during the rebellion, when any thing interesting occurred.

I don't regret having done so, as circumstances afterward occurred (Stanton's ill-conduct toward Sherman) which tended to cast odium on General Sherman for allowing such liberal terms to Jos. Johnston.

Could the conversation that occurred on board the Queen, between the President and General Sherman, have been known, Sherman would not, and could not, have been censured. Mr. Lincoln, had he lived, would have acquitted the general of any blame, for he was only carrying out the President's wishes.

My opinion is, that Mr. Lincoln came down to City Point with the most liberal views toward the rebels. He felt confident that we would be successful, and was willing that the enemy should capitulate on the most favorable terms.

I don't know what the President would have done had he been left to himself and had our army been unsuccessful, but he was then wrought up to a high state of excitement. He wanted peace on almost any terms, and there is no knowing what proposals he might have been willing to listen to. His heart was tenderness throughout, and, as long as the rebels laid down their arms, he did not care how it was done. I do not know how for he was influenced by General Grant, but I presume, from their long conferences, that they must have understood each other perfectly, and that the terms given to Lee after his surrender were authorized by Mr. Lincoln. I know that the latter was delighted when he heard that they had been given, and exclaimed, a dozen times, "Good!" "All right!"

"Exactly the thing!" and other similar expressions. Indeed, the President more than once told me what he supposed the terms would be: if Lee and Johnston surrendered, he considered the war ended, and that all the other rebel forces would lay down their arms at once.

In this he proved to be right. Grant and Sherman were both of the same opinion, and so was every one else who knew any thing about the matter.

What signified the terms to them, so long as we obtained the actual surrender of people who only wanted a good opportunity to give up gracefully? The rebels had fought "to the last ditch," and all that they had left them was the hope of being handed down in history as having received honorable terms.

After hearing General Sherman's account of his own position, and that of Johnston, at that time, the President expressed fears that the rebel general would escape south again by the railroads, and that General Sherman would have to chase him anew, over the same ground; but the general pronounced this to be impracticable. He remarked: "I have him where he cannot move without breaking up his army, which, once disbanded, can never again be got together; and I have destroyed the Southern railroads, so that they cannot be used again for a long time." General Grant remarked, "What is to prevent their laying the rails again?" "Why," said General Sherman, "my 'bummers' don't do things by halves. Every rail, after having been placed over a hot fire, has been twisted as crooked as a ram's-horn, and they never can be used again."

This was the only remark made by General Grant during the interview, as he sat smoking a short distance from the President, intent, no doubt, on his own plans, which were being brought to a successful termination.

The conversation between the President and General Sherman, about the terms of surrender to be allowed Jos. Johnston, continued. Sherman energetically insisted that he could command his own terms, and that Johnston would have to yield to his demands; but the President was very decided about the matter, and insisted that the surrender of Johnston's army must be obtained on any terms.

General Grant was evidently of the same way of thinking,

for, although he did not join in the conversation to any extent, yet he made no objections, and I presume had made up his mind to allow the best terms himself.

He was also anxious that Johnston should not be driven into Richmond, to reinforce the rebels there, who, from behind their strong intrenchments, would have given us incalculable trouble.

Sherman, as a subordinate officer, yielded his views to those of the President, and the terms of capitulation between himself and Johnston were exactly in accordance with Mr. Lincoln's wishes. He could not have done any thing which would have pleased the President better.

Mr. Lincoln did, in fact, arrange the (so considered) liberal terms offered General Jos. Johnston, and, whatever may have been General Sherman's private views, I feel sure that he yielded to the wishes of the President in every respect. It was Mr. Lincoln's policy that was carried out, and, had he lived long enough, he would have been but too glad to have acknowledged it. Had Mr. Lincoln lived, Secretary Stanton would have issued no false telegraphic dispatches, in the hope of killing off another general in the regular army, one who by his success had placed himself in the way of his own succession.

The disbanding of Jos. Johnston's army was so complete, that the pens and ink used in the discussion of the matter were all wasted.

It was asserted, by the rabid ones, that General Sherman had given up all that we had been fighting for, had conceded every thing to Jos. Johnston, and had, as the boys say, "knocked the fat into the fire;" but sober reflection soon overruled these harsh expressions, and, with those who knew General Sherman, and appreciated him, he was still the great soldier, patriot, and gentleman. In future times this matter will be looked at more calmly and dispassionately. The bitter animosities that have been engendered during the rebellion will have died out for want of food on which to live, and the very course Grant, Sherman, and others pursued, in granting liberal terms to the defeated rebels, will be applauded. The fact is, they met an old beggar in the road, whose crutches had broken from under him: they let him have only the broken crutches to get home with!

I sent General Sherman back to Newbern, North Carolina, in the steamer Bat.

While he was absent from his command he was losing no time, for he was getting his army fully equipped with stores and clothing; and, when he returned, he had a rested and regenerated army, ready to swallow up Jos. Johnston and all his ragamuffins.

Johnston was cornered, could not move without leaving every thing behind him, and could not go to Richmond without bringing on a famine in that destitute city.

I was with Mr. Lincoln all the time he was at City Point, and until he left for Washington. He was more than delighted with the surrender of Lee, and with the terms Grant gave the rebel general; and would have given Jos. Johnston twice as much, had the latter asked for it, and could he have been certain that the rebel would have surrendered without a fight. I again repeat that, had Mr. Lincoln lived, he would have shouldered all the responsibility.

One thing is certain: had Jos. Johnston escaped and got into Richmond, and caused a larger list of killed and wounded than we had. General Sherman would have been blamed. Then why not give him the full credit of capturing on the best terms the enemy's last important army and its best general, and putting an end to the rebellion?

It was a finale worthy of Sherman's great march through the swamps and deserts of the South, a march not excelled by any thing we read of in modern military history.

D. D. PORTER, Vice-Admiral.[4]

In 1885, 20 years after the events at City Point, Admiral Porter published his own memoir. The account in Porter's memoir is far more detailed than the memorandum included in Sherman's memoirs and probably the most comprehensive recounting of the topics discussed at the meeting aboard the *River Queen*:

Leaving General Schofield in command of the army, Sherman took the small steamer Russia from Morehead

4. Ibid., 328-331. Sherman's memoirs note that Porter wrote his account "in 1866, at the United States Naval Academy at Annapolis, Md., and mailed [it] to General Sherman at St. Louis, Mo."

City and proceeded in her to City Point, arriving on
March 27th. He was received on board the River Queen
by the President with that warmth of feeling which
always distinguished him when meeting any of the brave
men who had devoted their lives to crushing out the great
Rebellion.

General Sherman spent a long time with the President,
explaining to him the situation in his department, which
was very encouraging.

At this moment Sherman's army was holding General Joe
Johnston's forces in North Carolina in a position from
which he could not move without precipitating a battle
with some eighty thousand of the best troops in our
army. It was thought at that time that Johnston would
endeavor to make a junction with General Lee at
Richmond, which, in the light of subsequent events,
would have been an impossibility. Again, it was thought
that Lee would attempt to escape from Richmond and try
to affect a junction with Johnston. Quite as impossible as
the other move, for at that moment Sheridan was pushing
his cavalry across the James River from North to South,
and with this cavalry intended to extend his left below
Petersburg so as to meet the South Shore road, and, if
Lee should leave his fortified lines, Grant would fall on
his rear and follow him so closely that he could not
possibly fall on Sherman's army in North Carolina,
besides which Sherman felt confident that with his eighty
thousand men he could hold his own against Johnston
and Lee combined until Grant came up with the Army of
the James.

The morning after Sherman's arrival the President held a
council on board the River Queen, composed of General
Grant, General Sherman, and myself, and, as considerable
controversy was caused by the terms of surrender
granted to General Joe Johnston, I will mention here the
conversation which took place during this meeting in the
River Queen's cabin.

I made it a rule during the war to write down at night
before retiring to rest what had occurred during each day,
and I was particularly careful in doing so in this instance.

At this meeting Mr. Lincoln and General Sherman were
the speakers, and the former declared his opinions at
length before Sherman answered him. The President

feared that Lee—seeing our lines closing about him, the coast completely blockaded, his troops almost destitute of clothing and short of provisions—might make an attempt to break away from the fortified works at Richmond, make a junction with General Joe Johnston, and escape South or fight a last bloody battle.

Any one looking at the situation of the armies at that time will see that such an attempt would not have been possible.

Sherman had eighty thousand fine troops at Goldsboro, only one hundred and fifty miles from Richmond and one hundred and twenty miles from Greensborough, which latter place cut the Richmond and Danville Railroad, the only one by which Lee could escape.

The President's mind was made easy on this score, yet it was remarkable how many shrewd questions he asked on the subject, and how difficult some of them were to answer. He stated his views in regard to what he desired; he felt sure, as did every one at that council, that the end of the war was near at hand; and, though some thought a bloody battle was impending, all thought that Richmond would fall in less than a week.

He wanted the surrender of the Confederate armies, and desired that the most liberal terms should be granted them. "Let them once surrender," he said, "and reach their homes, they won't take up arms again. Let them all go, officers and all. I want submission, and no more bloodshed. Let them have their horses to plow with, and, if you like, their guns to shoot crows with. I want no one punished; treat them liberally all round. We want those people to return to their allegiance to the Union and submit to the laws. Again I say, give them the most liberal and honorable terms."

"But, Mr. President," said Sherman, "I can dictate my own terms to General Johnston. All I want is two weeks' time to fit out my men with shoes and clothes, and I will be ready to march upon Johnston and compel him to surrender; he is short of clothing, and in two weeks he would have no provisions at all."

"And," added the President, "two weeks is an age, and the first thing you will know General Johnston will be off South again with those hardy troops of his, and will keep the war going indefinitely. No, General, he must not get away; we must have his surrender at all hazards, so don't be hard on him about terms. Yes, he will get away if he can, and you will never catch him until after miles of travel and many bloody battles."

"Mr. President," said Sherman, "there is no possible way of General Johnston's escaping; he is my property as he is now situated, and I can demand an unconditional surrender; he can't escape."

"What is to prevent him from escaping with all his army by the Southern railroads while you are fitting out your men?" asked Grant.

"Because," answered Sherman, "there are no Southern railroads to speak of; my bummers have broken up the roads in sections all behind us—and they did it well."

"But," said Grant, "can't they relay the rails, the same as you did the other day, from Newbern and Wilmington to Goldsboro?"

Sherman laughed. "Why, no," he said, "my boys don't do things by halves. When they tore up the rails they put them over hot fires made from the ties, and then twisted them more crooked than a ram's horn. All the blacksmiths in the South could not straighten them out."

"Mr. President," said Sherman, turning to Mr. Lincoln, "the Confederacy has gone up, or will go up. We hold all the line between Wilmington and Goldsboro, where my troops are now fitting out from the transports. My transports can come up the Neuse River as far as Newbern. We could flood the South with troops and provisions without hindrance. We hold the situation, and General Johnston can surrender to me on my own terms."

"All very well," said the President, "but we must have no mistakes, and my way is a sure way. Offer Johnston the same terms that will be offered to Lee; then, if he is defiant, and will not accept them, try your plan. But as long as the Confederate armies lay down their arms, I don't think it matters much how it is done. Only don't let us have any more bloodshed if it can be avoided. General Grant is for giving Lee the most favorable terms."

To this General Grant assented.

"Well, Mr. President," said Sherman, "I will carry out your wishes to the letter, and I am quite satisfied that, as soon as Richmond falls, Joe Johnston will surrender also."

Sherman, at the end of that council, supposed he was acting under instructions, which he carried out, so far as I can understand it, pretty much as the President desired.

The council over, and the President being desirous that General Sherman should return to his command as soon as possible, the latter determined to return that afternoon by sea.

I gave him the naval steamer Bat to take him back again to his post—a vessel that could make sixteen knots an hour—and he was soon at his headquarters.

I shall never forget that council which met on board the River Queen. On the determinations adopted there depended peace, or a continuation of the war with its attendant horrors. That council has been illustrated in a fine painting by Mr. Healy, the artist, who, in casting about for the subject of an historical picture, hit upon this interview, which really was an occasion upon which depended whether or not the war would be continued a year longer. A single false step might have prolonged it indefinitely.

Even at the last, when the Confederates were known to be in most straitened circumstances—without food and clothing for their troops or forage for their animals, short at the same time of ammunition, without which their armies were useless—they had powerful forces in and about Richmond, which, if once united with General Johnston's army, would have made a most formidable array. Eighty thousand men, handled by such men as General Lee and General Johnston, would have been a hard army to beat.

We had had so many proofs during the war of the ability of those generals and soldiers to hold their own against superior numbers, that we knew very well what they could and would do when driven to desperation.

Though seemingly brought to the end of their tether, they were still able to fight one more bloody battle—so bloody that it would have brought sorrow to the hearthstones of very many thousands, North and South.

Mr. Lincoln saw all this; he often talked to me about it, and when he came to City Point it was with the intention to bring about a peace, even if he had to waive some point to the Confederate generals.

The kindness of his intentions was shown when he agreed to the late Justice Campbell's proposition to allow the Virginia Legislature to convene in the State-House at Richmond, as related in the last chapter.

Another proof of Mr. Lincoln's determination to bring about peace was that he would not permit any member of his Cabinet to join him at City Point.

Mr. Seward telegraphed several times to the President for an invitation to visit him at that place, with other members of the Cabinet; but Mr. Lincoln, on each and every occasion, positively declined to have them come there. He had his own views, and determined to carry them out, unhampered by the opinions of his advisers.

General Grant and the President were in perfect accord in all matters relating to the surrender of the Confederate forces; for, while the latter had the most implicit faith in General Grant's ability as a leader of armies, he had also great confidence in his good judgment and humane feelings.

Grant's most generous treatment of the Confederate army at Vicksburg, after its surrender, satisfied the President that he would be equally generous to Generals Lee and Johnston. I am quite sure that General Grant shared the convictions of the President, that we should deal with the Confederates in the most generous manner and thereby bring about a lasting peace.

I was present almost always at the interviews between the President and General Grant, and, though the former did most of the talking, General Grant agreed with him in his views of the situation.

Thus it was that Sherman, after his interview with the President on board the River Queen, became impressed with the latter's desire to terminate hostilities without further bloodshed, and that the most liberal terms should be conceded to his opponents.

Why it was that such a howl was sent up at the North when General Sherman entered into an agreement with General Johnston I don't know, especially as that agreement was to be submitted to the Government for confirmation.

There are points in those terms of capitulation which, it seems to me, should only have been decided upon by the Government itself, which, it will be perceived, is what General Sherman intended in the agreement drawn up between him and General Johnston. He had been so impressed with the President's views of concluding a peace that he desired only to carry out—after his death—what he supposed to be his policy, and which, if living, he felt certain Mr. Lincoln would have approved.

At least he would have considered it, and would not have "rejected it with the disdain" exhibited by the new President, Andrew Johnson, through his Secretary of War, Edwin M. Stanton.

It seemed to be the policy of the Secretary of War to lose no opportunity to throw a stone at those who had made themselves prominent in the Rebellion. Even if Sherman had made a mistake, his great services entitled him to better treatment than he received at the hands of Mr. Stanton.

How deeply he felt this treatment was shown when he arrived in Washington with his troops, and was invited upon the platform whence the President and his Cabinet were reviewing them. He deliberately refused to take Stanton's hand when the secretary stepped forward to greet him.

It is now twenty years since the interesting events referred to took place; most of the actors in those scenes have gone to their final resting places. The passions which animated men in high places have died out, but Grant and Sherman still live, and are gratefully remembered by their countrymen for the invaluable services they rendered during the most trying times of the Republic's existence.[5]

5. David Dixon Porter, *Incidents and Anecdotes of the Civil War* (New York: D. Appleton & Co., 1885), 313-318. Porter was born on June 8, 1813, in Chester, Pennsylvania. His grandfather was a naval officer in the Revolutionary War, and his father was Commodore David Porter, a hero of the War of 1812. He was raised with his adopted brother, Admiral David G. Farragut, and came from one of the most famous of American naval families. Porter began serving as a midshipman on his father's flagship, USS John Adams, at the age of 10 and served constantly for nearly 60 years. Porter served in the antebellum Navy and in the Mexican-American War. He served with great distinction throughout the Civil War. He was promoted to rear admiral on July 4, 1863, in recognition of his service during the Vicksburg Campaign, when his gunboats effectively blockaded Vicksburg and contributed to the siege that ultimately led to the city's collapse. After the Civil War, he was

Porter greatly admired and respected Lincoln, as well as Sherman and Grant. His vigorous defense of Sherman may seem a bit overstated, but, nevertheless, his point is well taken—when Sherman made his deal with Johnston on April 18, 1865, the general had good reason to believe that Lincoln would have approved the terms and that they were completely consistent with the president's wishes.

Grant, on the other hand, left no account of the March 28, 1865, meeting. However, Grant's staff officer Lt. Col. Horace Porter recorded his recollections of the conversation he had with Grant after the meeting ended:

> **The next morning (March 28) Admiral Porter came to headquarters, and in the course of his conversation said to Sherman: "When you were in the region of those swamps and overflowed rivers, coming through the Carolinas, didn't you wish you had my gunboats with you?" "Yes," answered Sherman; "for those swamps were very much like that Western fellow's Fourth of July oration, of which a newspaper said, 'It was only knee-deep, but spread out over all creation.' One day, on the march, while my men were wading a river which was surrounded for miles by swamps on each side, after they had been in the water for about an hour, with not much prospect of reaching the other side, one of them cried out to his chum: 'Say, Tommy, I'm blowed if I don't believe we've struck this river lengthways!'"**

---

superintendent of the U.S. Naval Academy and achieved the same rank, admiral, as his adopted brother, Farragut—admiral is the Navy's highest rank (Farragut was the Navy's first full admiral and Porter its second; Porter succeeded his adopted brother as the Navy's highest ranking officer). Porter died at the age of 77 on February 13, 1891, and was buried in Arlington National Cemetery. John H. Eicher and David J. Eicher, *Civil War High Commands* (Stanford, CA: Stanford University Press, 2002), 434-435. Secretary of the Navy Gideon Welles, under Lincoln, wrote about Porter in his diary in 1863: "Porter...has...stirring and positive qualities, is fertile in resources, has great energy, excessive and sometimes not over-scrupulous ambition, is impressed with and boastful of his own powers, given to exaggeration in relation to himself,—a Porter infirmity,—is not generous to older and superior living officers, whom he is too ready to traduce, but is kind and patronizing to favorites who are juniors, and generally to official inferiors. Is given to cliquism but is brave and daring like all his family." Morse, *The Diary of Gideon Welles*, 1:157. For a well-respected treatment of Porter's Civil War career, see Chester G. Hearn, *Admiral David Dixon Porter: The Civil War Years* (Annapolis: Naval Institute Press, 1996). For a full-length, but old, biography of Porter, see Richard Sedgewick West, *The Second Admiral: A Life of David Dixon Porter*, 1813-1891 (New York: Coward-McCann, 1937).

After spending a quarter of an hour together, General Grant said that the President was expecting them aboard his boat, and the two generals and the admiral started for the River Queen. No one accompanied them. There now occurred in the upper saloon of that vessel the celebrated conference between these four magnates, the scene of which has been so faithfully transferred to canvas by the artist Healy. It was in no sense a council of war, but only an informal interchange of views between the four men who, more than any others, held the destiny of the nation in their hands. Upon the return of the generals and the admiral to headquarters, they entered the general-in-chief's hut, where Mrs. Grant and one or two of us were sitting. The chief said to his wife: "Well, Julia, as soon as we reached the boat this morning I was particular to inquire after Mrs. Lincoln, and to say that we desired to pay our respects to her. The President went to her state-room, and soon returned, saying that she was not well, and asking us to excuse her." General Grant afterward told us the particulars of the interview. It began by his explaining to the President the military situation and prospects, saying that the crisis of the war was now at hand, as he expected to move at once around the enemy's left and cut him off from the Carolinas, and that his only apprehension was that Lee might move out before him and evacuate Petersburg and Richmond, but that if he did there would be a hot pursuit. Sherman assured the President that in such a contingency his army, by acting on the defensive, could resist both Johnston and Lee till Grant could reach him, and that then the enemy would be caught in a vise and have his life promptly crushed out. Mr. Lincoln asked if it would not be possible to end the matter without a pitched battle, with the attendant losses and suffering; but was informed that that was a matter not within the control of our commanders, and must rest necessarily with the enemy. Lincoln spoke about the course which he thought had better be pursued after the war, and expressed an inclination to lean toward a generous policy. In speaking about the Confederate political leaders, he intimated, though he did not say so in express terms, that it would relieve the situation if they should escape to some foreign country. Sherman related many interesting incidents which occurred in his campaign. Grant talked less than any one present. The President twice expressed some apprehension about Sherman being away from his army; but Sherman assured

him that he had left matters safe in Schofield's hands, and that he would start back himself that day.[6]

Apparently, the meetings were not important enough to Grant to discuss them in his own post-war memoir. His insights would be helpful.

As set forth in Chapter 6, Sherman had no idea that Lincoln had written and sent the letter of March 3, 1865, that instructed Grant not to treat with the Confederate authorities for peace. Nobody told Sherman about that important letter until after the deal with Johnston had been repudiated. Unaware of the letter and coupled with his interpretation of Lincoln's intentions divined from the March 28 meeting, Sherman's actions at Bennett Place on April 18, 1865, were both understandable and reasonable.

6. Horace Porter, *Campaigning with Grant* (New York: The Century Co., 1897), 422-424.

APPENDIX C

THE REMARKABLE CORRESPONDENCE BETWEEN PRESIDENT JEFFERSON DAVIS AND HIS REMAINING CABINET OFFICERS LEADING UP TO THE SURRENDER OF THE CONFEDERATE ARMIES AT BENNETT PLACE

As set forth in Chapter Five, Confederate President Jefferson Davis sought the specific written opinions of his remaining cabinet members as to whether to ratify the terms of the convention entered into by Sherman and Johnston at their meeting of April 18, 1865, and, if so, how best to do so. Each of the remaining cabinet members did as requested.[1] Those letters are below.

Secretary of State Judah P. Benjamin wrote:

> **CHARLOTTE, N. C., April 22, 1865.**
> **The PRESIDENT:**
>
> **SIR: I have the honor to submit this paper as the advice in writing which you requested from the heads of the Departments of the Government. The military convention made between General Johnston and General Sherman is in substance an agreement that if the Confederate States will cease to wage war for the purpose of establishing a separate government, the United States will receive the several States back into the Union with their State governments unimpaired, with all their constitutional rights recognized, with protection for the persons and property of the people, and with a general amnesty. The question is, whether, in view of the military condition of the belligerents, the Confederate States can hope for any better result by continuing the war; whether there is any reason to believe that they can establish their independence and final separation from the United States.**

1. For a detailed listing and biographies of all of the members of Davis' cabinet, including the five men to who remained at the end of the Civil War, see Dennis L. Peterson, *Confederate Cabinet Departments and Secretaries* (Jefferson, NC: McFarland & Co., 2016).

To reach a conclusion it is requisite to consider our present condition, and the prospect of a change for the better. The general-in-chief of the Armies of the Confederacy has capitulated, and his army, the largest and finest within our country, is irretrievably lost. The soldiers have been dispersed, and remain at home as paroled prisoners. The artillery, arms, and munitions of war are lost, and no help can be expected from Virginia, which is at the mercy of the conqueror. The army next in numbers and efficiency is known as the Army of Tennessee, and is commanded by Generals Johnston and Beauregard. Its rolls call for more than 70,000 men. Its last returns show a total present for duty of all arms of less than 20,000 men. This number is daily diminishing by desertion and casualties. In a recent conference with the cabinet at Greensborough Generals Johnston and Beauregard expressed the unqualified opinion that it was not in their power to resist Sherman's advance, and that as fast as their army retreated the soldiers of the several States on the line of retreat would abandon the army and go home.

We also hear on all sides and from citizens well acquainted with public opinion, that the State of North Carolina will not consent to continue the struggle after our armies shall have withdrawn farther south, and this withdrawal is inevitable if hostilities are resumed. This action of North Carolina would render it impossible for Virginia to maintain her position in the Confederacy, even if her people were unanimous in their desire to continue the contest. In the more southern States we have no army except the forces now defending Mobile and the cavalry under General Forrest. The enemy are so far superior in numbers that they have occupied, within the last few weeks, Selma, Montgomery, Columbus, and Macon, and could continue their career of devastation through Georgia and Alabama without our being able to prevent it by any forces now at our disposal. It is believed that we could not at the present moment gather together an army of 30,000 men by a concentration of all our forces east of the Mississippi River.

Our seacoast is in possession of the enemy, and we cannot obtain arms and munitions from abroad, except in very small quantities, and by precarious and uncertain means of transportation. We have lost possession in Virginia and North Carolina of our chief resources for the supply of powder and lead.

We can obtain no aid from the Trans-Mississippi Department, from which we are cut off by the fleets of gunboats that patrol the river.

We have not a supply of arms sufficient for putting into the field even 10,000 additional men, if the men themselves were forthcoming. The Confederacy is, in a word, unable to continue the war by armies in the field, and the struggle can no longer be maintained in any other manner than by a guerrilla or partisan warfare. Such a warfare is not, in my opinion, desirable, nor does it promise any useful result. It would entail far more suffering on our own people than it would cause damage to the enemy; and the people have been such heavy sufferers by the calamities of the war for the last four years that it is at least questionable whether they would be willing to engage in such a contest unless forced to endure its horrors in preference to dishonor and degradation. The terms of the convention imply no dishonor, impose no degradation, exact only what the victor always requires, the relinquishment by his foe of the object for which the struggle was commenced. Seeing no reasonable hope of our ability to conquer our independence, admitting the undeniable fact that we have been vanquished in the war, it is my opinion that these terms should be accepted, being as favorable as any that we, as the defeated belligerent, have reason to expect or can hope to secure. It is further my opinion that the President owes it to the States and to the people to obtain for them by a general pacification, rights and advantages which they would, in all probability, be unable to secure by the separate action of the different States. It is natural that the enemy should be willing to accord more liberal conditions for the purpose of closing the war at once than would be granted if each State should continue the contest till separate terms could be made for itself.

The President is the chief political executive of the Confederacy as well as the commander-in-chief of its armies. In the former capacity he is powerless to act in making peace on any other basis than that of independence. In the latter capacity he can ratify the military convention under consideration, and execute its provisions relative to the disbandment of the army, and the distribution of the arms. He can end hostilities. The States alone can act in dissolving the Confederacy and returning to the Union according to the terms of the convention. I think that if this convention be ratified by the United States, the President should, by proclamation, inform the States and the people of the Confederacy of the facts above recited; should ratify the convention so far as he has authority to act as commander-in-chief, and should execute the military provisions; should declare his inability, with the means remaining at his disposal, to defend the Confederacy or maintain its independence, and should resign a trust which it is no longer possible to fulfill. He should further invite the several States to take into immediate consideration the terms of this convention, with a view to their adoption and execution, as being the best and most favorable that they could hope to obtain by a continuance of the struggle.

Very respectfully, your obedient servant,
J. P. BENJAMIN,
Secretary of State.[2]

Postmaster General John H. Reagan, who had previously supported the idea of ending the war, wrote:

CHARLOTTE, N. C., April 22, 1865.
The PRESIDENT:

SIR: In obedience to your request for the opinions in writing of the members of the cabinet on the questions, first, as to whether you should assent to the preliminary agreement of the 18th instant, between General Joseph E. Johnston, of the Confederate Army, and Maj. Gen. W. T. Sherman, of the Army of the United States, for the suspension of hostilities and the adjustment of the difficulties between the two countries, and if so, second, the proper mode of executing this agreement on our part, I have to say that, painful as the necessity is, in view of the relative condition of the armies and resources of the belligerents, I must advise the acceptance of the terms of the agreement. General Lee, the general-in-chief of our armies, has been compelled to surrender our principal army, heretofore employed in the defense of our capital, with the loss of a very large part of our ordnance, arms, munitions of war, and military stores of all kinds, with what remained of our naval establishment. The officers of the civil government have been compelled to abandon the capital, carrying with them the archives, and thus to close, for the time being at least, the regular operations of its several departments, with no place now open to us

2. OR 47, 3:821-823.

at which we can re-establish and put these departments in operation with any prospect of permanency or security for the transaction of the public business and the carrying on of the Government. The army under the command of General Johnston has been reduced to fourteen or fifteen [thousand] infantry and artillery, and cavalry, and this force is, from demoralization and despondency, melting away rapidly by the troops abandoning the army and returning to their homes singly and in numbers large and small; it being the opinion of Generals Johnston and Beauregard that, with the men and means at their command, they can oppose no serious obstacle to the advance of General Sherman's army. General Johnston is of opinion that the enemy's forces now in the field exceed ours in number by probably ten to one. Our forces in the south, though still holding the fortifications at Mobile, have been unable to prevent the fall of Selma and Montgomery, in Alabama, and of Columbus and Macon, in Georgia, with their magazines, work-shops, and stores of supplies. The army west of the Mississippi is unavailable for the arrest of the victorious career of the enemy east of that river, and is inadequate for the defense of the country west of it. The country is worn down by a brilliant and heroic, but exhausting and bloody, struggle of four years. Our ports are closed so as to exclude the hope of procuring arms and supplies from abroad, and we are unable to arm our people if they were willing to continue the struggle. The supplies of quartermaster and commissary stores in the country are very limited in amount, and our railroads are so broken and destroyed as to prevent, to a great extent, the transportation and accumulation of those remaining.

Our currency has lost its purchasing power, and there is no other means of supplying the Treasury; and the people are hostile to impressments and endeavor to conceal such supplies as are needed for the army from the officers charged with their collection. Our armies in case of a prolongation of the struggle, will continue to melt away as they retreat through the country. There is danger, and I think I might say certainty, based on the information we have, that a portion and probably all of the States will make separate terms with the enemy as they are overrun, with the chance that the terms so obtained will be less favorable to them than those contained in the agreement under consideration, and the despair of our people will prevent a much longer continuance of serious resistance unless they shall be hereafter urged to it by unendurable oppressions. The agreement under consideration secures to our people, if ratified by both parties, the uninterrupted continuance of the existing State governments, the guarantees of the Federal Constitution and of the constitutions of their respective States, the guarantee of their political rights and of their rights of person and property, and immunity from future prosecutions and penalties for their participation in the existing war, on the condition that we accept the Constitution and Government of the United States and disband our armies by marching the troops to their respective States and depositing their arms in the State arsenals, subject to the future control of that Government, but with a verbal understanding that they are only to be used for the preservation of peace and order in the respective States. It is also to be observed that the agreement contains no direct reference to the question of slavery, requires no concession from us in regard to it, and leaves it subject to the Constitution and laws of the United States and of the several States just as it was before the war. With these facts before us and under the belief that we cannot now reasonably hope for the achievement of our independence, which should be dearer than life if it were possibly attainable, and under the belief that a continuance of the struggle with its sacrifices of life and property and its accumulation of sufferings, without a reasonable prospect of success, would be both unwise and criminal, I advise that you assent to the agreement as the best you can now do for the people who have clothed you with the high trusts of your position. In advising this course I do not conceal from myself nor would I withhold from Your Excellency, the danger of trusting the people who drove us to war by their unconstitutional and unjust aggressions, and who will now add the consciousness of power to their love of dominion and greed of gain.

It is right also for me to say that, much as we have been exhausted in men and resources, I am of opinion that if our people could be induced to continue the contest with the spirit which animated them during the first years of the war our independence might yet be within our reach- but I see no reason to hope for that now. On the second question, as to the proper mode of executing the agreement, I have to say that whatever you may do looking to the termination of the contest by an amicable arrangement which may embrace the extinction of the Government of the Confederate States must be done without special authority to be found in the Constitution; and yet I am of opinion that, charged as you are with the duty of looking to the general welfare of the people, and without time or opportunity under the peculiarity and necessities of the case to submit the whole question to the States for their deliberation and action without danger of losing material advantages provided for in the agreement, and as I believe that you, representing the military power and authority of all the States, can obtain better terms for them than it is probable they could obtain each for itself, and as it is in your power, if the Federal authorities accept this agreement, to terminate the ravages of war sooner than it can be done by the several States, while the enemy is still unconscious of the full extent of our weakness, you should, in case of the acceptance of the terms of this agreement by the authorities of the United States, accept them on the part of the Confederate States and take steps for the disbanding of the Confederate armies on the terms agreed on. As you have no power to change the government of the country or to transfer the allegiance of the people, I would advise that you submit to the several States, through their governors, the question as to whether they will, in the exercise of their own sovereignty, accept, each for itself, the terms proposed. To this it may be said that after the disbanding of our armies and the abandonment of the contest by the Confederate Government they would have no alternative but to accept the terms proposed, or an unequal and hopeless war, and that it would be needless for them to go through the forms and incur the trouble and expense of assembling a convention for the purpose. To such an objection, if urged, it may be answered that we entered into the contest to maintain and vindicate the doctrine of State rights and State sovereignty and the right of self-government, and that we can only be faithful to the Constitution of the United States and true to the principles in support of which [we] have expended so much blood and treasure by the employment of the same agencies to return into the old Union which we employed in separating from it and in forming our present Government, and that if this should be an unwelcome and enforced action by the States, it would not be more so on the part of the States than on the part of the President if he were to undertake to execute the whole agreement, and while they would have authority for acting, he would have none. This plan would at least conform to the theory of the Constitution of the United States and would, in future, be an additional precedent to which the friends of State rights could point in opposing the doctrine of the consolidation of powers in the central government; and if the future shall disclose a disposition (of which I fear the chance is remote) on the part of the people of the United States to return to the spirit and meaning of the Constitution, then this action on the part of the States might prove to be of great value to the friends of constitutional liberty and good government.

In addition to the terms of agreement an additional provision should be asked for, which will probably be allowed without objection, stipulating for the withdrawal of the Federal forces from the several States of the Confederacy, except a sufficient number to garrison the permanent fortifications and take care of the public property, until the States can call their conventions and take action on the proposed terms. In addition to the necessity for this course, in order to make their action as free and voluntary as other circumstances will allow, it would aid in softening the bitter memories which must necessarily follow such a contest as that in which we are engaged. Nothing is said in the agreement about the public debt, and the disposition of our public property beyond the turning over of the arms to the State arsenals. In the final adjustment we should endeavor to secure provisions for the auditing of the debt of the Confederacy, and for its payment in common with the war debt of the United States. We may ask this on the ground that we did not seek this war, but only sought peaceful separation to secure our people and States from the effects of unconstitutional encroachments by the other States, and because on the principles of equity, allowing that both parties had acted in good faith and gone to war on a misunderstanding which admitted of no other solution, and now agree to a reconciliation, and to a burial of the past, it would be unjust to compel our people to assist in the payment of the war debt of the United States, and for them to refuse to allow such of the revenues as we might contribute to be applied to the payment of our creditors. If it should be said that this is a liberality never extended by the conqueror to the conquered, the answer is, that if the object of the pacification is to restore the Union in good faith and to reconcile the people to each other, to restore confidence and faith and prosperity and homogeneity, then it is of the first importance that the terms of reconciliation should be based on entire equity, and that no just ground of grief or complaint should be left to either party; and to both parties, looking not only to the present, but to the interest of future generations, the amount of money which would be involved, though large, would be as nothing when compared with a reconciliation entirely equitable, which should leave no sting to honor, and no sense of wrong to rankle in the memories of the people, and lay the foundation for new difficulties and for future wars. It is to this feature, it seems to me, the greatest attention should be given by both sides. It will be of the highest importance to all, for the present as well as for the future, that the frankness, sincerity, and justice of both parties shall be as conspicuous in the adjustment of past difficulties as their courage and endurance have been during the war, if we would make peace on a basis which would be satisfactory and might be rendered perpetual. In any event, provisions should be made which will authorize the Confederate authorities to sell the public property remaining on hand, and to apply the proceeds, as far as they will go, to the payment of our public liabilities, or for such other disposition as may be found advisable. But if the terms of this agreement should be rejected or so modified by the Government of the United States as to refuse a recognition of the right of local self-government, and our political rights and rights of person and property, or as to refuse amnesty for past participation in this war, then it will be our duty to continue the struggle as best we can, however unequal it may be; as it would be better and more honorable to waste our lives and substance in such a contest than to yield both to the mercy of a remorseless conqueror.

I am, with great respect,
Your Excellency's obedient servant,
JOHN H. REAGAN,
Postmaster-General[3]

Attorney General George Davis weighed in next.

---

3. Ibid., 823-826.

CHARLOTTE, N. C., April 22, 1865.

The PRESIDENT:

SIR: The questions submitted by you to the members of your cabinet for their opinion are: First. Whether the convention agreed upon on the 18th instant by and between General Johnston, commanding the Confederate forces, and Major-General Sherman, commanding the forces of the United States in North Carolina, should be ratified by you. Second. If so, in what way it should be done.

The terms of that convention are substantially as follows: That the armies of the Confederate States shall be disbanded and their arms surrendered. That the several State governments shall be recognized by the Executive of the United States, upon their officers and legislatures taking the oaths prescribed by the Constitution of the United States, and where there are conflicting State governments the question to be referred to the decision of the Supreme Court. That all political rights and franchises, and all rights of person and of property, shall be respected and guaranteed. That a general amnesty be granted and no citizen be molested in person or property for any acts done in aid of the Confederate States in the prosecution of the war. Taken as a whole, the convention amounts to this: That the States of the Confederacy shall re-enter the old Union upon the same footing on which they stood before seceding from it. These States, having in their several conventions solemnly asserted their sovereignty and right of self-government, and having established for themselves and maintained through four years of bloody war a government of their own choosing, no loyal citizen can consent to its abandonment and destruction as long as there remains a reasonable hope of successful resistance to the arms of the United States. The question, therefore, whether the terms of the military convention should be accepted will depend upon whether the Confederate States are in a condition further to prosecute the war with a reasonable hope of success, and this question will be answered by a brief review of our military situation.

The Army of Northern Virginia, for four years the pride and boast of the Confederacy, under the lead of the general-in-chief whose name we have been accustomed to associate with victory, after having been defeated and reduced to a mere remnant by straggling and desertion, has capitulated to the enemy. All who were not embraced in the capitulation have thrown away their arms and disbanded, beyond any hope of reorganization. Our only other army east of the Mississippi, the Army of Tennessee, contains now about 13,000 effective men, of infantry and artillery, and is daily melting away by desertion. It is confronted by one of the best armies of the United States, 50,000 strong. Manifestly it cannot fight, and if it retreats the chances are more than equal that, like the Army of Northern Virginia, it will dissolve and the remnant be forced to capitulate. If it should retreat successfully, and offer itself as a nucleus for reorganization it cannot be recruited. Volunteering is long since at an end, and conscription has exhausted all its force. East of the Mississippi, scattered through all the States, we have now about 40,000 organized troops. To oppose these the enemy have more than 200,000. Persevering efforts for many months passed have failed to overcome the obstacles to the removal of troops from the west to the east of the Mississippi. We can, therefore, look for no accession of strength from that quarter if a returning sense of duty and patriotism should bring back the stragglers and deserters in sufficient numbers to form a respectable army, we have not the means of arming them. Our supply of arms is very nearly exhausted, our means of manufacturing substantially at an end, and the blockade of our ports prevents their introduction from abroad except in small quantities, and at remote points. In view of these facts our two generals highest in command in the field have expressed, in decided terms, our inability longer to continue the struggle. Observation has satisfied me that the States of Virginia and North Carolina are finally lost to our cause. The people of the latter are utterly weary of the war, broken and despairing in spirit, and eager to accept terms far less liberal than the convention proposes. In the absence of a general arrangement, they will certainly make terms for themselves. Abandoned by our armies, the people of Virginia will follow their example, and it will be impossible to arrest the process of disintegration thus begun. This melancholy array of facts leaves open but one conclusion. I am unhesitatingly of the opinion that the convention ought to be ratified. As to the proper mode of ratification greater doubt may be reasonably entertained. The Confederate Government is but the agent of the States, and as its Chief Executive you cannot, according to our governmental theory, bind the States to a government which they have not adopted for themselves. Nor can you rightfully, without their consent, dissolve the government which they have established. But there are circumstances so desperate as to override all constitutional theories, and such are those which are pressing upon us now. The Government of the Confederate States is no longer potent for good. Exhausted by war in all its resources to such a degree that it can no longer offer a respectable show of resistance to its enemies, it is already virtually destroyed, and the chief duty left for you to perform is to provide as far as possible for the speedy delivery of the people from the horrors of war and anarchy. I therefore respectfully advise that upon the ratification of the convention by the Executive of the United States you issue your proclamation, plainly setting forth the circumstances which have induced you to assent to the terms proposed, disbanding the armies of the Confederacy, resigning your office as Chief Magistrate, and recommend to the people of the States that they assemble in convention and carry into effect the terms agreed on.

GEORGE DAVIS.[4]

Next to write was Maj. Gen. John C. Breckinridge, the Secretary of War. As a former Vice President of the United States and presidential candidate, Breckinridge keenly understood the political implications and stated them succinctly.

CHARLOTTE, N. C., April 23, 1865.
His Excellency the PRESIDENT:

SIR: In obedience to your request I have the honor to submit my advice as to the course you should take upon the memorandum or basis of agreement made on the 18th instant, by and between General J. E. Johnston, of the C. S. Army, and Maj. Gen. W. T. Sherman, of the U. S. Army, provided that paper shall receive the approval of the Government of the United States. The principal army of the Confederacy was recently lost in Virginia. Considerable bodies of troops not attached to that army have either disbanded or marched toward their homes accompanied by many of their officers. Five days ago the effective force, in infantry and artillery, of General Johnston's army, was but 14,770 men, and it continues to

4. Ibid., 827-830.

diminish. That officer thinks it wholly impossible for him to make any head against the overwhelming forces of the enemy. Our ports are closed and the sources of foreign supply lost to us. The enemy occupy all the greater part of Kentucky, Tennessee, Virginia, and North Carolina, and move almost at will through the other States to the east of the Mississippi. They have recently taken Selma, Montgomery, Columbus, Macon, and other important towns, depriving us of large depots of supplies and of munitions of war. Of the small force still at command many are unarmed, and the ordnance department cannot furnish 5,000 stand of small-arms. I do not think it would be possible to assemble, equip, and maintain an army of 30,000 men at any point east of the Mississippi River. The contest, if continued after this paper is rejected, will be likely to lose entirely the dignity of regular warfare. Many of the States will make such terms as they may, in others separate and ineffective hostilities may be prosecuted, while the war, wherever waged, will probably degenerate into that irregular and secondary stage, out of which greater evils will flow to the South than to the enemy.

For these and for other reasons, which need not now be stated, I think we can no longer contend with a reasonable hope of success. It seems to me that the time has arrived when, in a large and clear view of the situation, prompt steps should be taken to put an end to the war.

It may be said that the agreement of the 18th instant contains certain stipulations which you cannot perform. This is true, and it was well understood by General Sherman that only a part could be executed by the Confederate authorities. In any view of the case grave responsibilities must be met and assumed. If the necessity for peace be conceded, corresponding action must be taken. The modes of negotiation, which we deem regular and would prefer, are impracticable. The situation is anomalous and cannot be solved upon the Principles of theoretical exactitude. In my opinion you are the only person who can meet the present necessities. I respectfully advise: First, that you execute, so far as you can, the second article in the agreement of the 18th instant; second, that you recommend to the several States the acceptance of those parts of the agreement upon which they alone can act; third, having maintained with faithful and intrepid purpose the cause of the Confed-

erate States, while the means of organized resistance
remained, that you return to the States and the people the
trust which you are no longer able to defend. Whatever
course you pursue opinions will be divided. Permit me to
give mine. Should these or similar views accord with your
own, I think the better judgment will be that you can have
no higher title to the gratitude of your countrymen and
the respect of mankind than will spring from the wisdom
to see the path of duty at this time, and the courage to
follow it regardless alike of praise or blame.

Respectfully and truly, your friend,
JOHN C. BRECKINRIDGE,
Secretary of War.[5]

Secretary of the Navy Stephen H. Mallory was the last one to
weigh in. Mallory had been encouraging Davis to surrender since the
first conference with Johnston and Beauregard on April 12. He
remained consistent in his opinion.

CHARLOTTE, N. C., April 24, 1865.

MR. PRESIDENT: In compliance with your suggestion,
I have the honor briefly to present the following views
upon the propositions discussed in cabinet council yesterday: These propositions, agreed upon and signed by
Generals Joseph E. Johnston and W. T. Sherman, may
fairly be regarded as providing for the immediate
cessation of hostilities, the disbandment of our armies,
and the return of our soldiers to the peaceful walks of
life, the restoration of the several States of our Confederacy to the old Union, with the integrity of their State
governments preserved, the security of their people and
inhabitants in their rights of person and property under
the Constitution and the laws of the United States,
equally with the people of any other State, guaranteed,
and a general amnesty for and on account of any participation in the present war. The very grave responsibility
devolved upon you by these propositions is at once
apparent. To enter at all upon their discussion is to admit
that independence, the great object of our struggle, is
hopeless. I believe and admit this to be the case, and
therefore do I advise you to accept these propositions, so
far as you have the power to do so; and my conviction is
that nine-tenths of the people of every State of the
Confederacy would so advise if opportunity were

5. Ibid., 830-832.

presented them. They are weary of the war and desire peace. If they could be rallied and brought to the field, a united and determined people might even yet achieve independence; but many circumstances admonish us that we cannot count upon their cordial and united action.

The vast army of deserters and absentees from our military service during the past twelve months, the unwillingness of the people to enter the armies, the impracticability of recruiting them, the present utter demoralization of our troops consequent upon the destruction of the Army of Virginia, the rapid decrease by desertion of General Johnston's army, which, as it retreats south, if retreat it can, will retain in its ranks but few soldiers beyond the by-paths and cross-roads which lead to their homes, together with the recent successes of the enemy, the fall of Selma, Montgomery, Columbus, and Macon, his forces in the field, and his vast resources, all dictate the admission I have made. I do not believe that by any possibility we could organize, arm, and equip, and bring into the field, this side of the Mississippi, 15,000 men within the next sixty days; and I am convinced that both General Beauregard and General Johnston are utterly hopeless of continuing the contest. A guerrilla warfare might be carried on in certain portions of our country for a time, perhaps for years; but while such a warfare would be more disastrous to our own people than it could possibly be to the enemy, it would exercise little or no influence upon his military operations or upon his hold upon the country. Conducted upon our own soil, our own people would chiefly feel its evils, and would afford it neither countenance nor support. Guerrilla warfare never has been, and never can be, carried on by and between peoples of a common origin, language, and institutions.

Our sea-board and our ports being in the enemy's hands, we cannot rely upon supplies of arms and other munitions of war from abroad, and our means of producing them at home, already limited, are daily decreasing. The loss of Selma and of Columbus, where much valuable machinery for the construction of ordnance and ordnance stores was collected, must materially circumscribe our ability in this respect.

Our currency is nearly worthless, and will become utterly so with further military disasters, and there is no hope that we can improve it. The arms of the United States have rendered the great object of our struggle hopeless; have conquered a reconstruction of the Union; and it becomes your duty to secure to the people, as far as practicable, life, liberty, and property. The propositions signed by the opposing generals are more favorable to these great objects than could justly have been anticipated. Upon you, with a more thorough knowledge of the condition of our country, the character and sentiments of our people, and of our means and resources than is possessed by others, is devolved the responsibility of promptly accepting or of promptly rejecting them. I advise their acceptance, and that, having notified General Johnston of your having done so, you promptly issue, so soon as you shall learn the acceptance thereof by the authorities of the United States, a proclamation to the people of the Confederate States, setting forth clearly the condition of the country, your inability to resist the enemy's overwhelming numbers, or to protect the country from his devastating and desolating march; the propositions submitted to you, and the reasons which, in your judgment, render their acceptance by the States and the people wise and expedient. You cannot, under the Constitution, dissolve the Confederacy and remit the States composing it to the Government of the United States. But the Confederacy is conquered; its days are numbered; Virginia is lost to it, and North Carolina must soon follow; and State after State, under the hostile tread of the enemy, must re-enter the old Union. The occasion, the emergency, the dire necessities and misfortunes of the country, the vast interests at stake, were never contemplated by those who framed the Constitution. They are all outside of it; and in the dissolution of the Confederacy and the wreck of all their hopes the States and the people will turn to you, whose antecedents and whose present position and powers constitute you more than any other living man the guardian of their honor and their interests, and will expect you not to stand upon constitutional limitations, but to assume and exercise all powers which to you may seem necessary and proper to shield them from useless war and to save from the wreck of the country all that may [be] practicable of honor, life, and property.

If time were allowed for the observance of constitutional forms I would advise the submission of these propositions to the executives of the several States, to the end that, through the usual legislative and conventional action, the wills of the people of the States, respectively, might be known. But in the present condition of the country such delay as this course would involve would be the deathblow to all hopes founded upon them. The pacification of the country should be as speedy as practicable, to the end that the authorities of the States may enter upon the establishment and maintenance of law and order. Negotiations for this purpose can more appropriately follow upon the overwhelming disaster of General Lee than at a future time. The wreck of our hopes results immediately from it. I omit all reference to the details, which must be provided for by the contending parties to this agreement, for future consideration.

Very respectfully, your obedient servant,

S. H. MALLORY,
Secretary of the Navy.[6]

Faced with the unanimous opinion and opposition of his remaining cabinet officers to any attempt to continue the war, Davis reluctantly followed their advice and wisely elected to approve the convention of April 18, 1865. Sadly, the assassination of Abraham Lincoln made its acceptance by the government of the United States impossible and set the stage for Johnston to disobey a direct order from Davis in deciding to surrender all of the remaining Confederate forces east of the Mississippi River on April 26.

---

6. Ibid., 832-834.

APPENDIX D

WADE HAMPTON'S SAGA

Lieutenant General Wade Hampton had every reason to be unhappy. At the outbreak of the Civil War, Hampton was reputedly the wealthiest man in the South, having assembled numerous plantations scattered throughout the antebellum region. Major General William T. Sherman's troops burned his lovely plantation Millwood to the ground, and by the end of the war, he had lost everything. Hampton had suffered several severe wounds in combat during the course of the war. His brother Lieutenant Colonel Frank Hampton was mortally wounded at the June 9, 1863, Battle of Brandy Station, in Virginia, and his 21-year-old son Lieutenant Preston Hampton was killed in action outside Petersburg, Virginia, in August 1864. The general's son Wade Hampton IV was severely wounded while trying to drag his brother to safety. Aside from Hampton's personal losses, he was infuriated the most by Sherman blaming him for burning, Columbia, South Carolina, his hometown.

On April 16, Col. J. Fred Waring, commander of the Jeff Davis Legion Cavalry, noted in his diary, "Gen. Hampton visited the Brigade to-day & made us an address. The men cheered him heartily. No surrender in him."[1] Waring's observations were absolutely accurate.

Consequently, Hampton decided that he was unwilling to surrender his command along with the rest of General Joseph E. Johnston's army, even though he had been an ideal subordinate throughout the course of his service during the Civil War. This time, he had no intention of obeying Johnston's order to surrender. After the debacle at the Bennett house, where he and the Union cavalry commander, Bvt. Maj. Gen. Judson Kilpatrick, nearly came to blows, Hampton wrote to Confederate President Jefferson Davis:

HILLSBOROUGH, April 19, 1865.
His Excellency President Davis:

---

1. Waring diary, entry for April 16, 1865.

MY DEAR SIR:

Having seen the terms upon which it is proposed to negotiate, I trust that I may be pardoned for writing to you in relation to them. Most of our officers look only at the military side of the picture at present, but you will regard it in other aspects also. The military situation is very gloomy, I admit, but it is by no means desperate, and endurance and determination will produce a change. There are large numbers of the Army of Northern Virginia who have escaped, and of these many will return to our standard if they are allowed to enter the cavalry service. Many of the cavalry who escaped will also join us if they find that we are still making head against the enemy. There are now not less than 40,000 to 50,000 men in arms on this side of the Mississippi; on the other there are as many more. Now the question presents itself, shall we disband these men at once, or shall we endeavor [to] concentrate them? If we disband we give up at once and forever all hope of foreign intervention. Europe will say, and say justly, Why should we interfere if you choose to re-enter the Union? But if we keep any organization, however small, in the field, we give Europe the opportunity of aiding us. The main reason urged for negotiation is to spare the infliction of any further suffering on the people. Nothing can be more fallacious than this reasoning. No suffering which can be inflicted by the passage over our country of the Yankee armies can equal what would fall on us if we return to the Union. In this latter event I look for a war between the United States and England and France, when we of the South, under a more rigorous conscription than has yet obtained here, shall be forced to fight by the side of our own negroes and under Yankee officers. We shall have to pay the debts incurred by the United States in this war, and we shall live under a base and vulgar tyranny. No sacrifice would be too great to escape this train of horrors, and I think it far better for us to fight to the extreme limits of our country rather than to reconstruct the Union upon any terms. If we cannot use our infantry here, let it disband, calling upon them for volunteers for the cavalry, collect all our mounted force, and move toward the Mississippi. When we cross that river we can get large accessions to the cavalry, and we can hold Texas. As soon as forces can be organized and equipped, send this heavy cavalry force into the country of the enemy, and they will soon show that we are not conquered. If I had 20,000 mounted men here I could force Sherman to retreat in twenty days. Give me a good force of cavalry and I will take them safely across the Mississippi, and if you desire to go in that direction it will give me great pleasure to escort you. My own mind is made up as to my course. I shall fight as long as my Government remains in existence; when that ceases to live I shall seek some other country, for I shall never take the "oath of allegiance". I am sorry that we paused to negotiate--for to my apprehension no evil can equal that of a return to the Union. I write to you, my dear sir, that you may know the feelings which actuate many of the officers of my command. They are not subdued, nor do they despair. For myself I beg to express my heartfelt sympathy with you, and to give you the assurance that my confidence in your patriotism has never been shaken. If you will allow me to do so, I can bring to your support many strong arms and brave hearts—men who will fight to Texas, and who, if forced from that State, will seek refuge in Mexico rather than in the Union.

With my best wishes, I am, very respectfully and truly, yours,

WADE HAMPTON.[2]

While Hampton's bellicosity was understandable, his belief that 20,000 men could drive Sherman's hordes from North Carolina was little short of the fantastic musings of an angry man. When his letter did not get a prompt response, Hampton made his way to Greensboro, North Carolina, in the hope of finding Davis to meet with him in person. However, Davis and what remained of his cabinet were already on their way to Charlotte, North Carolina. Frustrated, Hampton penned another letter.

GREENSBOROUGH, April 22, 1865.
His Excellency President DAVIS:

MY DEAR SIR:

I came here intending to go to Salisbury to see you, but hearing that you are not there I am not able to reach you at present. My only object in seeing you was to assure you that many of my officers and men agree with me in thinking that nothing can be as disastrous to us as a peace founded on a restoration of the Union. A return to the Union will bring all the horrors of war, coupled with

---

2. *OR* 47, 3:813-814.

all the degradation that can be inflicted on a conquered people. We shall be drawn into war with Europe, and under a rigorous conscription we shall, alongside of our own negroes, be forced to fight for the Yankees, under Yankee officers. If, under the first great reverse, we go back to the Union, Europe may well say that she cannot interfere. We give up our only hope of foreign intervention. But if we still keep some organization in the field we cannot only hope for intervention, but we may hope for some reaction in public sentiment. If you should propose to cross the Mississippi I can bring many good men to escort you over. My men are in hand and ready to follow me anywhere. I cannot agree to the terms which are proposed, and I shall seek a home in some other country. If Texas will hold out, or will seek the protectorate of Maximilian, we can still make head against the enemy. I write hurriedly, as the messenger is about to leave. If I can serve you or my country by any further fighting you have only to tell me so. My plan is to collect all the men who will still stick to their colors, and to get to Texas. I can carry with me quite a number, and I can get there.

With my best wishes for yourself, I am, very respectfully and truly, yours,
WADE HAMPTON.[3]

In short, Hampton had proposed to bring his entire 5,000-man cavalry force with him in an effort to link up with Davis and go to the Trans-Mississippi or Mexico, continuing the war from either location. Davis recognized that such a large escort would attract attention and invite pursuit, and it would not be sufficiently nimble and mobile enough to meet threats.[4] Davis responded to the general:

CHARLOTTE, N.C., April 26, 1865.
General WADE HAMPTON,
Greensborough, N.C.:

If you think it better you can, with the approval of General Johnston, select now, as proposed for a later period, the small body of men and join me at once, leaving General Wheeler to succeed you in the command of the cavalry.

JEFF'N DAVIS.[5]

3. Ibid., 829-830.
4. Edward L. Wells, *Hampton and Reconstruction* (Columbia, SC: The State Co., 1907), 66.
5. *OR* 47, 3:841.

In other words, Davis wanted only a small body of men that could effectively act as an escort.

Hampton tracked down Davis in Charlotte. The beleaguered Confederate president and the sizable South Carolinian met, and Davis approved Hampton's plan. Davis gave the general a letter—it authorized Hampton, and all the men willing to volunteer, to join Davis and take as many artillery and wagon-horses for mounts that might be deemed advisable. With Davis's authorization in hand, Hampton left for Hillsborough, North Carolina, to carry out the agreed-upon plan; he arrived in town at 11:00 p.m., April 26, only to find, to his great disappointment, that the army had surrendered.[6]

Davis had ordered Hampton to obtain Johnston's consent to continue fighting, so Hampton wrote to the commander:

> **HEADQUARTERS, April 26, 1865.**
> **General J. E. JOHNSTON,**
> **Commanding:**
>
> **GENERAL: On my return tonight I was notified that your army had been surrendered. Yesterday the honorable Secretary of War ordered me to move to South Carolina, where the enemy were threatening some portion of the State and I was carrying out this order when I was notified of your surrender. This fact, and the additional one of my absence during all the late negotiations, relieve me from the surrender, and I beg most respectfully to say that I do not regard myself as embraced in the capitulation. It is due to you, as well as myself, that this explanation should be made. I will add that if the Secretary of War regards me as embraced in your terms, or desires me to accept them, I shall at once disband my men.**
>
> **I am, very respectfully, yours,**
> **WADE HAMPTON,**
> **Lieutenant-General.**[7]

After making his case, there was little to do but wait for a response.

Hampton also tried to communicate with Maj. Gen. John C. Breckinridge, the Confederate secretary of war, hoping to receive further instructions.

---

6. Wells, *Hampton and Reconstruction*, 66.
7. *OR* 47, 3:841.

CHESTER, April 27, 1865.
General YORK:
Forward following dispatch by courier to General Breckinridge:
Hon. J. C. BRECKINRIDGE,
Company's Shops:

Some time ago I notified General Johnston not to include me in any surrender. You gave me orders to move on 25th. On return I find army surrendered. I think I am free. What is your decision? Answer here and Greensborough.
WADE HAMPTON,
Lieutenant-General.
WILLIAM P. JOHNSTON.[8]

Impatient, Hampton sent a second dispatch at 11:00 p.m. that night:

GREENSBOROUGH, N.C., April 27, 1865 11 p.m.
General JOHN C. BRECKINRIDGE:

You gave me orders on the 25th to move. On my return on 26th I found military convention. I think I am free from its terms by your previous order. Have notified General Johnston that I will abide by your decision. Am ready to move as ordered. Answer here or Lexington.
WADE HAMPTON,
Lieutenant-General.[9]

Thoroughly frustrated, Hampton wrote again to Johnston on April 27, looking for guidance. Hampton suggested that Breckinridge should decide whether he was included in the surrender convention, and he agreed to be bound by that decision.

HEADQUARTERS, April 27, 1865.
General J. E. JOHNSTON, Commanding:

GENERAL: On the 25th instant, by order of the honorable Secretary of War, I was charged with a duty which transferred to another field of service. Returning with this order on the 26th to report to you, I found that a convention had been entered into between Major-General Sherman and yourself. In this condition of affairs I beg most respectfully to submit the case to the Secretary of

8. Ibid., 845. Major William P. Johnston served in the 2nd Kentucky Mounted Infantry of the Army of Tennessee. He was not related to Joseph E. Johnston. Instead, he was the son of Gen. Albert Sidney Johnston and Aide-de-camp to Jefferson Davis
9. Ibid.

War for his decision. Should he determine that his order of the 25th instant is still in force, I cannot avail myself of the terms of the convention entered into, but if he considers me as still on duty here, I shall of course consider myself as embraced in the terms of this convention. His decision shall be forwarded to you as soon as received.

I am, very respectfully, yours,
WADE HAMPTON,
Lieutenant-General[10]

Major General Matthew C. Butler's cavalry division—formerly Hampton's division—was camped around Hillsborough. "Wright says he will not surrender this Brigade unless they desire it," Colonel Waring recalled. "They shall all have the opportunity of getting away. Six of my men have gone home to avoid the humiliation of surrender."[11]

Word spread that the Confederate army had been surrendered en masse, and the men began making preparations to go home. Colonel Gilbert J. "Gib" Wright, of the Cobb Legion Cavalry and who commanded Hampton's old brigade, "came out the camp as fast as his horse could bring him" and had the men assemble. Wright told the soldiers that they would not be surrendered without their consent, that the men should not disgrace themselves by just riding off, and that they would only do so over his dead body. "That settled it," a trooper of the Cobb Legion noted, "for the whole brigade was more afraid of him than of the Yankees." Those men who had saddled up, quietly unsaddled and made their way back to camp.

Later that day, Wright ordered his brigade to move out in the direction of Greensboro, North Carolina. The Confederates arrived at a small town known as Company Shops, about 22 miles from Hillsborough, about 11:00 p.m. When the entire column had arrived, Wright had the men dismount and gather around him. He told the troopers that they had at least a 30-mile head start on Kilpatrick's troopers, as well as plenty of supplies. If they wanted to move out for the Trans-Mississippi, Kilpatrick said he would be pleased to go with them as either a commander or as a private. He wanted the men to decide for themselves, though.[12]

Colonel Waring remarked, "Wright in a speech laid the matter before the Brigade, whether they would try to get away without a

10. Ibid.
11. Waring diary, entry for April 26, 1865.
12. Charles P. Hansell, "Surrender of Cobb's Legion." *Confederate Veteran* 25 (October, 1917): 463.

parole, or stay and accept the parole. I advised my men to stay and accept the terms offered by Sherman. My officers & myself I considered bound in honor to take the fate of the army."[13]

After learning about the movement of Butler's division, which had been included in Johnston's surrender agreement, Johnston sent Hampton a command. As Maj. Gen. Jacob D. Cox observed, "Johnston, feeling that his honor as a commander was involved, sent peremptory orders to Hampton to march back to the position near Hillsborough which he had abandoned. He gave Wheeler similar orders."[14] It was a stinging rebuke and shut down Hampton's plan to join Davis.

> **GREENSBOROUGH, April 27, 1865 1 p.m.**
> **Lieut. Gen. WADE HAMPTON, Commanding Cavalry:**
>
> **GENERAL: The following telegram has just been received at these headquarters from Brig. Gen. H. H. Anderson, commanding Company's Shops:**
>
> **General Hampton has left here with Butler's division.**
>
> **General Johnston directs that you cause this division to return immediately to the position near Hillsborough, in which it has been serving under his orders.**
>
> **I have the honor to be, &c.,**
> **A. ANDERSON,**
> **Assistant Adjutant-General.**[15]

Hampton swung into his saddle and set out to obey the order. When he found Wright's camp, Hampton ordered the men to be formed and moved out. They proceeded a short distance toward Greensboro before Hampton had them dismount and go into camp. Private J. M. Thomasson, who served in Company K of the 7th Confederate Cavalry of Wheeler's corps, watched as Hampton and his staff galloped up. "The General was on his horse—brave and majestic as ever, though the tears were streaming down his cheeks," Thomasson remembered. The men formed around Hampton. Removing his hat, Hampton gave an impromptu farewell speech to the dumbstruck troopers. "I have been riding three days and nights trying to get you out of here," he declared. "But you know there is a higher authority than I am. I never knew until this morning that we were surrendered. I do not know on what terms we were surrendered," the general continued. "I advise you to go to Greensboro with [Colonel] Wright

13. Waring diary, entry for April 27, 1865.
14. Cox, *Military Reminiscences*, 2:522.
15. *OR* 47, 3:846.

and you will find out all about it. I advise you to go home by companies as much as possible. Do not scatter about. I hope you will get home to your families safely and may God be with you."

Despite his gloom, the burly South Carolinian remained defiant. Certainly, he had not lost his fighting spirit. Hampton continued speaking:

> There is a day coming when we will meet and fight again. Those that deserted and ran to the woods will come up and fight with us. I ask today if there is one man, or five men, or 50 men who will go with me. I mean single men, not men with families. I will ride by their side and will fight as long as there is a drop of blood in my veins. I will say one thing for this brigade: I never ordered you to dismount from your horses and to take your arms to a trial but you did. I never ordered you to draw sabers and charge the enemy but you went.[16]

"He first told them of the very high reputation the brigade had won for itself and many things that touched the hearts of those seasoned veterans, so there was hardly a dry eye in the crowd," a trooper of the Cobb Legion Cavalry recalled. "He wound up telling us that he had worked hard to have the cavalry excepted from the terms of surrender, and if it was he was ready to go with us anywhere we wanted to go, but that if we were included in the agreement to surrender it was our duty to surrender, and he knew we would do our duty."[17]

A trooper of the Charleston Light Dragoons, which was also known as Company K, 4th South Carolina Cavalry, described the scene:

> Learning that a large part of his men had refused to surrender and had left the camp, he sent a courier after them with orders to halt, until he could come up with them, and at twelve o'clock midnight left his headquarters, accompanied by several of his staff, and seventeen scouts and couriers. At sunrise he came up with the men to whom he had sent orders halt, and besought them to prove themselves then, as they had done throughout the war, good soldiers, by obeying the command of General Johnston by whom they had been surrendered, as part of his army. He assured them in most affecting words, that he knew they were ready to

16. J. M. Thomasson, "Hampton's Farewell to His Gallant Men," *The State*,
    May 11, 1908.
17. Hansell, "Surrender of Cobb's Legion," 463.

share his fate, but that this they could not honorably do, as they had been surrendered with the army, but that he himself was acting under the orders of the commander-in-chief, and could therefore join him. The writer was not present, but has been informed by those, who were there, that it was a most impressive and pathetic scene, old soldiers with tears streaming down their faces, and many sobbing like children, the General's eyes wet and his voice shaking with emotion.[18]

Hampton's farewell stunned the horsemen into silence. The war was over? All they could do was watch as an emotional Hampton bowed and rode off. "You could have heard a pin drop while he spoke. It was a sad occasion for all of us, but we felt a thrill of pride in our fearless general," Thomasson concluded.[19]

Before departing the camp, Hampton took a few minutes to prepare some final official correspondence. First, he responded to Johnston:

> QUARTERMASTER'S OFFICE, BUTLER'S CAVALRY DIVISION,
> April 27, 1865 9:45 p.m.
> General J. E. JOHNSTON:
>
> GENERAL: Your letter has just reached me, and I beg to assure you that my misapplication of the terms, of which you complain, was entirely accidental and by no means intended to reflect upon you. My ignorance of the proper distinction in these terms led me into the error I committed, and that there may be no misunderstanding of my position in this matter, I withdraw the letter handed to you by General Logan. I inclose one which I beg to substitute for the one withdrawn.
>
> I wish solely to have my own record right, and if you will consider the position in which I find myself placed, you will see how great is my embarrassment. By your advice I went to consult with the President, the armistice having been annulled. After full conference with him, a plan was agreed on to enable him to leave the country. He charged me with the execution of this plan, and he is now moving in accordance with it. On my return here I find myself not only powerless to assist him, but placed myself in a position of great delicacy. I must either leave him to his fate, without an effort to avert it, or subject myself to

18. Wells, *Hampton and Reconstruction*, 66-67.
19. Thomasson, "Hampton's Farewell to His Gallant Men."

possible censure by not accepting the terms of the convention you have made. If I do not accompany him I shall never cease to reproach myself; and if I go with him I may go under the ban of outlawry. I choose the latter, because I believe it to be my duty to do so. But I leave my command to abide the terms, as I shall not ask a man to go with me. Should any join me, they will be stragglers like myself and, like myself, willing to sacrifice everything for the cause and for our Government. The letter I sent--and the one now inclosed--I had and have but one object--to save you from any misconstruction on account of my action in this matter. Hoping that this end may be obtained,

I am, very respectfully, yours,
WADE HAMPTON,
Lieutenant-General.[20]

Hampton then wrote to Wheeler that Johnston had surrendered Wheeler's command and, with his command included in the surrender, Hampton advised Wheeler that Hampton had no authority to give any orders:

APRIL 27, 1865 11 p.m.
Maj. Gen. J. WHEELER,
Salisbury or Charlotte:

Military convention has been entered into. Terms equivalent to those discussed before. Will write fully. Can give you no orders.

WADE HAMPTON,
Lieutenant-General.[21]

Wheeler responded an hour later.

SALISBURY, COMPANY'S SHOPS, April 27, 1865 12 m.
Lieutenant-General HAMPTON:

Am moving my command as directed.

J. WHEELER,
Major-General.[22]

On his own, and now a man without a country, Wade Hampton took leave of his old command, many of whom had been with him since the heady days of 1861. He mounted his horse and set out for Charlotte, accompanied by only a small cavalry escort. When he reached Charlotte on the night of April 28, he learned that Davis had

---

20. *OR* 47, 3:846.
21. Ibid., 847.
22. Ibid.

already left for Yorkville, South Carolina, about 35 miles away. Hampton found a fresh mount—the escort's horses were played out—and left his escort at Charlotte, pressing on alone to Yorkville. His horse swam the Catawba River during the night, and Hampton arrived at Yorkville about 2:00 a.m. on April 30, only to find that Davis was already in Abbeville, South Carolina.

A former comrade in arms said, "Thus disappointed in overtaking Mr. Davis and not knowing his plans of route, Hampton dispatched a letter to him by General Wheeler, whom he met at Yorkville, and also sent two couriers with communications for him, but all these failed of reaching him." He continued, "Thus, faithful to the last, but hearing nothing further from Mr. Davis, General Hampton eventually accepted a parole in accordance with General Lee's views that resistance was to cease, and, from that moment, there was no man, South or North, more sincere in accepting the legitimate results of the war, or in using his influence more conscientiously to bring about a Union restored in good faith and fraternal feeling."[23]

When Wheeler reached Yorkville, he called upon Hampton. "I was shocked at the appearance of my fellow officer," Wheeler wrote. "He was harassed in mind and worn in body, and the story of his march from Greensboro made it plain to us all how sadly his fortunes had fallen." With Wheeler's encouragement and the pleas of Hampton's wife, Mary, Hampton decided to lay down his sword and tend to his family, which had also been devastated by the war. Wheeler explained, "He had a family, and his vast business interests, which had been left to others for four years, demanded his attention. I explained that it was very different with me, as I had no such obligations. He finally yielded."[24] Wade Hampton's distinguished military career ended, and he accepted his parole and swore the oath of loyalty to the United States.

On May 10, Hampton sent a letter to a friend. "I was not included in the late convention (as I was absent), but the command was. Those however who were absent, can either accept or reject the terms," he wrote. "Nothing can be done at present, either here or elsewhere, so I advise quiet for a time. If any opportunity offers, later, we can avail ourselves of it."[25] Even at this late date, Hampton still held out hope that he would get an opportunity to continue the fight.

23. Wells, *Hampton and Reconstruction*, 67-68.
24. Dodson, *Campaigns of Wheeler and His Cavalry*, 358-362. Wheeler eventually surrendered and was imprisoned at Fort Delaware until June 8, 1865, when Secretary of War Edwin Stanton ordered that he be released and paroled under the terms of Johnston's convention with Sherman.
25. Charles E. Cauthen, ed., *Family Letters of the Three Wade Hamptons 1782-1901* (Columbia: University of South Carolina Press, 1953), 114.

He eventually mellowed, however. "Wade Hampton was the Moses of his people," an admirer proclaimed, "the God-given instrument to help them free themselves from their enemies."[26] Hampton accepted the Democratic nomination for governor of South Carolina in 1865 and narrowly lost a disputed election to a handpicked Radical Republican. He vigorously opposed Radical Republican Reconstruction policies and disputed the harsh treatment meted out to South Carolina, in particular, which most Northerners viewed as the cradle of rebellion.

Hampton ran for governor again in 1876, winning the election. He espoused equal rights for the freed slaves, who comprised the majority of South Carolina's population, and an end to the Federal army's occupation of the last three states of the former Confederacy—South Carolina, Louisiana, and Florida—under President Ulysses S. Grant. Hampton's policies earned him the proud title of the "Savior of South Carolina." President Rutherford B. Hayes withdrew the remaining Federal troops from South Carolina in 1877, marking the official end of Reconstruction in the Palmetto State, as well as Louisiana and Florida. Hampton was re-elected to a second two-year term without opposition in 1878, but he resigned in 1879 to take a seat in the Senate, which he held for 12 years. His political career was marked not by the pugnacity of his military personality but by his advocacy of racial inclusiveness. In 1881, President James A. Garfield, another Civil War veteran, nominated Hampton's enemy Judson Kilpatrick for U.S. ambassador to Chile—such nominations require the advice and consent of the Senate. Demonstrating that time had, indeed, healed all wounds, Senator Wade Hampton placed his former rival's name before the Senate, which unanimously approved Kilpatrick's nomination.[27] For Hampton and Kilpatrick, at least, the bitterness and rancor of their row at Bennett Place on April 17, 1865, was finally forgotten.

After being defeated for a third Senate term in 1892, Hampton served as U.S. railroad commissioner for four years before retiring to private life in his beloved hometown, Columbia. A monument honoring Hampton stands outside the Capitol building in Columbia, a token showcasing the esteem in which his fellow citizens held him.

In 1899, an accidental fire destroyed Hampton's home. He was 82 years old and could not afford to rebuild it. Friends and admirers raised money to erect a house for the aging warrior-politician, and they presented it to him despite his protests. Hampton spent the last years of his life in the new home. He died on April 11, 1902. Reportedly, his last words were, "God bless all my people, black and white." Hampton

26. Mrs. Julia Porcher Wickham, "Wade Hampton, the Cavalry Leader, and His Times," *Confederate Veteran* 36 (1928), 448.
27. *Sussex Independent*, February 1, 1918.

lay in repose in the South Carolina Capitol before 20,000 mourners followed his casket to its gravesite.[28]

28. Manly Wade Wellman, *Giant in Gray: A Biography of Wade Hampton of South Carolina* (New York: Charles Scribner's Sons, 1949), 193-334.

BIBLIOGRAPHY

PRIMARY SOURCES

NEWSPAPERS:

Durham Herald
Evening Star (Washington, D.C.)
Frank Leslie's Illustrated Newspaper
Harper's Weekly
National Tribune
New York Herald
New York Times
Ohio Statesman (Columbus, Ohio)
Philadelphia Inquirer
Philadelphia Weekly Times
Raleigh State Journal
The Daily Standard (Raleigh, North Carolina)
The Scranton Republican
The State (Columbia, South Carolina)
The Sun (New York, New York)
Sussex Independent
Western Democrat (Charlotte, North Carolina)

MANUSCRIPT SOURCES:

Archives, American Civil War Museum, Richmond, Virginia:
  Joseph E. Johnston Papers

Archives, Bennett Place State Historic Site, Durham, North Carolina:
  Arthur C. Menius, III, "Bennett Place," 1979 unpublished manuscript
  W. S. Tarleton, "Report on the Bennett House Restoration," unpublished
    research report, North Carolina Department of Archives and History,
    August 27, 1959

Archives, Bentonville Battlefield, Four Oaks, North Carolina:
Mark Bradley Collection
Peter Eltinge letter to his father, May 5, 1865
"Henry" letter to his sister, April 20, 1865

Illinois Archives and Manuscripts Department, Chicago Historical Society, Chicago, Illinois:
Thomas Benton Roy Diary

Archives, Detroit Public Library, Detroit, Michigan:
Alpheus S. Williams Papers

Special Collections, Perkins Library, Duke University, Durham, North Carolina:
James Bennitt Papers
"Address of Vice-President Hubert H. Humphrey, Bennett Place Commemoration, Durham, North Carolina," April 25, 1965
Ferdinand F. Boltz Papers
Bradley T. Johnson Papers
John Johnson Family Papers
Joseph M. Stetson Letters

Manuscripts Division, Library of Congress, Washington, D.C.:
Salmon P. Chase Papers
Alexander H. Stephens Papers

Manuscripts Division, New York Historical Society, New York, New York:
"Notes Personal of Lieut. Col. Alex Robt. Chisholm Relative to the War of Secession"

Tennessee State Library and Archives, Nashville, Tennessee:
Confederate Collection
H. M. Pollard Diary
Tom E. Sloan Diary

Southern Historical Collection, Wilson Library, University of North Carolina, Chapel Hill, North Carolina:
Southern Historical Collection:
    Munson Monroe Buford Diary
    Campbell Family Papers
    Elizabeth Collier Diary 1861-1865
    Anne Cameron Collins Papers
    Hezekiah M. Corkle Diary
    William M. Gordon Collection
    Moore & Gatling Law Firm Papers
    J. Frederick Waring diary for 1864-1865
    John Taylor Wood Papers

North Carolina Collection:
> Richard R. Sacchi and Terry H. Erlandson, "An Intensive Archaeological Survey of the Bennett Place"

Special Collections, Hesburgh Library, University of Notre Dame, South Bend, Indiana:
> William T. Sherman Papers

Special Collections, University of Washington Libraries, Seattle, Washington:
> Manning F. Force Papers

Archives, Western Reserve Historical Society, Cleveland, Ohio:
> Regimental Papers of the Civil War
> Walker Letters (South Carolina)

PUBLISHED SOURCES:

"A 10th Ohio Cavalryman," "Campaign Through the Carolinas. With Kilpatrick from Goldsboro to the End of the War. Lee's Surrender. Joy in Sherman's Ranks at the Glorious News. The Grand Roundup. Scenes with Wheeler's Cavalry when They Surrendered," *National Tribune*, May 12, 1892.

Andersen, Mary Ann, ed. *The Civil War Diary of Allen Morgan Geer Twentieth Regiment, Illinois Volunteers*. Denver, CO: R. C. Appleman, 1977.

Basler, Roy, ed. *Collected Works of Abraham Lincoln*. 8 vols. New Brunswick, NJ: Rutgers University Press, 1953.

Becker, L. F. "Campaigning with a Grand Army. Some of the 104th Ohio's Service in the Latter Part of the War," *National Tribune*, November 23, 1899.

Blackburn, J. K. P. "Reminiscences of the Terry Rangers." Included in Thomas W. Cutrer, ed., *Terry Texas Ranger Trilogy*. Austin, TX: State House Press, 1996: 85-181.

Boies, Andrew J. *Record of the Thirty-Third Massachusetts Volunteer Infantry, From Aug. 1862 to Aug. 1865*. Fitchburg, MA: Sentinel Printing Co., 1880.

Boyle, John Richards. *Soldiers True: The Story of the One Hundred and Eleventh Regiment Pennsylvania Veteran Volunteers, and of Its Campaigns in the War for the Union 1861-1865*. New York: Eaton & Mains, 1903.

Boynton, H V. *Sherman's Historical Raid. The Memoirs in the Light of the Record. A Review Based Upon Compilations from the Files of the War Office*. Cincinnati: Wilstach, Baldwin & Co., 1875.

Brooks, Ulysses R. *Butler and His Cavalry in the War of Secession 1861-1865*. Columbia, SC: The State Company, 1899.

----------------------, ed. *Memoirs of the War of Secession from the Original Manuscripts of Johnson Hagood, Brigadier-General*, C.S.A. Columbia, SC: The State Co., 1910.

Brown, Norman, ed. *One of Cleburne's Command: The Civil War Reminiscences and Diary of Capt. Samuel T. Foster, Granbury's Texas Brigade, CSA*. Austin: University of Texas Press, 1980.

Bryant, Edwin E. *History of the Third Regiment of Wisconsin Veteran Volunteer*

Infantry, 1861-1865. Madison, WI: Veterans Association of the Regiment, 1891.

Byrne, Frank L., ed. *The View from Headquarters: Civil War Letters of Harvey Reid*. Madison: Wisconsin Historical Society, 1965.

"Captain Ridley's Journal," *Confederate Veteran* 3 (1895): 99.

Carter, George E., ed. *The Story of Joshua D. Breyfogle, Private, 4th Ohio Infantry (10th Ohio Cavalry) and the Civil War*. Lewiston, NY: Edward Mellen Press, 2001.

Cauthen, Charles E., ed. *Family Letters of the Three Wade Hamptons 1782-1901*. Columbia: University of South Carolina Press, 1953.

Clausewitz, Carl von. *On War*. Trans. by Michael Howard and Peter Paret. Princeton, NJ: Princeton University Press, 1976.

Coleman, William D. "Jefferson Davis' Week at Danville," *Philadelphia Weekly Times*, May 28, 1881.

Conyngham, David P. *Sherman's March Across the South with Sketches and Incidents of the Campaign*. New York: Sheldan & Co., 1865.

Cox, Jacob D. *Reminiscences of the Civil War*. 2 vols. New York: Charles Scribner's Sons, 1900.

Cutrer, Thomas W., ed. *A Terry Texas Ranger: The Life Record of H. W. Graber*. Austin, TX: State House Press, 1987.

Davis, Jefferson. *The Rise and Fall of the Confederate Government*. 2 vols. New York: D. Appleton & Co., 1881.

Davis, Theo R. "With Sherman in His Army Home." *The Cosmopolitan* 12 (December 1891): 195-205.

Dodson, W. C. *Campaigns of Wheeler and His Cavalry 1862-1865*. Atlanta: Hudgins Publishing Co., 1899.

Donald, David, ed. *Inside Lincoln's Cabinet: The Civil War Diaries of Salmon P. Chase*. New York: Longmans, Green & Co., 1954.

Dougherty, Dave, ed. *Making Georgia Howl! The 5th Ohio Cavalry in Kilpatrick's Campaign and the Diary of Sgt. William H. Harding*. Point Pleasant, NJ: Winged Hussar Publishing, 2016.

DuBose, John Witherspoon. *General Joseph Wheeler and the Army of Tennessee*. New York: Neale Publishing Co., 1912.

Evans, J. W. "Reminiscences of J. W. Evans in the War Between the States." Included in *Confederate Reminiscences and Letters 1861-1865*. Vol. 10. Atlanta: Georgia Division, United Daughters of the Confederacy, 1999: 19-23.

Fore, Mrs. James A. "Last Meeting of Confederate Cabinet Held in Charlotte," *Raleigh State Journal*, March 2, 1917.

Fremantle, Arthur J. L. *Three Months in the Southern States*. Edinburgh: William Blackwood & Sons, 1863.

"From Gen. Sherman's Army: Sherman's Conference with Johnston. Interesting Particulars of the Interview. Johnston Informs Sherman Where Wilson is Raiding and Wants Him Stopped," *New York Times*, April 27, 1865.

"From North Carolina. The Surrender of Johnston," *Evening Star*, May 1, 1865.

"From Washington: The Grand Review of the Armies (Official). Details of the Great Review. Revision of Our Revenue System. Deserved Promotion," *New York Times*, May 18, 1865.

Garber, Michael C., Jr. "Reminiscences of the Burning of Columbia, South Carolina," *Indiana Magazine of History*, Vol. 11, No. 4 (1915): 285-300.

"Gen. Joseph E. Johnston," *The Scranton Republican*, March 24, 1891.

Grady, Henry W. "An Interview with General Longstreet." Included in Peter Cozzens, ed. *Battles and Leaders of the Civil War.* Vol. 5 Urbana: University of Illinois Press, 2002: 686-695.

Granger, Arthur O. "The 'Fifteenth' at General Joe Johnston's Surrender." Included in Charles H. Kirk, ed. *History of the Fifteenth Pennsylvania Volunteer Cavalry.* Philadelphia: Historical Committee of the Society of the Fifteenth Pennsylvania Cavalry, 1906: 589-595.

Grant, Ulysses S. *Personal Memoirs of U. S. Grant.* 2 vols. New York: Charles L. Webster & Co., 1892.

Guild, George B. *A Brief Narrative of the Fourth Tennessee Cavalry Regiment, Wheeler's Corps, Army of Tennessee.* Nashville: n.p., 1913.

Hagood, Johnson. *Memoirs of the War of Secession, from the Original Manuscripts of Johnson Hagood.* Columbia, SC: The State Company, 1910.

Halliburton, Lloyd, ed. *Saddle Soldiers: The Civil War Correspondence of General William Stokes of the 4th South Carolina Cavalry.* Orangeburg, SC: Sandlapper Publishing Co., 1993.

Hampton, Wade. "An Effort to Rescue Jefferson Davis. Statement of General Wade Hampton as to the Connection of Himself and Command Therewith." *Southern Historical Society Papers* 27 (1899): 132-136.

--------------------. "The Battle of Bentonville." Included in Robert U. Johnson and Clarence C. Buel, eds. *Battles and Leaders of the Civil War.* 4 vols. New York: Century Publishing Co., 1884-1889, 4:700-705.

Hansell, Charles P. "Surrender of Cobb's Legion." *Confederate Veteran* 25 (October, 1917): 463-464.

Harwell, Richard and Philip N. Racine, eds. *The Fiery Trail: A Union Officer's Account of Sherman's Last Campaigns.* Knoxville: University of Tennessee Press, 1986.

Hatcher, Edmund M. *The Last Four Weeks of the War.* Columbus, OH: Edmund N. Hatcher, 1891.

Hedley, F. Y. *Marching Through Georgia: Pen-Pictures of Every-Day Life in General Sherman's Army, From the Beginning of the Atlanta Campaign Until the Close of the War.* Chicago: M. A. Donohue & Co., 1884.

Hinkley, Julian Wisner. *A Narrative of Service with the Third Wisconsin Infantry.* Madison: Wisconsin History Commission, 1912.

Hinman, Wilbur F. *The Story of the Sherman Brigade. The Camp, the March, the Bivouac, the Battle; and How "the Boys" Lived and Died During Four Years of Active Field Service.* Self published, 1897.

Hoar, Jay S., ed. "'General' James Reid Jones: Last Witness to Bennett Place

Surrender," *Blue & Gray* Vol. 2, No. 11 (April-May, 1985), 57-58.

Howard, Oliver O. *Autobiography of Oliver Otis Howard*. 2 vols. New York: Baker & Taylor Co., 1907.

----------------------. "General Howard's Address." Included in *Report of the Proceedings of the Society of the Army of the Tennessee at the Twenty-Eighth Meeting, Held at St. Louis, Mo., November 18-19, 1896*. Cincinnati: Press of F. W. Freeman, 1898: 67-81.

Howard, Wiley C. *Sketch of Cobb Legion Cavalry and Some Incidents and Scenes Remembered*. Atlanta: Atlanta Camp, United Confederate Veterans, 1901.

Howe, M. A. DeWolfe, ed. *Home Letters of General Sherman*. New York: Charles Scribner's Sons, 1909.

-------------------------------. *Marching with Sherman: Passages from the Letters and Campaign Diaries of Henry Hitchcock, Major and Assistant Adjutant General of Volunteers November 1864-May 1865*. New Haven: Yale University Press, 1927.

Jamison, Matthew H. *Recollections of Pioneer and Army Life*. Kansas City, MO: Hudson Press, 1911.

"Joe Johnston," *New York Herald*, May 10, 1865.

Johnston, Joseph E. "My Negotiations with Sherman." *North American Review* 143 (August 1886): 183-197.

----------------------. *Narrative of Military Operations, Directed, During the Late War Between the States*. New York: D. Appleton & Co., 1874.

Jordan, A. L. "Surrender of Johnston's Army." *Confederate Veteran* 28 (1920): 425.

Kittinger, Joseph. *Diary, 1861-1865*. Buffalo, NY: Kittinger Co., 1979.

Loop, Myron B. *The Long Road Home: Ten Thousand Miles Through the Confederacy With the 68th Ohio*. Ed. by Richard A. Baumgartner. Huntington, WV: Blue Acorn Press, 2006.

Mallory, Stephen R. "The Last Days of the Confederate Government." Included in Peter Cozzens, ed. *Battles and Leaders of the Civil War*. Vol. 5. Urbana: University of Illinois Press, 2002: 666-684.

McClellan, Henry B. "The Campaign of 1863—A Reply to Kilpatrick," *Philadelphia Weekly Times*, February 7, 1880.

McMurray, W. J. *History of the Twentieth Tennessee Regiment Volunteer Infantry, C.S.A.* Nashville, TN: Regimental Publication Committee, 1904.

McSwain, Eleanor D., ed. *Crumbling Defenses or Memoirs and Reminiscences of John Logan Black, Colonel C.S.A.* Macon, GA: The J. W. Burke Co., 1960.

Morse, John T., ed. *The Diary of Gideon Welles, Secretary of the Navy Under Lincoln and Johnson*. 3 vols. New York: Houghton-Mifflin, 1911.

Mowris, J. A. *A History of the One Hundred Seventeenth N. Y. Volunteers (Fourth Oneida) from the Date of Its Organization, August 1862, till that of Its Muster Out, June 1865*. Hartford, CT: Case, Lockhart & Co., 1866.

"Mr. E. D. Wesftall's Dispatch," *New York Herald*, April 27, 1865.

"Mr. O. F. Howe's Dispatches," *New York Herald*, April 27, 1865.

"Mr. Theodore C. Wilson's Dispatch," *New York Herald*, May 10, 1865.

Nichols, George Ward. *The Story of the Great March, from the Diary of a Staff Officer.* New York: Harper & Bros., 1865.

Ninety-Second Illinois Volunteers. Freeport, IL: Journal Steam Publishing House and Bookbindery, 1875.

"North Carolina—Sherman and Johnston," *Philadelphia Inquirer*, April 28, 1865.

Oeffinger, John C., ed. *A Soldier's General: The Civil War Letters of Major General Lafayette McLaws.* Chapel Hill: University of North Carolina Press, 2002.

"On His Way to His Rest. New-York's Sad Farewell to the Great Soldier," *New York Times*, February 21, 1891.

Pepper, George W. *Personal Recollections of Sherman's Campaigns in Georgia and the Carolinas.* Zanesville, OH: Hugh Dunne, 1866.

--------------------. *Under Three Flags: or, The Story of My Life as Preacher, Captain in the Army, Chaplain, Consul, with Speeches and Interviews.* Cincinnati: Curtis & Jennings, 1899.

Porter, David Dixon. *Incidents and Anecdotes of the Civil War.* New York: D. Appleton & Co., 1885.

Porter, Horace. *Campaigning with Grant.* New York: The Century Co., 1897.

Quaife, Milo M., ed. *From the Cannon's Mouth: The Civil War Letters of General Alpheus S. Williams.* Detroit: Wayne State University Press, 1959.

Ratchford, J. W. *Some Reminiscences of Persons and Incidents of the Civil War.* Reprint edition. Austin, TX: Shoal Creek Publishers, 1971.

Reagan, John H. *Memoirs with Special Reference to Secession and the Civil War.* New York: Neale Publishing Co., 1906.

Rennolds, Edwin H. *A History of Henry County Commands Which Served in the Confederate States Army, Including Rosters of the Various Companies Enlisted in Henry County, Tenn.* Jacksonville, FL: Sun Publishing Co., 1904.

Ridley, Bromfield. *Battles and Sketches of the Army of Tennessee.* Mexico, MO: Missouri Printing and Publishing Co., 1906.

Roman, Alfred. *The Military Operations of General Beauregard in the War Between the States 1861-1865.* New York: Harper & Bros., 1884.

Schofield, John M. *Forty-Six Years in the Army.* New York: The Century Co., 1897.

Schurz, Carl. *The Reminiscences of Carl Schurz.* 4 vols. London: John Murray, 1909.

"Sherman and Breckinridge," *New York Times*, April 27, 1865.

"Sherman-Johnston." Included in *Report of the Joint Committee on the Conduct of the War at the Second Session, Thirty-Eighth Congress.* Washington, DC: Government Printing Office, 1865: 3-23.

Sherman, William T. *Memoirs of Gen. W. T. Sherman.* 2 vols. New York: Charles L. Webster & Co., 1891.

"Sherman's Army; Gen. Sherman Negotiating with Gen. Johnston. His Action Repudiated by the President and the Cabinet. Hostilities to Commence at Once. President Lincoln's Instructions to be Carried Out. Lieut.-Gen. Grant Hastens to the Scene of Action. Sherman's Order Suspending Hostilities. Great

Dissatisfaction Created by it in the Army," *New York Times*, April 24, 1865.

"Sherman's Scheme of Peace and our Great Calamity," *New York Times*, April 25, 1865.

Simpson, Brooks D. and Jean V. Berlin. *Sherman's Civil War: Selected Correspondence of William T. Sherman, 1860-1865*. Chapel Hill: University of North Carolina Press, 1999.

Slocum, Henry W. "Final Operations of Sherman's Army." Included in Robert U. Johnson and Clarence C. Buel, eds. *Battles and Leaders of the Civil War*. 4 vols. New York: Century Publishing Co., 1884-1889, 4:734-738.

"Sorrow at the Capital: Formal Announcement by the President—Eulogies in the Senate," *New York Times*, February 15, 1891.

Spencer, Cornelia Phillips. *The Last Ninety Days of the War in North Carolina*. New York: Watchman Publishing Co., 1866.

Stevenson, Thomas M. *History of the 78th Regiment O.V.V.I., From Its "Muster-In" to Its "Muster-Out"*. Zanesville, OH: Hugh Dunne, 1865.

Stewart, Nixon B. *Dan McCook's Regiment: 52nd O.V.I.-1865. A History of the Regiment, Its Campaigns and Battles. From 1862 to 1865*. Alliance, OH: Review Print, 1900.

Story of the Service of Company E, and of the Twelfth Wisconsin Regiment, Veteran Volunteer Infantry, in the War of the Rebellion. Milwaukee, WI: Swain & Tate Co., 1893.

Supplement to the Official Records of the Union and Confederate Armies. 100 vols. Wilmington, NC: Broadfoot Publishing, 1994.

"The Astounding News from General Sherman—His Rash Armistice and the Consequences," *New York Herald*, April 24, 1865.

"The Bennett House," *Philadelphia Inquirer*, May 8, 1865.

"The Final Collapse. Confederate Papers Captured at the End of the War," *The Sun*, February 14, 1886.

"The North Carolina Campaign; Occupation of Smithville and Capture of Raleigh. The Negotiation Between Sherman and Johnston. Their Commencement and Ending. Clayton Reached--Skirmishing. Raleigh Occupied by Kilpatrick--The Colors of the Fifth Ohio Cavalry the First in the Capital. The Delegation to Sherman--The Proposed Surrender of the State--Wade Hampton Opposed to the Movement--Gov. Vance-- Newspapers--The Legislature," *New York Times*, April 30, 1865.

The War of the Rebellion: A Compilation of the Official Records of the Union and Confederate Armies. 128 volumes in 3 series. Washington, D.C.: United States Government Printing Office, 1889.

Thomasson, J. M. "Hampton's Farewell to His Gallant Men," *The State*, May 11, 1908.

Watkins, Sam R. *"Co. Aytch," Maury Grays, First Tennessee Regiment; or, A Side Show of the Big Show*. Chattanooga, TN: Times Printing Co., 1900.

Wells, Edward L. *A Sketch of the Charleston Light Dragoons, From the Earliest Formation of the Corps*. Charleston, SC: Lucas, Richardson & Co., 1888.

——————. *Hampton and His Cavalry in '64*. Richmond, VA: B. F. Johnson Publishing Co., 1899.

——————. *Hampton and Reconstruction*. Columbia, SC: The State Co., 1907.

White, William Lee and Charles Denny Runion, eds. *Great Things Are Expected of Us: The Letters of Colonel C. Irvine Walker, 10th South Carolina Infantry, C.S.A.* Knoxville: University of Tennessee Press, 2009.

Wickham, Mrs. Julia Porcher. "Wade Hampton, the Cavalry Leader, and His Times," *Confederate Veteran* 36 (1928): 448-450.

Wills, Charles W. *Army Life of an Illinois Soldier*. Washington, DC: Globe Printing Co., 1906.

Wilson, Theodore C. "Johnston's Surrender," *New York Herald*, May 9, 1865.

Wise, John S. *The End of an Era*. Boston: Houghton-Mifflin & Co., 1901.

Worsham, W. J. *The Old Nineteenth Tennessee Regiment, C.S.A. June 1861-April 1865*. Knoxville, TN: Press of Paragon Printing Co., 1902.

SECONDARY SOURCES:

Andrew, Rod, Jr. *Wade Hampton: Confederate Warrior to Southern Redeemer*. Chapel Hill: University of North Carolina Press, 2009.

Andrews, R. McCants. *John Merrick: A Biographical Sketch*. Durham, NC: The Seeman Printery, 1920.

Barefoot, Daniel W. *General Robert F. Hoke: Lee's Modest Warrior*. Winston-Salem, NC: John F. Blair, 1996.

Boyd, William Kenneth. *The Story of Durham: City of the New South*. Durham, NC: Duke University Press, 1925.

Bradley, Mark L. *The Battle of Bentonville: Last Stand in the Carolinas*. Mason City, IA: Savas Publishing, 1996.

——————. *This Astounding Close: The Road to Bennett Place*. Chapel Hill: University of North Carolina Press, 2000.

Bush, Bryan S. *Terry's Texas Rangers: The 8th Texas Cavalry*. Paducah, KY: Turner Publishing, 2002.

Coffman, Richard M. *Going Back the Way They Came: The Phillips Georgia Legion Cavalry Battalion*. Macon, GA: Mercer University Press, 2011.

Connelly, Thomas Lawrence. *Autumn of Glory: The Army of Tennessee, 1862-1865*. Baton Rouge: Louisiana State University Press, 1971.

Daniel, Larry J. *Soldiering in the Army of Tennessee: A Portrait of Life in a Confederate Army*. Chapel Hill: University of North Carolina Press, 1991.

Davis, William C. *Breckinridge: Statesman, Soldier, Symbol*. Baton Rouge: Louisiana State University Press, 1974.

——————. "John Cabell Breckinridge." Included in William C. Davis and Julie Hoffman, eds. *The Confederate General*. 6 vols. New York: National Historical Society, 1991, 1:126-127.

Dawson, George Francis. *Life and Services of General John A. Logan as Soldier and Statesman*. Washington, DC: *National Tribune*, 1884.

Dunkerly, Robert M. *The Confederate Surrender at Greensboro: The Final Days of the Army of Tennessee, April 1865*. Jefferson, NC: McFarland, 2013.

Eicher, John H. and David J. Eicher. *Civil War High Commands*. Stanford, CA: Stanford University Press, 2002.

Flood, Charles Bracelen. *Grant and Sherman: The Friendship That Won the Civil War*. New York: Farrar, Straus and Giroux, 2005.

Fonvielle, Chris E. *The Wilmington Campaign: Last Rays of Departing Hope*. Mason City, IA: Savas Publishing, 1997.

Gallagher, Gary W. "Pierre Gustave Toutant Beauregard," Included in William C. Davis and Julie Hoffman, eds. *The Confederate General*. 6 vols. New York: National Historical Society, 1991, 1:84-93

Govan, Gilbert E. and James W. Livingood. *A Different Valor: The Story of General Joseph E. Johnston, C.S.A*. Indianapolis: Bobbs-Merrill, 1956.

Green, John. "Henry Hitchcock." *American Antiquarian Society* 17 (October 1895): 253-262.

Hartley, Chris J. *Stoneman's Raid, 1865*. Winston-Salem, NC: John F. Blair, 2010.

Hearn, Chester G. *Admiral David Dixon Porter: The Civil War Years*. Annapolis: Naval Institute Press, 1996.

Hoole, William Stanley. *Alabama Tories: The First Alabama Cavalry, U.S.A., 1862-1865*. Tuscaloosa, AL: Confederate Publishing Co., 1960.

Hopkins, Donald A. *The Little Jeff: The Jeff Davis Legion, Cavalry, Army of Northern Virginia*. Shippensburg, PA: White Mane, 1999.

Hughes, Nathaniel Cheairs, Jr. *Bentonville: The Final Battle of Sherman and Johnston*. Chapel Hill: University of North Carolina Press, 1996.

------------------------------------. *General William J. Hardee: Old Reliable*. Baton Rouge: Louisiana State University Press, 1965.

Kelly, William Milner. "A History of the Thirtieth Alabama Volunteers (Infantry) Confederate States Army," *The Alabama Historical Quarterly*, Vol. 9, No. 1 (Spring 1947):115-189.

Lay, Maxwell G. *Ways of the World: A History of the World's Roads and of the Vehicles that Used Them*. New Brunswick, NJ: Rutgers University Press, 1992.

Longacre, Edward G. *Worthy Opponents: William T. Sherman and Joseph E. Johnston: Antagonists in War-Friends in Peace*. New York: Thomas Nelson, 2006.

Lundberg, John R. *Granbury's Texas Brigade: Diehard Western Confederates*. Baton Rouge: Louisiana State University Press, 2012.

Mahon, John K. and Romana Danysh. *Infantry Part I: Regular Army*. Washington, DC: Office of the Chief of Military History, United States Army, 1972.

Martin, Samuel J. *Kill-Cavalry: Sherman's Merchant of Terror: The Life of Union General Hugh Judson Kilpatrick*. Madison, NJ: Fairleigh-Dickinson University Press, 1996.

Marszalek, John F. *Sherman: A Soldier's Passion for Order*. New York: Free Press,

1993.

McDonough, James Lee. *William Tecumseh Sherman: In the Service of My Country. A Life.* New York: W. W. Norton, 2016.

McMurry, Richard M. "Joseph Eggleston Johnston." Included in William C. Davis and Julie Hoffman, eds. *The Confederate General.* 6 vols. New York: National Historical Society, 1991, 3:192-197.

McWhiney, Grady and Judith Ann Hallock. *Braxton Bragg and Confederate Defeat.* 2 vols. Tuscaloosa: University of Alabama Press, 1991.

Menius, Arthur C., III. "James Bennitt: Portrait of an Antebellum Yeoman," *North Carolina Historical Review* 58 (October 1981): 305-326.

Mesic, Harriett Bey. *Cobb's Legion Cavalry: A History and Roster of the Ninth Georgia Volunteers in the Civil War.* Jefferson, NC: McFarland & Co., 2009.

Moore, Mark Anderson. *Moore's Historical Guide To The Battle of Bentonville.* New York: DaCapo, 1997.

"Over Five Barricades." Included in W. F. Beyer and O. F. Keydel, eds. *Deeds of Valor.* 2 vols. Detroit, MI: The Perrien-Keydel Co., 1907, 1:463-465.

Peterson, Dennis L. *Confederate Cabinet Departments and Secretaries.* Jefferson, NC: McFarland & Co., 2016.

Rosa, J. G. "George Ward Nichols and the Legend of Wild Bill Hickock," *Arizona and the West,* Vol. 19, No. 2 (Summer 1977): 135-162.

Rowell, John W. *Yankee Cavalrymen: Through the Civil War with the Ninth Pennsylvania Cavalry.* Knoxville: University of Tennessee Press, 1971.

Schmiehl, Eugene D. *Citizen-General: Jacob Dolson Cox and the Civil War Era.* Athens, OH: Ohio University Press, 2014.

Simms, William Gilmore. *A City Laid Waste: The Capture, Sack, and Destruction of the City of Columbia.* Columbia: University of South Carolina Press, 2005.

Slocum, Charles Elihu. *The Life and Services of Major-General Henry Warner Slocum.* Toledo, OH: The Slocum Publishing Co., 1913.

Smith, Mark A. and Wade Sokolosky. *"No Such Army Since the Days of Julius Caesar": Sherman's Carolinas Campaign from Fayetteville to Averasboro, March 1865.* El Dorado Hills, CA: Savas-Beatie, 2017.

Sokolosky, Wade and Mark A. Smith. *"To Prepare for Sherman's Coming": The Battle of Wise's Forks, March 1865.* El Dorado Hills, CA: Savas-Beatie, 2015.

Sprunt, James. *Chronicles of the Cape Fear River 1660-1916.* Raleigh: Edwards & Broughton, 1916.

Symonds, Craig L. *Joseph E. Johnston: A Civil War Biography.* New York: W. W. Norton, 1992.

Tap, Bruce. *Over Lincoln's Shoulder: The Committee on the Conduct of the War.* Lawrence: University Press of Kansas, 1998.

Todd, Glenda McWhirter. *First Alabama Cavalry USA: Homage to Patriotism.* Bowie, MD: Heritage Books, 1999.

Trout, Robert J. *They Followed the Plume: The Story of J.E.B. Stuart and His Staff.* Mechanicsburg, PA: Stackpole Books, 1993.

Trudeau, Noah Andre. *Lincoln's Greatest Journey: Sixteen Days that Changed a*

Presidency, March 24 – April 8, 1865. El Dorado Hills, CA: Savas-Beatie, 2016.

----------------------------. *Southern Storm: Sherman's March to the Sea*. New York: Harper, 2007.

Vatavuk, William M. *Dawn of Peace: The Bennett Place State Historic Site, Durham, North Carolina*. Wake Forest, NC: The Scuppernong Press, 2014.

Warner, Ezra J. *Generals in Blue: Lives of the Union Commanders*. Baton Rouge: Louisiana State University Press, 1964.

Webb, Mena. *Jule Carr: General Without an Army*. Chapel Hill: University of North Carolina Press, 1987.

Wellman, Manly Wade. *Giant in Gray: A Biography of Wade Hampton of South Carolina*. New York: Charles Scribner's Sons, 1949.

Wert, Jeffry D. "Wade Hampton," Included in William C. Davis and Julie Hoffman, eds. *The Confederate General*. 6 vols. New York: National Historical Society, 1991, 3:50-53.

West, Richard Sedgewick. *The Second Admiral: A Life of David Dixon Porter, 1813-1891*. New York: Coward-McCann, 1937.

Williams, T. Harry *P.G.T. Beauregard: Napoleon in Gray*. Baton Rouge: Louisiana State University Press, 1955.

Wise, Jim. *On Sherman's Trail: The Civil War's North Carolina Climax*. Charleston, SC: The History Press, 2008.

Wittenberg, Eric J. *The Battle of Monroe's Crossroads and the Civil War's Final Campaign*. El Dorado Hills, CA: Savas-Beatie, 2006.

Yates, Richard E. "Zebulon B. Vance as War Governor of North Carolina, 1862-1865," *Journal of Southern History*, Vol. 3, No. 1 (February 1937): 43-75.

WEBSITES:

"A Brief History of the Bennett Family."
http://www.bennettplacehistoricsite.com/history/bennett-family/

"Bennett Place: Facilities."
http://www.nchistoricsites.org/bennett/facilities.htm

Civil War (A-F) Medal of Honor Recipients.
http://www.history.army.mil/moh/civilwar_af.html#ALBER

Joseph E. Johnston letter to Edward W. Bok of February 21, 1882.
https://www.abaa.org/book/577806772

Index

Photograph by Scott Cunningham

About the Author

Eric J. Wittenberg is an award-winning Civil War historian, speaker and tour guide. A native of southeastern Pennsylvania, he has been hooked on the Civil War since a third-grade trip to Gettysburg. Wittenberg is deeply involved in battlefield preservation efforts with the Civil War Trust. He is a graduate of Dickinson College and the University of Pittsburgh School of Law. He is an attorney in private practice in Columbus, Ohio, where he resides with his wife Susan and their three golden retrievers.

Made in the USA
Middletown, DE
21 November 2018